INCONVENIENCE GONE

The Short Tragic Life Of Brandon Sims

DIANE MARGER MOORE

WILDBLUE
PRESS

WildBluePress.com

INCONVENIENCE GONE published by:
WILDBLUE PRESS
P.O. Box 102440
Denver, Colorado 80250

WILDBLUE PRESS is registered at the U.S. Patent and Trademark Offices.

ISBN 978-1-947290-83-9 Trade Paperback
ISBN 978-1-947290-82-2 eBook

Interior Formatting/Book Cover Design by Elijah Toten
www.totencreative.com

7-2-2022

To Kevin,
A great house guest,
friend and Swiss
~~embassador~~

INCONVENIENCE
GONE

Diane Menger Moore

Michelle went on with life not like anything was wrong, like everything was okay, just an *inconvenience gone*. She went to work. She went to parties. She went to gatherings. She lived her life.

— Saundra Holiday

TABLE OF CONTENTS

INTRODUCTION

Where is Brandon Sims? The four-year-old child had not been seen since July 3, 1992, when he attended a birthday party with his twenty-year-old mother, Michelle Engron Jones. Michelle Jones was confident, talented, smart, assertive, and involved in many community activities in Indianapolis, Indiana. She had a great job at Eli Lilly, a major pharmaceutical company. In contrast, when he was last seen, Brandon Sims, her only child, was a serious, quiet, thin child, who rarely maintained eye contact with his mother. After that night, he was never seen again. His body has never been found.

Michelle Jones knows where she buried Brandon. She has never truthfully revealed where Brandon's remains are located. Brandon's father and paternal grandmother have never been able give Brandon a proper burial.

Michelle Engron was fourteen years old when she became pregnant. She was intelligent and pretty: petite and dark skinned with round dark eyes and straight white teeth. Her mother was less than pleased. The two had difficulties before the pregnancy but this was too much for the single woman who was attempting to raise her. Michelle would later describe her mother as having beaten her with a board when she told her about the pregnancy. Child services believed that this was not the first instance of abuse Michelle experienced at the hands of her mother. Whether that was true or not was never determined, but she was removed from the home and placed in a group home where she would remain until she was eighteen years old.

The father of her unborn child was Kevin Lamarr Sims, also a teen. He, however, had a loving mother, who, while disappointed in her son's actions, was pleased to welcome another child into her heart. Michelle named the infant Brandon Sims.

After the baby was born, Arlene Blevins, Kevin's mother, took the baby into their home to raise while Michelle was living at the group home and finishing high school. Arlene kept in contact with Michelle and brought Brandon to visit his mother frequently.

During this time, Michelle was offered an incredible opportunity – to intern at Eli Lilly in Indianapolis. Eli Lilly was considered the best employer in the area and it was an honor to be selected. When Brandon was nearly three years old, Michelle insisted that Arlene return him to her custody. She complied but begged Michelle to keep in touch and allow her to help with the child. She offered to babysit, provide daycare and do anything that Michelle needed for the child. Despite Arlene's love for Brandon and her offers of assistance, Michelle claimed she was interfering in the "bonding" between her and Brandon. She cut off all contact between Brandon and his grandmother.

Except for a couple of chance meetings, Michelle never allowed Arlene to see her grandson Brandon again. Arlene heard that Michelle had married a man named Jones, a member of the Nation of Islam, but was unable to find out more about the toddler she had come to love.

Kevin Sims, while a nice guy and a loving father to Brandon, had gotten into some trouble and was incarcerated for burglary. When he was released, he and his mother searched for Brandon and Michelle. Finally, Kevin knocked on the door of a friend of Michelle's with whom she was living. He explained why he was there. The friend was shocked. She knew the shy, thin boy, larger than his age, who had accompanied Michelle to dance practices and rehearsals a few times. Kevin asked where he could find Brandon. Michelle's friend recoiled.

"I haven't seen Brandon for nearly two years," she responded. "Michelle said that she sent Brandon to live with you."

CHAPTER ONE

SGT. MICHAEL CROOKE GOES TO MIDTOWN MENTAL HEALTH

Michael Crooke joined the Indianapolis Police Department in the late 1960s. By 1994, he had pretty much seen and heard it all. He had done his time on the streets in various divisions and worked his way up to the prestigious homicide unit. Despite the importance of the work done there, the unit was located in a large cluster of rooms with most of the desks pushed up against each other, little natural light, and no decoration of any kind. Metal desks, metal chairs, black telephones, grungy-looking printers, and fax machines.

He was at his desk in the unit on January 7, 1994, when a uniformed IPD officer entered the unit to report an unusual situation to the detective in charge. Crooke listened as Officer Frank Ingram described what he had just learned about a Michelle Engron Jones. It would be the beginning of more than two years of investigation, working leads, literally digging the earth, pressing for the truth, and ultimately charging Jones for the murder of her four-year-old son Brandon.

Officer Ingram told Sgt. Crooke that he had been dispatched to Midtown Mental Health, which was a unit of the county hospital known as Wishard. It's not unusual for an officer to be sent to Midtown to investigate the cause of a hospitalization, especially if the patient claims to have been abused, assaulted, or is self-harming. When he arrived, Ingram met with Toni Goffredo, a clinical crisis counselor, who had interviewed Jones when she appeared at the facility earlier in the day. Goffredo told Ingram that Jones checked in due to "stress" caused by taking her deceased child, dropping him off somewhere, and failing to have a proper burial for the child. What on Earth? These statements could be the vivid imagination of a mentally disturbed woman, describe an accidental death, abandonment, or an intentional killing. Crooke immediately returned to Midtown with Ingram but learned that Jones had been heavily sedated and was unable to meet with law enforcement.

Three days later, Sgt. Crooke spoke with Jones' social worker at Midtown. The social worker told Crooke that Jones was able to coherently describe what had happened and invited Crooke to come meet with her. They arranged for an interview on January 13, 1994. By then, Jones had been in the unit for nearly a week and had received several visitors.

Crooke, dressed in plain clothes but having identified himself as a detective, met with Michelle Jones in a room designated by the floor nurse. The nurse led Crooke into a small conference room and brought Jones into the room. She told Crooke that she wanted to be called by her maiden name, Engron. She explained that she gave birth to a boy on November 11, 1987. She told Crooke that she named him Brandon Lamarr Sims and that the father was Kevin Sims.

Jones appeared to understand all of Crooke's questions and gave coherent and accurate (when later confirmed) answers to most of his questions. She volunteered much of what she told him, including that she and Brandon had lived at the Georgetown Apartments at the time of his death. She was articulate and seemed high functioning.

Crooke would later quote much of what she told him that day in an affidavit in support of her arrest:

Michelle Engron Jones said that two years prior (1992) she was taking large doses of medication and drugs. She left her son at home, unattended, for approximately one week. She thought this was in July or August of 1992. When she returned home, the child was dead. She placed him in her vehicle and drove to police headquarters to report the death. Because of her religious beliefs at that time she felt a lack of trust for people of the white race. When she arrived at police headquarters she only saw white people. She left and went to a cemetery where she was going to bury him, but no one was there. She drove north on I-65 to what she believed was the Attica exit. Somewhere near that exit, she placed the body at the bottom of an embankment. She said she was sure she could take us to the location of the body.

Crooke would later relate that she never referred to the child by his name. He tried to comprehend the detachment he observed. It seemed to him that Jones was more concerned about what her friends thought of her than the absence of her son.

Crooke told Jones that he wanted her to take him to find Brandon's body. She agreed, saying that she was willing to do so. Crooke made arrangements to meet so that she could direct him to the area where she claimed to have put Brandon's body. When he returned to Midtown, Jones advised him, through the floor nurse, that she had hired a lawyer, Mark Earnest. She refused to speak to Crooke and did not take him to Brandon's body. Michelle Engron Jones was twenty-one years old.

CHAPTER TWO

A NEEDLE IN A HAYSTACK

Crooke returned to the unit believing that something had happened to Brandon Sims. But would he ever be able to prove it? Was there even a child named Brandon Sims? Without a body, it would be nearly impossible to prove that the child was dead. Besides that, Crooke had to convince himself that Brandon was a real, live child. Then he had to figure out if the child was dead. And then he would have to learn how the child died.

Was Jones hiding the child from his father? Was the child staying with relatives? Had she sold the child? Crooke needed to know a lot more about Brandon Sims.

Within twenty-four hours of his first meeting with Michelle Jones, Sgt. Crooke located and met with Kevin Sims and Arlene Blevins. Kevin told Crooke that he and Arlene had been searching for Brandon for months. They provided a well-worn photograph of Kevin and his son. Crooke saw a pudgy, smiling toddler in the arms of Kevin. Both were grinning and pointing, relaxed and happy. He learned that the photograph was taken while Arlene was caring for Brandon, before she had returned him to his mother.

Kevin and his mother gave tape-recorded statements to Crooke. They wanted Brandon back. Crooke did not share what Jones had told him.

How could he tell these family members that Brandon was dead when he didn't know if it was true? He just couldn't be sure. Was Michelle Jones credible? Crooke decided that the child was, at the least, missing. He filed a missing person report with that unit of IPD. He needed help looking for and finding Brandon Sims. Maybe the child would be found alive. Maybe.

On January 27, 1994, Sgt. Crooke gathered police resources to search for Brandon Sims. This would prove to be the first of many attempts by the Indianapolis Police Department to locate Brandon if he was indeed dead. Crooke and Lt. Mark Rice met with the Indiana State Police at the Attica exit off I-65 to try to find little Brandon's body. It was freezing cold in Indiana but a group of officers, detectives, and troopers (some on their own time as volunteers) searched for baby Brandon Sims.

They searched the woods surrounding the exit and on-ramps of the Attica exit on I-65 and the surrounding area. They dug up any ground that looked like it had been disturbed. They tried to identify children's clothing or blankets that may have been left or buried with Brandon, since parents who killed their children, especially a young child, were known to wrap the body in the child's favorite blankets, leave their stuffed animals or some other comforting item from the child's life with the body. The officers spent hours looking for a body. They found nothing.

There are thirty-one exits on I-65 heading toward Chicago from the I-465 northern loop of Indianapolis. The Attica exit, onto State Road 28, is the eighth. Crooke wondered why Jones would have chosen the Attica exit. He found no connection between her and Attica. It was not particularly isolated or wooded. Was this really where she left Brandon's body? Although it had been a while since he died, evidence of his body should have remained if it was "laid" or buried there as she had told him.

Frustrated, Crooke searched the records for unidentified bodies that may have been found in the area for the preceding three years. There were no bodies found. It was becoming a mystery that haunted him. A four year old left alone in life and, if Jones was to be believed, in death.

So Crooke dug in. He was determined to find out what had happened to the smiling toddler from the photograph. He tracked down a birth certificate proving that Brandon Lamarr Sims had been born to Michelle Engron and Kevin Sims. He obtained Brandon's medical records from Wishard Hospital where Brandon had been born and Riley Children's Hospital where Brandon had been seen by pediatricians. He located welfare records for Brandon and even obtained the birth announcement that Arlene Blevins had saved. He knew that Brandon was a real child, not the figment of Jones' imagination.

All the while, Michelle Jones, who had left Midtown, was back to her life. No charges had been filed against her. She continued working, dancing, dating, and living with friends. Crooke knew little about her but was bound and determined to know everything he could about this seemingly dispassionate woman who had abandoned her child.

Crooke tracked down Mae Engron, Michelle's mother. Mae was brusque. She had been injured while working for the US Postal Service and had been living on disability for years. She had not had any contact with her daughter since she was placed in the group home, nearly eight years earlier. Mae gave Crooke names and contact information for other members of the family. Crooke methodically tracked each down, but Jones had lost touch or not been in contact for years. Her family knew that Brandon had been born but had no idea where he was. No one had seen him in more than two years.

Crooke continued searching for evidence. Months went by. No child's body had been uncovered. Michelle Engron Jones had "lawyered up" and was not going to speak with the police or anyone else about the case. Despite her earlier admission, she resumed her life as if nothing had happened to her only child. She returned to work at Eli Lilly. Kevin and Arlene were becoming increasingly frantic to find Brandon. Crooke was getting nowhere.

CHAPTER THREE

A CROOKE AT THE DOOR

There was a knock on my door. I didn't get many formal visitors in my closet-sized office at the Marion County Prosecutor's Office. The guys from the Fire Investigation Unit just walked in, assuming I would be there or in court and not really caring if they interrupted me. But this knock was more tentative.

"Come in." Wow, I was in a gracious mood allowing anyone into my space — where I spent more time than I cared to admit.

A man slowly opened the door. Apparently, he knew the general size of a prosecutor's office. My small rolling chair, one metal desk placed flush up against the window, nearly hidden by my computer screen and stacks of files, a narrow window sill with my children's photographs, one battered gray metal file cabinet and one metal chair for "guests." He looked at me without much enthusiasm.

He was middle aged, maybe a bit younger than I was, but he looked tired and worn down. His hair was dark with some grey growing in. *Did he use Brylcreme?* I wondered. (*Did that hair product still exist? Probably replaced by some newer sounding name, hair goo all the same.*) He was wearing a tweed jacket that had seen better days, a pair of wrinkled khaki pants, some form of cotton shirt stretched tight over his slightly protruding belly and a tie that seemed colorless. I knew instantly that he was a detective. It was the universal look of a plainclothes cop. I bit my lip to refrain from smiling when the comparison of my visitor and the stereotypical southern sheriff came to mind.

"Diane Moore?" he asked, despite the obvious name plate on my door. He did not have a southern accent. I kept a straight face. There was something about his eyes. There was still some intensity. Actually, a lot of intensity, disguised by the minutely slumped posture and schleppy clothing.

"No. Diane *Marger* Moore," I replied emphasizing the maiden name that I had incorporated into my married name. That always aggravated them. My nonhyphenated double last name.

"Uh huh. I'm Sergeant Mike Crooke, IPD, *homicide*," he retorted.

"Are you lost?"

I was the chief arson prosecutor for Marion County, Indiana, which included all of Indianapolis and some of the small townships outside of Indy. So, other than arson detectives and their fire investigation counterparts, I had few contacts with other Indianapolis Police Department detectives or Marion County Sheriff's Department deputies.

My cases were different. I was assigned to work with the fire investigation unit and would go to the scenes of fires to help determine, on the spot, whether a crime was committed. I could screen and file my cases without going through the screeners, but then I would handle the cases through the investigation and prosecution. It did not always make me popular. Actually, I wasn't popular for many reasons better left for later discussion. But if I filed a case, then I would handle the case regardless of politics, difficulties, or anything else so long as I was convinced of the defendant's guilt. If a detective's evidence couldn't convince me, then I could not "sell" the case to a jury and I declined to file it.

Most of the other prosecutors received case assignments after a detective had met with a screening prosecutor. These screeners were a group of very experienced prosecutors who did nothing else. The screener would consider the evidence, consult the criminal laws that might have been broken and file charges if they found sufficient evidence. In some instances, the screeners might direct a detective to obtain further evidence before they would file the case. Sometimes they told the officers that no case would be filed. The detectives could do the extra work, suggest additional or different charges, or, most commonly, accept the decline of prosecution.

Once a case was screened and filed, it would go to the clerk of court for a random assignment to one of the criminal courts that handled that level of crime. For serious felonies, there were six courts to which a case could be assigned. After the case was sent to a particular court, the felony court supervisor in that court would assign the case to one of the deputy prosecutors who worked there.

So why was this detective standing in my office? I wondered. He wasn't an arson investigator; by then I had met all or most of them. Arson detectives were a different species. Besides, he'd said he was homicide.

"No. Van Buskirk said I should speak with you," he said flatly.

Van Buskirk was a homicide detective with whom I was working on an entirely circumstantial arson murder case: the murder of an eight-week-old infant. Despite an inauspicious start, Van B and I had become friends. Van B tended to be possessive of her cases and of me, as "her" prosecutor. Had she "loaned" me to another homicide detective? Who was this guy? I asked him to sit out of respect for Van Buskirk. If she had sent him to me, then I would at least hear him out.

Crooke explained his dilemma. The case posed issues similar to a law school examination. How to reach a goal with legal land mines galore standing in the way of justice. I was already overextended with an enormous caseload of circumstantial and complicated arson cases. I really didn't have time to get involved in another case. Especially one that was not in my bailiwick.

This case involved the possible death of a four-year-old child. Was the child really dead? How could death be proven without a corpse? The law might not allow Crooke to use Michelle Jones' statements against her. That is because Indiana is one of the few states that severely limits the use of confessions, like "I left my four year old home alone for a week and he died." Confessions were not admissible without extrinsic proof that a crime had been committed.

Complicating the issue of proof further, the person making the statements was in a mental hospital at the time she confessed. Before her admissions could be used, the prosecution had to have independent proof that a crime was committed, and that the confessor had perpetrated the crime.

As Crooke described what he knew of the child, I began to picture him in my mind: dark brown face, long eyelashes, brown nearly black eyes, a quiet nearly silent demeanor, much taller than the average four-year-old child, bright, and very thin. My vision of Brandon Sims was sadly compelling.

Crooke told me that he had been working on the case for nearly a year, but no one in our office was willing to file charges. He explained that he had spoken several times with the head screening deputy prosecuting attorney. She was smart and experienced and had told him that there was not enough evidence to prosecute the case. I appreciated Crooke's candor. He admitted the problems of proof. But he explained that this was one of those cases, he just couldn't let it go. He needed to either find the child alive or the child's body, and get justice for the child and his father and grandmother. He had nearly exhausted all the resources with which he was familiar. He wanted to file neglect charges against Jones. He wanted to discover enough proof to charge and convict her. That was refreshing. Many times, detectives sought only enough evidence to close their case, regardless of whether it was sufficient for prosecution. That was the screener's job, not the detective's, many thought.

Crooke was different. That was a great sign. At the very least, he wanted some suggestions as to where to look next. I looked down at my watch. We had been discussing Michelle Engron Jones for more than two hours. I was late for court. I had hearings scheduled in Criminal Court 5 and Judge Gary Miller did not tolerate latecomers. Besides, I needed to think about this situation. I also wanted to speak with Van Buskirk. Crooke held the door for me as I ran out of my office, arms overloaded with files, nearly running to the elevators.

CHAPTER FOUR

MENTAL BREAKDOWN OR EMERGING DEFENSE?

Crooke had explained how he learned about the death of Brandon Sims. He told me that in January 1994, he was informed about a patient at Midtown Mental Health who described leaving her four-year-old child at home for several days. The patient admitted that when she returned home, the child was dead. She was claiming to have had a sort of "breakdown" as a result of having to tell her friends about the death.

Midtown at Wishard was the Marion County, Indiana, hospital with a trauma unit, psych ward, and other services. It was well known as the facility that treated most of the gunshot wounds in the county. Crooke had described his meeting with Jones, his attempt to get her to show him where she dumped Brandon's body, and her lawyering up.

I wondered about Crooke's impressions of the young woman, her confession, and her hospitalization. Smart move to claim "stress" caused you to be mentally disturbed when the child had been dead, according to her account, for nearly two years. Why would it stress her now that Brandon's father and grandmother were tracking her down? Was something else going on here? What did she actually confess? There wasn't enough in what she said to call it a murder.

In the months since he learned of Brandon, Crooke had obtained a good deal of additional information about

Michelle Jones but all of it together did not add up to a solid case. Her statements were possibly inadmissible because of her mental state at the time she made them. She had admitted herself to a mental ward. *Good strategy*, I thought to myself. Either this is one smart cookie (my grandfather's words) or she had received good legal advice. But why did she speak to the police at all? Maybe not so clever.

Okay, I must admit that I talk to myself. A lot. I also practice closing arguments in the shower and my children claim to have seen me gesturing as if making a jury argument while driving them to school. I deny the latter ... mostly.

Whatever the reason that she checked herself into Midtown, her admission was the basis for some serious investigation. The only question now was whether I would be involved in the case. I felt certain that Sgt. Crooke would never just drop the case.

CHAPTER FIVE

JUST MY KIND OF CASE

I wanted to know a lot more about Sgt. Mike Crooke before I made a decision. I spoke with several detectives about the man, including Leslie Van Buskirk. Each of them described Crooke as a "legend." Although the detectives each had a different story about Crooke, they all considered him one of the finest homicide investigators in the state, if not the country. High praise from usually critical and cynical detectives.

I learned that Crooke had been the lead detective assigned to the I-70 killer case. The serial murderer had not been caught, but it wasn't for lack of trying. The murders all took place along the I-70 corridor of the Midwest, with the first being the murder of 26-year-old Robin Fuldauer, who was killed as she worked in a shoe store near Indianapolis. The killer would take five more lives in Indiana, Missouri, and Kansas. Although he had not solved the case, Crooke's dedication to the victims and the search was laudable.

Crooke had solved the case of Tracy Poindexter, a fifteen-year-old child who was killed in 1985. She had been bound and sexually assaulted before her death. For more than seven years, Crooke wouldn't let the case go. In 1992, DNA evidence became more widely available and Crooke obtained a DNA match for the killer.

There were many more cases that Crooke had solved, but it was his persistence and determination to solve cases that impressed me. And I couldn't get the picture of the little chubby boy out of my mind. Crooke was the kind of detective I wanted to work with. And this — nearly impossible, legally challenging situation — was my kind of case.

It was obvious to me that leaving a four-year-old child home alone for several days was neglect. But I had never prosecuted a neglect case, never set foot in juvenile court. I just felt that no mother could leave a *four-year-old child* home alone for days without being culpable of some crime. Why hadn't she called Arlene Blevins to babysit? Why hadn't she taken Brandon wherever she had gone? As a mother of two young children, the thought of leaving my four year old home alone was not possible. No way. No matter how angry, frustrated, or tired I had become, it was not possible. **NO.**

I called Crooke on the main homicide line, since he had not given me his cell phone number. I told him that we needed to discuss his case further. I wasn't ready to commit to a case that would be tough to prove and time consuming. We agreed to meet in my office the next day.

Before Crooke arrived for our second meeting, I did some research. Always go to the law, I had been taught. It will lead you to justice. What were the elements of neglect? Elements are the facts that had to be proved to convict someone of that crime. I read the law that criminalized neglect. When a parent neglected a child, they could be pulled into juvenile court where the primary issue would be the child's welfare. But neglect was also a crime. The criminal courts focused on punishing criminal behavior.

I learned that the crime of neglect of a dependent was a felony, but there were less serious and more serious types of neglect. A person having the care of a dependent, who knowingly or intentionally abandons or cruelly confines a dependent commits neglect of a dependent, a Class D Felony. A Class D Felony had a minimum sentence of one year and a maximum sentence of three years. This is the charge that would apply to Michelle Engron Jones if we couldn't prove that Brandon Sims was seriously injured or had died. If we could prove that Brandon was seriously injured or dead, then the crime of neglect would be a Class B Felony. The maximum sentence for a B Felony was twenty years. But the sentence could be suspended, or probation ordered. Finally, and making this case even more serious, the law provided that if the perpetrator was more than eighteen years old and the victim was under fourteen years old, then the crime was a Class A Felony. A sentence of up to fifty years could be imposed for neglect as a Class A Felony.

I needed to understand and consider each of the elements that the State would have to prove. One: Did Michelle Jones have legal custody of Brandon at the time he died? It seemed obvious, but I started taking notes. We needed the birth certificate, sure, but also the legitimation petition, if there was one. In the 1990s, when a child was born out of wedlock, if the mother hoped to get welfare benefits and child support, she would file a paternity petition establishing her rights to the child. A father could also file a petition to acknowledge and legitimate the child, but with both parents teenagers themselves, I was doubtful that Kevin had filed a petition. Still, it was an item that had to be checked. Maybe these two children had filed a petition to protect Brandon. Otherwise, we would have to rely on the fact that a mother is the "natural guardian" of her child.

Gotta be some benefit from those stretch marks, weight gain, and tender nipples, I thought.

The second element was going to be a bit more challenging to prove: that the neglectful acts by Michelle Engron Jones were done knowingly or intentionally. So she had to recognize the danger in leaving her son alone for a week. Did she leave him food and water? Would that be enough? Was their apartment safe? These were all things that a good defense lawyer could argue to show that she did not have the mental intent to harm Brandon. We would have to prove that she had the intellect, the common sense, and the experience to know or intend to neglect the child.

The next element was to prove the extent of the harm to Brandon. This is where the case fell apart. Did her abandoning him endanger his life? It would depend on how long she left him and under what conditions.

Note to self: put mothers on the jury. I wouldn't leave my four year old home alone for any longer than it took me to walk to my mailbox. Was that too long? Was it safe? If the State proved only that Jones' abandonment of Brandon could have endangered Brandon, without more, then a mother who allowed her child to die while she was away could only be punished for a D Felony. That was a maximum three-year sentence. With no prior criminal history, she would walk. There was no question.

If Crooke could prove that her neglect had resulted in serious bodily injury or death, serious prison time could be imposed. How does one punish a mother for leaving her child home alone for a week? What about if the child is just four years old?

The last element was crucial. Since the State could not compel Jones to talk to the police again, she could change her story with little chance of impeachment. She had to know that. Why wouldn't she give Kevin Sims and Arlene Blevins the relief of burying this beloved little boy? Later, Crooke and I speculated that she did not want us to find the body for a reason. We discussed how to track down the little corpse.

It really didn't matter what class of felony she had committed because her statements were inadmissible. Crooke did not have enough evidence to charge her with anything. It had been a year since she told Crooke about the death of Brandon. Jones may have believed that she would never be punished.

We needed more, I thought. Much more. Then I realized that I had already included myself in "we." Didn't I have my hands full with difficult and complex arson cases to prosecute? How would I make time to work on this case? I put those thoughts aside for the moment. This was my kind of case. Nearly impossible, mostly circumstantial, complex. I was hooked. I wanted justice for Brandon.

Sgt. Crooke arrived for our scheduled appointment. I had a head full of thoughts and instructions. Without preamble, I started telling him what I wanted him to do. One might wonder if I had been a drill sergeant in a prior life. In order to prove this case, we would need to put together a puzzle with no missing pieces. Before we could prove that Brandon was dead, we had to prove he had been alive. I had some definite ideas about how to prove that. Then we needed to show that Michelle Engron Jones had sole custody of Brandon when he died. She could have given custody of the child to someone else, including his father, grandmother, a friend, or family member. So long as she had not "sold" the child, she had the right to place him with any competent adult. We had to prove that Brandon was living with her and was in her "custody" when he died. That was a tall order. Finally, we had to prove that he was dead and that she had abandoned him in their apartment. I had spent some serious time thinking about how to do it.

I told Crooke that we needed Brandon's birth certificate, any paternity or legitimation records, and his medical records. Without taking a breath, I told him to try to find Brandon's school records. Then I said, "And get the school records from other cities nearby." I had barely given this experienced detective a second to interject.

"Add that to the list, Sergeant Crooke," I directed.

He gave me a look.

"Please," I added.

Police departments are paramilitary organizations. IPD was no different. Hierarchy is important. Crooke had a lot of seniority. He was in a specialized and high-powered unit. He was a sergeant, which meant that he was a supervisor of other highly-qualified detectives in an elite unit. He expected respect.

I, on the other hand, had been a prosecutor for about a year. I had successfully prosecuted a couple of arson cases and one arson murder case. While I had a decent reputation as an arson prosecutor, I was not exactly a "star" in the office. I had been a lawyer for nearly fifteen years before I joined the prosecutors' office. My first trial, in 1979, was a death penalty multiple murder case that I defended with my dad. I had tried a number of high-profile cases in Georgia and Florida. But in Indiana, aside from my cases as a deputy attorney general, I always downplayed my trial experience. Better to have defense lawyers underestimate me. Unfortunately, so did some of my colleagues in the office. And detectives who had not been in trial with me.

"Sergeant, let's see if we can get her tax returns too. Maybe she listed Brandon as a dependent." I tried to tone my demands down to requests.

We talked about other documentation that might prove Michelle Jones' sole custody. Crooke agreed to obtain any records that he could from Eli Lilly, including all of their insurance records.

Crooke and I talked about how we could obtain evidence to prove intent. Even just her high school records might help us prove that she understood that leaving Brandon alone endangered his life.

"Even if we make a case, Michelle Engron Jones may get probation or a suspended sentence. It seems to be her first offense and we don't know what happened to Brandon," I told Crooke. He nodded his head in agreement.

He and I spent the afternoon discussing possibilities. How to obtain evidence to discover the truth when the person who knows the most is constitutionally protected from telling it to us? How to get to the truth when the law stands in the way? I did some more legal research. Always the key: go to the law. It will help you find the way to justice.

How to determine whether there really was a crime committed by Michelle Jones? Crooke needed to prove that Brandon was dead. The only person who knew this truth with certainty was Jones. We discussed a strategy to collect the evidence that we needed to prove neglect of a dependent causing serious bodily injury or death. We had to satisfy ourselves first that the child was dead. Then we would have to prove it in court.

The first step: prove that Brandon is actually dead. Jones could testify at any time that he was alive and well and living in Alaska with her third cousin. Since we, as the State, had the burden of proof, we needed to be able to convince a jury beyond a reasonable doubt that the child was dead. Crooke and I discussed what we needed to do that. While I believed the sergeant's sincerity, I wasn't sure that a case could be made against Michelle Jones. She might just get away with it. I didn't want to be the one to tell Mrs. Blevins or Kevin Sims that potential truth.

CHAPTER SIX

DISCOVERY AND COERCED CONFESSIONS

When I graduated from the University of Georgia's Lumpkin Law School in 1978, I became one of about three female criminal defense lawyers in the state. I wanted to be a defense lawyer because the law did not protect the innocent accused. Especially in a racially divided southern state. As a female, sometimes viewed as a less than equal person with my male counterparts, I wanted to change that. I wanted to equalize the playing field.

At the time, there was almost no discovery in criminal cases. A majority of criminal defendants were African American. Confessions were frequently introduced to prove the defendant's guilt. Innocent people went to prison.

A criminal defendant wasn't even entitled to obtain a copy of his own statement until the time of trial. No depositions, no Miranda warnings ("you have a right to remain silent, to have legal representation," etc.). The justice system had been tainted by forced confessions, many times beaten from minority suspects and completely unreliable. Those abuses were finally brought to light in the 1950s and 1960s when the United States Supreme Court mandated protections to ensure that force or other forms of coercion played no part in admissible confessions. More well-known protections included warning suspects about their legal rights, including their right to counsel, to remain silent, and the use of any statement made by the accused. The courts were determined to ensure the fairness of the system. Most of these changes were the result of the "liberal," or more accurately described "personal rights," Warren Supreme Court. Earl Warren, a former three-term California governor, was Chief Justice of the Supreme Court from 1953 until he retired in 1969. Protecting an accused's rights was too long in coming. Starting in the federal courts and later spreading to state courts, most of the information collected by police must be provided to the defendant long before his case comes to trial. Defendants are entitled to take the deposition (sworn statement) of the State's witnesses before trial, to hire and use expert witnesses and other privileges that were once only available to the prosecution. Compelled confessions or those that are not voluntary must be excluded and suppressed.

But some criminal defendants through counsel and courts went too far, allowing the accused to abuse these protections. The prosecution was prohibited from admitting into evidence "compelled" confessions. Some of these statements were not trustworthy. For example, a confession obtained by beating a suspect, starving him, isolating him, or telling him what to say is not reliable. This is true for both oral and written confessions. In this example, it doesn't change the conclusion when the police order the beaten, starved, isolated accused to write down a confession dictated by the police. In such a situation, the confession is not only compelled but there is a strong likelihood that the confession is false.

Other compelled confessions are trustworthy but may still be inadmissible. For example, a person suspected of a crime walks into a police station. He says he wants to confess. He is sitting in a room alone with police who already suspect him of a crime. They would not have let him leave even if he had refused to speak with them. The man starts talking, without being asked questions, but he was not read his Miranda warnings. His statement is probably inadmissible. But it is likely trustworthy.

When Crooke walked into my office, I had been a prosecutor for a short time. I had spent more than ten years as a criminal defense lawyer, federal public defender, and writer/lecturer on the personal rights encompassed in the United States Constitution. My dad had been, since the year of my birth, a criminal defense lawyer. I believed. Really believed in personal rights. Nothing about my current job altered that. But it was inexplicable that Michelle Jones could abandon and neglect her child, tell the police about it, and be free from punishment.

My quick research reminded me that a court can compel a person to testify against themselves so long as that testimony is not used against them. But the person cannot then lie to the court with impunity. The Supreme Court said, "Evidence that has been illegally obtained ... is *in*admissible on the prosecution's direct case, or otherwise, as substantive evidence of guilt." However, the Court concluded that permitting the use of such illegally obtained evidence to impeach a defendants' testimony would further the goal of truth-seeking by preventing defendants from perverting the exclusionary rule into a license to use perjury by way of a defense. So the Court concluded that the balance of values underlying the exclusionary rule justified an exception covering impeachment of a defendant's testimony.

I told Crooke that a criminal case was premature. First, he needed to determine whether Brandon was alive.

"How can you do that, Sergeant?" I asked.

We were both getting tired. It had been a long day. He looked at me inquiringly.

"Do you believe this child, Brandon, if he is alive, may he be *in need of services?*" I asked.

"What?" he responded blankly.

Think. Think, Crooke, you've been around. I don't want to tell you what to do nor be involved in compelling Michelle to say anything. But we need to know if Brandon is really dead, I thought, never speaking a word, just looking at him.

Crooke stared at me blankly and then a more knowing look slowly crossed his face.

I agreed to work with him to try to build a case for neglect against Michelle Engron Jones. He had to prove that Brandon was dead. Crooke left my office.

I was going to try my best to get the face of that adorable baby out of my mind.

CHAPTER SEVEN

WORKING THE CASE

Sgt. Crooke and I began to meet fairly often to work on the case. Crooke had obtained the Eli Lilly records. Michelle Jones had listed Brandon as a dependent on her personnel records when she had been hired at Eli Lilly's. In fact, Brandon and Damon Jones, her husband, had been listed as her dependents on her tax forms, insurance forms, and in other places in her personnel records. Damon Jones had been removed when she divorced him.

Those same records revealed that after August 1992, she changed her records, removing Brandon Sims from her W-2 and insurance documents. She no longer paid for dependent coverage on her medical policy. This was a powerful indication to me that Brandon was dead. It was evidence that Jones knew he was dead. But we needed more.

As I reviewed the records, Brandon Sims would have been nearly six years old, a first grader. Crooke obtained records from the Marion County School Board. No Brandon Sims had ever been enrolled in school. Crooke checked the surrounding school systems. Brandon had never been enrolled in Head Start, kindergarten, or first grade.

Next, I wanted to know about the apartment where Brandon had lived when he was abandoned. Crooke told me that he had visited the apartment complex. He had asked for the records for Jones' apartment. He had been told that the records had been destroyed. Crooke hiked his shoulders, shrugging.

"They were not very cooperative. That's what they told me," Crooke explained.

I didn't believe them. He looked like he didn't believe them either. My actual reaction to Crooke telling me that was a reference to cow patties. So we decided to drive over to the apartment complex.

Knowing that Van Buskirk had a car that could only be described as a wreck, I wondered what Crooke drove. When he picked me up in front of the City-County Building where we both worked, he was driving a white nondescript something. It was not marked but any criminal worth their salt could have identified it as a cop car from a mile away. It was a limo compared to Van Buskirk's unmarked clunker. Apparently being a sergeant had its benefits. I hopped in and we drove the short distance to the complex.

The Georgetown Apartments consisted of a group of brick buildings meandering around in a series of circular drives. There were sidewalks in front of every building. I liked that. There were plenty of kids in the complex. Most of the buildings were two stories with a single common entrance. Some of the first-floor apartments had a small concrete slab patio in the back with sliding doors leading outside. I had never been to the complex before, so Crooke and I looked around before parking in front of the office and going in. I suspected that some of the apartments were subsidized low-income housing, but the buildings were in pretty good shape and it seemed well maintained.

Crooke was not in uniform, but he wore his standard detective attire. Wrinkled khakis, button-down shirt, colorless tie, and some kind of worn tweed blazer. I was in a suit, which I guess was my prosecutor garb. At the time, I was also carrying my identification and a badge that I had purchased.

Indiana prosecutors are designated as law enforcement officers. (Right, as if I was going to chase a suspect! Not in this lifetime. I was fortyish, a mother of two, in middle-aged shape - not like those Hollywood middle-aged beauties usually wearing high heels. Just not gonna happen.) I was entitled to have a badge, but the office didn't give them to us. There was a small shop that catered to "cops" near downtown. It engraved and sold badges, holsters, and all sorts of police paraphernalia. One of my arson detectives, William Wilson, had taken me there early in my career. He assured me that the badge would simplify my life as I arrived at crime scenes. I even bought the black case with the nifty velvet divider which held both my identification and the badge. The badge was gold with the words chief arson prosecutor and Marger Moore engraved on it. I had only used it a few times but made sure to bring it with me on this expedition.

Crooke parked outside the office and we walked in. The gal who greeted us seemed friendly enough. She immediately started telling us about the available apartments. Her wide smile retreated into an unfriendly grimace when we told her who we were. We asked for the manager and she said she was "acting manager." I did the talking. No need to flash my badge. Shucks.

"We want the entire rental file for Michelle Engron Jones," I told her. "She lived here in the summer of 1992."

Her response was nearly automatic. "We don't retain rental records for that long. Sorry." She didn't look sorry. Her attitude screamed annoyance and a hostility toward law enforcement.

"Really?" I asked in my nicest prosecutorial tone. "That's against the law. You are required to maintain rental records for at least six years. You could get in trouble for destroying them," I bluffed. Well, it may have been against the law, it should be against the law, but what did I know? I didn't do rental enforcement.

"Besides, I bet you can find them if you look," I added firmly.

She looked like a kid whose hand had been found in the proverbial cookie jar. She frowned but said nothing.

"Look, we are trying to find a missing child. *A child.* We need those records. Can you find them?" I asked.

"They are in storage. All the boxes are a mess. They are just thrown together," she grudgingly replied.

"Where are they? I'll go through them myself. Just hand over the boxes." My heart was beating faster now. This was exciting. Maybe we were getting closer. I looked at Crooke. He was deadpan.

She seemed to be thinking for a few minutes and then told us that the boxes were upstairs in the office. My heart was beating more quickly.

"What's the name of the tenant you're looking for?"

We told her the name: Michelle Engron Jones. She lived here with her son Brandon. Summer 1992.

With a fake, weary sigh (she was maybe twenty-eight or twenty-nine years old), she got up to go look for the file. She wasn't exactly hurrying, but we would be patient.

While Crooke and I waited, my excitement was nearly uncontrollable. I hoped the file would give us some information because otherwise, we were at a standstill. It took only a few minutes for her to return with a slim manila file folder in her hands. She gave it to me after telling me that I couldn't take it out of the building. We sat on a small sofa in the office and I read the file.

The file showed that Michelle Jones had leased a two-bedroom apartment. The occupants were listed as Michelle and Brandon. (The apartment number was listed.) It was a ground floor apartment.

I carefully read the "move-in" inspection sheet. I hated those when I rented apartments. They have you sign them the day you move in, excited and hopeful. This one showed that the apartment was clean, all appliances were working, the carpets were clean without stains, the windows worked, and a variety of other things noted on a long check list. Each box was checked and then the document had what looked like the signature of Michelle Jones. Crooke was reading over my shoulder.

I kept reading. There was a move-out check list and handwritten notes. Before long, I was both ecstatic and deeply saddened. The document showed that upon move-out, there was a large brown stain on a significant portion of the smaller bedroom carpet. The notation included a hand-drawn diagram of the room and the area of the stain. It was large. This had to be Brandon's room. The rest of the apartment had been in good shape. Jones had moved out on January 1, 1993, months before her lease expired.

We questioned the Georgetown representative at length. She had not worked at the apartments in 1992. The former manager, Janet Norris, was the person who conducted the move-out inspection. She did not have Janet Norris' contact information. She told us that the apartment had been rented twice since Jones moved out and that the carpet had been cleaned each time someone moved out. She agreed to show us the apartment.

We drove the very short distance to the building. It was close to the front of the property. We parked about ten feet from the apartment building. Only a sidewalk and a few feet of grass and shrubs separated us from a first-floor window. The acting manager told us that the window was in the smaller bedroom of the apartment. The window was close to the ground, maybe only three or four feet above the grass.

We walked in the entrance. It led to a hallway and doors. There was also a staircase leading up from the foyer. We entered and moved to the right of the stairs. The apartment employee opened the door and we entered a sunlit living area. I immediately noticed that there was a sliding door to a small patio that consisted of a slab of concrete separated from the neighbor's slab by a brick wall. Behind this particular unit was a large, deep, empty lot. I didn't notice any lighting behind the buildings and there was no patio furniture.

The apartment was vacant. Crooke and I walked the open living area, small rooms, kitchen, and bath. When we wandered into the small bedroom, I had to hold my breath. There was something eerie here. I'm not known to be a drama queen. But walking into a room where I knew a small child had died affected me. It was terrible and worrisome. How had he died?

The small bedroom was brightly lit by the incoming sunshine. There was a large window, lower than most. It was facing the parking area in front of the building. The secondary bedroom was just across the hall from the bathroom. There was a large closet with folding doors nearly the width of the bedroom at the far side, perpendicular to the window. We could not detect where the stain had been, but compared the drawing on the move-out sheet with the bedroom to better visualize it. It was in the bedroom near the closet and covering most of the room, except where a twin bed may have been against the wall. It looked like some of the move-out drawing showed the stain inside the closet.

I whispered to Crooke, "We need to take a sample for testing." From the look on his face, I could tell that he was way ahead of me. I suspected a crime scene tech would be dispatched.

Neither of us had a camera, so no photographs were taken, but we walked around the apartment enough to memorize its size, shape, and the locations of rooms. The forensic unit of the Marion County Crime Lab met us at the apartment. They were permitted to take a sample of the carpet from the closet and smaller samples from the area designated on the move-out sheet as having a brown stain.

I kept returning to the sliding glass doors. It would have been easy to carry a small body out through those doors in the middle of a dark night and bury it in the large, deserted field.

I suspected we had located the place where Brandon's body had been hidden. Perhaps I was being overly optimistic. I just wanted to find him so that the family who loved him, Kevin Sims and Arlene Blevins, could bury him. Crooke and I agreed that we would organize a group to search the field for Brandon Sims' body.

CHAPTER EIGHT

MANY DEAD ENDS

Although we were making progress — the move-out sheet showing what I assumed might be a very large blood stain, Eli Lilly's records showing Brandon had been removed from Jones' health insurance and as a dependent, and no school records — we needed to try to find the body of the missing child. It had been two years, but forensic pathology would be able to tell us how Brandon died, if he was indeed dead. I still had some doubts. Crooke was tenacious and kept working the case, but he did not share his thoughts or expectations with me. He was very hard to read. Not quite stoic, but really close.

While months passed, Crooke, Lt. Mark Rice, and many others with the IPD searched the most promising sites. I went to help on most of the digs. My first frustrating and feeble effort was in the empty field behind Jones' apartment. It was a huge area. Police officers in uniform and in jeans, many on their day off, spread out over the area and began to look for the body. A cadaver dog arrived. I had never seen such a dog in action. Unlike other dogs, like the blood hounds most of us have heard about, this dog was trained specifically to find deceased bodies, cadavers. The dog was far more methodical than we were.

But he found nothing. Neither did we.

We returned to the exit off I-65 with helicopter support and more dogs.

Nothing.

We worked every angle and looked at exits before and after the one that Jones had identified.

Nothing.

Indiana, while not one of the largest states, started seeming endless. There were too many places to search and too few leads.

CHAPTER NINE

THE JUVENILE COURT CHINS ACTION

The Marion County Prosecutor's Office, with elected prosecutor Scott Newman, was broken down into several divisions. There was the criminal division — divided into Major Felony, C and D Felony — and misdemeanor subdivisions, all housed in the City-County Building. There was a child support division housed elsewhere that prosecuted parents who failed to pay support; the sex crimes division, also in a separate building, prosecuted the rapes, sexual assaults, and child molestation cases. There was a community prosecutor and later several additional prosecutors assigned to prosecute street crimes in other areas of Marion County. (I was assigned to the sheriff's jurisdiction for a while.) There was also the juvenile division, which was in another building out on I-70 near the juvenile court.

Judges were elected to the bench by political party. Democrats and Republicans would each nominate a slate of incumbent or potential judges whose names were placed on the ballot. There were an unequal number of judges elected. Half of the judges were Democrats and half Republicans. The additional judge was elected from either party depending on the number of votes obtained. The nominee from either party with the lowest number of votes was not elected. The political party with the additional judge was in control of the court until the next election. All of the elected judges voted for the presiding judge who administered the courts.

The presiding judge assigned judges to various courts and courtrooms. Most of the judges had courtrooms in the main courthouse, the City-County Building in downtown Indianapolis. Traffic court and juvenile court had their own courthouses outside of the downtown area.

At the time, the juvenile court was run with an "iron hand" by Judge James Paine. Paine had ruled over the proceedings and the assigned magistrates of the juvenile court for more than twenty years with his own sense of fairness, but without much concern for the formalities. He not only controlled the court, but the entire juvenile justice system, running the detention center and juvenile probation. It was a distant planet from the criminal courts where our cases were controlled by laws, rules, and precedent.

Juvenile court was a whole different world. I had never and never intended to enter that universe. The rules were different. Most decisions were based upon the "best interests of the child," making it a place where a judge would control life and death decisions regarding families based upon what he or she thought was best. Judge Marilyn Moores was quoted as saying, when she took over the juvenile court in 2006, "One of the things they did not do here was practice law."

Juvenile proceedings are confidential. Secret. It is a closed club. In most instances, only the child, the child's parents, the attorneys, guardian *ad litem*, court staff, and judge(s) know what is going to or has occurred. Only when the court permits the courtroom to be opened to the public can we know what is occurring there. It is rare.

Juvenile courts hear a variety of cases, including delinquency (children's crimes), paternity, and what are known as CHINS actions. The acronym stands for Child In Need of Services. Most of the CHINS cases are initiated by the Department of Children's Services (known sometimes as the Department of Families and Children) after receiving a complaint of some sort. The department's investigation may have concluded that the child needs to be removed from the home or is in imminent danger of neglect or abuse. Sometimes a family member will initiate a CHINS action.

Judge James Paine was no nonsense. He got to the heart of the matter and did not suffer fools. I knew him by reputation but had never met him. I never would. But as I read the *Indianapolis Star* newspaper one day in early August 1995, a smile crept over my face. There was the haunting photograph of Brandon Sims sitting with Kevin Sims. The headline read **Mom Spurs Trail of Questions**. And beneath that headline, it read, "Woman, who detective says confessed to neglecting child missing for three years, may be ordered by the court to produce the boy." Crooke had gotten it. Brandon was a "child in need of services," meaning that Crooke had gotten a juvenile prosecutor to open a case to determine the health and well-being of Brandon Sims. Judge Paine had kept the high-profile case.

I read with interest the painful statements from Arlene Blevins. "I see kids that might be his age and I look at them and wonder, could that be him? If he's dead, there's no way of knowing what kind of hell he went through. I want to find out one way or another so that I can grieve. The not knowing is the hard part."

The article also suggested that Sgt. Crooke harbored a growing suspicion that Brandon may have been murdered. Darn straight! (Okay, I may have said something stronger ... but this is the gist of it.) Crooke hadn't said a word to me. He had done what was necessary to prove that Brandon was dead. In juvenile court, the judge could order a parent to bring the child to court or send the parent to jail for failure to comply. To avoid jail, Michelle Jones would have to produce Brandon or swear that he was dead.

While I had hoped for the juvenile court order, I hadn't considered that there would be publicity about the case. The press, and their coverage, could either help the case or make it more difficult. As a prosecutor, I never spoke with the press before a trial. It could taint the jury and result in a mistrial. But the article I read that summer was going to help. Hopefully, some of Jones' friends or family who knew something about Brandon would come forward and tell the police what they knew. We needed a break to get justice for Brandon.

I called Crooke and asked him what was going on in the juvenile case. He told me what he could. He couldn't, and didn't, share much. Calls were coming in about the missing child. Leads. Real leads. He and I would soon begin to speak with every friend, contact, and relative we could find regarding what had happened to Brandon Sims.

Michelle Jones was represented in the juvenile court matter by Mark Earnest, the same lawyer who had apparently told her to refuse to speak with the police more than a year and a half earlier. It was rumored that Mark Earnest had been dating one of the nurses at Midtown and that was how he had come into contact with Jones. I didn't know and really, it didn't matter at all. What mattered was whether she could produce Brandon.

Naturally, I followed every newspaper and television account of the juvenile case with interest. My source of information was abruptly halted when, only about ten days later, at Earnest's request, the juvenile judge entered a gag order. A gag order is what the name implies. No one was allowed to discuss the case outside of the courtroom. No statements were to be given, no news coverage, and sanctions could be imposed for any violation. There would be no further press about the case. By then, the court had ordered Jones to produce Brandon Sims or his body. She did neither.

On September 7, 1995, or around that time, when the court threatened her with contempt, she admitted that Brandon was dead. As the court ordered, she took law enforcement to a location where she claimed that Brandon was buried. They found nothing. No trace of Brandon, or any evidence that a small body had been placed in the area. The judge was satisfied that she had "tried" to show the police where the body was buried. She was allowed to leave the courtroom. There would be no finding of contempt. No body had been found.

Information concerning Jones' confession and the search for Brandon's body was plastered on the front page of the City/State section of the *Indianapolis Star*. I didn't know how or whether the gag order had been lifted. I had never considered the possibility that information from the juvenile proceeding would be made public. I had no way of assessing the effect this would have on our investigation or prospective jurors.

How can a young woman forget where she left her dead child? *Impossible*, I thought. She doesn't want that body to be found. Crooke never said a word about that search. Never.

CHAPTER TEN

MICHELLE JONES IS CHARGED WITH TWO COUNTS OF NEGLECT

With proof by way of her confession to Judge Paine that Brandon was dead, as reported in the newspaper, and the other accumulated information we had collected, there was finally enough evidence to file charges. Her confession that Brandon was dead made to Judge Paine and the juvenile court was not admissible, but if Jones tried to claim that the child was in Alaska with her third cousin, her sworn statement to Judge Paine would be admissible to impeach her.

Crooke and I agreed that we still did not have enough evidence to charge her with murder. So she was charged with two counts of neglect of a dependent. My greatest fear was that a smart lawyer would plead her guilty to those charges immediately. With her good looks, good job, and lack of criminal record, most judges would have let her off with probation. Maybe a year or two. But she pled not guilty. Jones challenged the State to prove that Brandon was dead. Apparently, she believed, despite her confession to Crooke and Judge Paine, she could get off.

Michelle Jones was arrested, and Mark Earnest entered an appearance on her behalf. He would be her lawyer for the trial of the case. Because the maximum sentence for Neglect as a B Felony was twenty years, and because of her lack of a criminal record, her bond was set at twenty thousand dollars. By the time Earnest filed a motion to get the bond reduced, she had already bonded out of jail. She left her job at Eli Lilly and went to live in the northern part of Indiana.

CHAPTER ELEVEN

"AIN'T GONNA RAISE NO FREAK"

Michelle Jones had burned many bridges with her friends who had helped her in the years since Brandon's death. Several of these women called and spoke with Crooke or called the prosecutor's office. Crooke and I interviewed many of those friends, and the picture of a selfish, fun-loving, talented, smart woman with questionable parenting skills emerged.

We learned that, for a while, she had brought Brandon with her to rehearsals for shows she produced, danced in, or was otherwise involved in making happen. Several of these maternal-seeming women described Brandon as very thin and shy. A child who kept to himself. The description was in stark contrast to the photographs and stories Arlene Blevins had shared of the fun-loving, plump, curious little boy who had lived with her for most of his life.

Crooke obtained Brandon's medical records and determined that the toddler suffered from a disease with a lengthy medical diagnosis but commonly called "precocious puberty." As a result, although Brandon was only four years old at the time of his death, he was much taller than his stated age. Brandon was the height of an average seven year old. He also had hair under his arms and in his genital area, and his sexual organ and testes were more developed. We asked Arlene, a substantial source of information about Brandon, how his mother reacted to Brandon's diagnosis. Arlene said that Jones told her once, "I ain't gonna raise no freak."

Michelle Jones' trial for the neglect charges was set for October 21, 1996. Crooke and I had never stopped trying to accumulate evidence. One of her friends had hinted that Jones had struck and killed her son, but she wouldn't come straight out and say it. So the charges remained: Neglect of a Dependent, two counts. Jones showed up for her court appearances and never said a word in court (at least not so the court or anyone in the courtroom, except perhaps Mark Earnest, could hear her). I kept expecting her lawyer to discuss a plea, but he never said a word.

Because we only charged her with neglect, if she had pled guilty to the neglect charge, the prosecutor's office could not have charged her with murder later, even if Brandon's body was found, other witnesses contacted us or were identified — not for any reason at all. That is because of double jeopardy. This constitutional prohibition against subjecting a person to jeopardy twice for the same crime would have barred a subsequent prosecution. The neglect charge included serious bodily injury to Brandon. For that reason, if Michelle Jones had pled guilty to the neglect charge, the most serious one, a B Felony, she could not have been charged with murder. She probably would have received a probated sentence.

Jones brazenly pled not guilty to neglecting Brandon. Instead, she insisted, as was her right, on a jury trial.

CHAPTER TWELVE

SOME WEIRD STUFF GOING ON

As the trial was getting closer, Crooke and I had driven away from Indianapolis to interview a witness. We had a working relationship and nothing more. He did not share his thoughts and feelings, only facts regarding the case. As we drove in his unmarked car, he got a call on the radio. It was all in the numeric code that police officers and dispatchers use to confuse the rest of us. I watched Crooke's face. He had gone pale. Really ghostly white. He seemed highly disturbed. He illuminated his blue and red lights for the first and only time while I was with him. He put his foot on the gas and we sped through the light traffic.

"What was that?" I asked, stunned by the obvious concern that showed on his face. He ignored me, but I persisted. "Where are we going? What's the hurry?"

Crooke said nothing for a few seconds and then told me that we were heading to Crown Hill Cemetery. "What for? Has someone found Brandon's body?" I asked hopefully.

"No."

We rode the rest of the way in silence.

Crown Hill Cemetery is the oldest and largest cemetery in Indianapolis. It was first opened in 1863. It was enormous. James Whitcomb Riley, the famous Hoosier writer and poet, was the first person buried in the cemetery in 1917. A lot of famous and infamous people are buried at Crown Hill, including John Dillinger, the bank robber, and James Baskett, the famous actor who played Uncle Remus in the controversial Disney film *Song of the South.* Part of the cemetery lines 38th Street, an east/west thoroughfare in Indianapolis. I had passed it as I drove on 38th Street but had never been on the property.

Crooke drove like a maniac. Fast. Weaving in traffic. Eyes straight ahead on the road. He pulled into one of the driveways that entered the cemetery and headed for a white building. I saw other police cars and the crime lab vehicles already there. I followed him into the building. Several officers, including some with stars and bars on their collars, circled around a table with a brown paper bag on top. Crooke spoke quietly to some of the officers and then cautiously approached the bag and looked in. I stood right behind him.

Crooke told me that some remains or body parts had been left at the cemetery and discovered shortly before he received the call. He added that in the bag with the human flesh, or whatever it was, there was a note. On the note, several names were scrawled in pencil, including his. All the names were of people involved in the prosecution of Michelle Engron Jones.

"Who are the other names?" I asked.

Crooke said, "Your boss, Scott Newman, the prosecutor, for one. Many of the investigating officers."

"Was my name there?"

"No."

Did he sound disappointed? I wondered to myself. I watched the room. It was clear that the find was disturbing to many of the police officers there. I asked if I could look into the bag. "Suit yourself," Crooke said. "Just don't touch anything inside the bag."

I looked into the bag. There was a red, bloody, meaty-looking object with spices and twigs on it. I thought I saw some dirt too. All of it was wrapped in a black cheesecloth strewn with nails and needles. I tried to turn it over. I thought I recognized the contents. I wanted to tell Crooke, but he and the others were in no mood to hear from me. They were on edge. The note had caused consternation, and the meat was some scary stuff. The bag had been found under a tree in the children's section of the cemetery. As a kid, I was raised in Haiti. I love that country and enjoyed every minute we lived there. My sister and I had a horse and went riding in Kenscoff, the mountainous area where there was plenty of air, terrain, and cooler weather than in Port-au-Prince. We frequently saw items that could not be explained. A bottle carefully placed against a tree with a stick coming out of the neck, or clearly sorted pieces of wood placed in an unusual pattern with nails in it. Our friend (the one who took us riding) told us that we were not to disturb those things — they were Voodoo.

The herbs and sticks and other stuff in the brown bag looked like Voodoo to me. And the meaty object looked like something I recognized. Okay, I didn't learn about the particular item I thought was in the bag in Haiti; I got that from Katz's Deli in New York. Beef tongue is a delicacy to us Jewish folks. It's served cold or just slightly warm in a sandwich in the city's better delis. Add mustard.

I giggled. Very juvenile for a forty-three-year-old prosecutor. But I couldn't help myself. There was so much genuine apprehension from the officers that perhaps it was a defense mechanism. Still, I thought it a bit much. So I giggled, but very quietly with my back turned to the others. I hoped to avoid being shot.

Despite knowing what the bag contained, I kept all of this to myself. Maybe I was wrong. Anyway, it was up to the detectives to find out what this was, who placed it there, and what it meant. Crooke caught my slight smile. He said, "Your name wasn't on the paper. Easy for you to smile."

Crooke took me back to the City-County Building. A decision was made to keep this piece of information away from the press and the public. There was no way to connect it to Michelle Jones, but it was evident: she was the only defendant in Marion County who was being investigated by the named officers and prosecuted by Scott Newman's office. The belief this was related to the Jones case was instantaneous and unanimous.

High-ranking officers of the IPD were tasked with telling my boss and the others whose names appeared on the list. Scott Newman never mentioned the list or the beef tongue to me.

About a week later, Crooke told me their investigation concluded that it was a tongue in the bag. I did not smile outwardly. We never discussed it again. Not until nearly a year later. Then the whole incident became key to accrediting a witness who came forward nearly too late.

CHAPTER THIRTEEN

TRIAL PREPARATIONS

The Michelle Engron Jones case was assigned to Judge Jane Magnus-Stinson. The judge had served as chief counsel to Governor Evan Bayh. She was very politically active and effective. She was also an excellent judge who knew and followed the law. I had only appeared in her court once before. This judge had a reputation of being fair but perhaps a smidge defense oriented. She and Scott Newman were of different political parties.

There had been a few routine hearings in the case, but nothing out of the usual. That was all about to change. The State had provided discovery to defense counsel in the normal course. When the various witnesses were interviewed, most of them had already been interviewed by the defense team.

In the months I had been working with Mike Crooke on the case, I had met many of Jones' former friends. I say *former* because after her arrest and release from jail, she left all of these women behind. All of them were African American, involved in the community, and very proud of their heritage. They were dancers, producers, activists, and mothers. As I met these women, I was impressed by their intelligence and integrity. This was especially true of the friend with whom Jones was living at the time of her "breakdown" and Midtown hospitalization.

Whether they wanted to or not, each of these exceptional women had given heartfelt statements to us about her. These women had cared for Michelle Jones. But they had also cared about Brandon. I could detect no reason for them to have lied or exaggerated or withheld information.

As time passed, we did not find Brandon's body. We had heard rumors that when asked if she killed Brandon by beating him, Jones had shrugged and said, "I guess so." While this information made it possible that Brandon's death was murder, the shrugged statement was just too vague. While Crooke and I believed the rumor, it was not enough to charge her with murder.

The defense moved to suppress the confession given by Michelle Jones to Sgt. Crooke while she was at the hospital. Her lawyers wanted to keep her Midtown statement out of evidence so the jury could not consider it.

Crooke testified at length about the conversation that resulted in her admitting to leaving Brandon, a four-year-old child, home alone for about a week. He testified about her saying Brandon was dead when she returned. But most of the hearing was about the conditions under which the statement was taken. Although Jones was in the hospital, she was able to understand Crooke's questions and provide accurate responses. She recalled Brandon's date of birth, the address where they lived at the time of his death, his father's name, the type of vehicle that she was driving. Crooke explained the nurse had chosen the room, had locked the door, and retained the key. He admitted he had not given any Miranda warnings, because she was not in custody. She was a walk-in patient who was free to leave the room and the hospital at any time. And Robbie Flippin, the nurse, was a neutral witness who was present for the entire statement.

The Court found that the statement was voluntarily given. It would be admissible. That was great news.

I listened to Crooke's testimony and was impressed. Unlike many officers I have heard testify, Crooke did not seem defensive when he was cross-examined. He seemed very truthful. But on cross-examination, he was asked whether Michelle Jones was sobbing as she spoke with him that first time. Crooke said that she was sobbing. At times, Jones pulled into what her lawyer described as the "fetal position" while speaking with the detective. This contrasted with his impression that she was cold and unemotional. I made a note to ask Crooke about that later.

Jones' lawyers also asked that the State be prevented from accessing the juvenile court records. They did not want me, the criminal prosecutor, knowing what had taken place in the juvenile court. More importantly, they did not want me to be able to obtain the sworn testimony of the witnesses who had testified, including Jones. So even if I knew what she had said and done, I would be unable to prove it.

The State purchased the transcripts of the juvenile court hearings when we learned (from reading the newspaper) that Jones had been ordered to produce Brandon's body and, in failing to do so, also testified that he was dead. We needed that transcript to prevent the defense from denying it. But Judge Magnus-Stinson disagreed. She ordered that the State was not permitted to obtain the transcript. This was a major victory for the defense.

The upcoming trial was highly publicized, as the case had been since Michelle Jones was first called into juvenile court. With the press coverage, more witnesses contacted the police department and our office. Crooke was shaking every bush that he could and had received cooperation from many of Jones' former and current friends.

CHAPTER FOURTEEN

AN IMPORTANT LEAD

With the trial only a month away, Cale Bradford, chief trial counsel in the Marion County Prosecutor's Office and another one of my supervisors, received a phone call. It was September 20, 1996. Brandon had been missing for more than four years. The woman did not give her name or any contact information at all. What she did tell him was that she knew "Malikia." She explained that Malikia also went by Michelle Jones. The caller told Bradford that she had prepared the cow's tongue. She said that Jones had confessed that she (Michelle/Malikia) had *beaten* Brandon to death. The caller also said that Malikia had told her, when asked to show the police where Brandon's body was buried, Malikia misled them. The caller hung up, stating that she just wanted to tell the truth about Malikia and Brandon but did not want to get involved.

Cale Bradford was incredulous. How could a witness drop such incriminating information in his lap but "not want to get involved"? He immediately contacted me.

"Michelle finally told someone the rest of the story," Bradford said when I came into his office.

I could hardly wait to tell Crooke. He had really worked hard on this case and deserved to know right away about the new evidence. When Crooke got to the prosecutor's office, Bradford repeated what he had been told in detail. An anonymous telephone tip might otherwise be discounted. I mean, the case had been all over the papers and television newscasts. But it was the cow's tongue that gave the witness credibility. No one knew about that. It still riled the police officers. Maybe Scott Newman too, but he never said a word about it to me.

"What's her name and phone number?" Crooke asked him. Crooke seemed ready to drive to wherever she was and take her statement. That's when Bradford explained the situation. Nonetheless, our telephone system recorded the telephone numbers of incoming calls. He jumped into the case. He waited a day and then called the number and spoke with an older woman. Apparently, the telephone number was for a Lillian P. Teamer, in Gary. She claimed that she had never called our office but would check with her daughter.

A few days later, Bradford's telephone rang and this time the caller identified herself as Clarissa Dunlap. Clarissa Dunlap repeated what she had told him in the first telephone call: Michelle Jones admitted that she beat Brandon to death and left him to die. Dunlap recounted additional details of her conversations with Malikia. She seemed to have insight and evidence of what happened to little Brandon Sims.

Bradford learned that Clarissa Dunlap, the caller, was a nurse who had worked for the Indiana Department of Corrections, a mother, and a Santeria Vodun priestess. He convinced her to travel to Indianapolis, on a bus ticket purchased by our office, to give her statement. She arrived on October 7, 1996. Her statements resulted in dramatic changes in the case.

After spending nearly all day with Clarissa Dunlap, Sgt. Crooke, Lt. Mike Rice, and Margo Jones, a paralegal from the prosecutor's office, I finally satisfied myself that Michelle Jones had murdered her son. A decision was made about the future of the case. The next day, I discussed this with Scott Newman and Cale Bradford.

While Bradford, who had spoken directly with Clarissa Dunlap was enthusiastic, Newman was hesitant. He was a politician and elected official. He worried about public perception, and the result of a failure to convict. He knew that I was certain about Michelle Jones' guilt, but he was worried about whether I could convince a jury of her guilt. Despite his reservations, he gave me permission to proceed.

CHAPTER FIFTEEN

MURDER CHARGE FILED

On October 22, 1996, the State of Indiana filed a new charging Information against Michelle Engron Jones. Michelle had just turned twenty-four years old.

In some states, only a grand jury can charge a person with murder. The grand jury considers the evidence presented to it by the prosecution. If the grand jury finds insufficient evidence, it can "no bill" an indictment. However, since the prosecution presents evidence to the grand jury and the accused is not permitted to provide contradictory evidence, an indictment is fairly easy to procure. Usually when a grand jury investigation results in a "no bill" or failure to indict, it is because that was the direction the prosecutor wanted to go. That way, the grand jury could be blamed in politically-charged cases. When a grand jury issues such a charge, it is called an indictment. One sitting judge famously concluded "a grand jury would 'indict a ham sandwich,' if that's what [the prosecutor] wanted."

In Indiana, prosecutors did not have to go to the grand jury to charge a person with murder or other major crimes. Grand juries were used more to investigate ongoing, long term, criminal conduct and political corruption. Instead prosecutors would file an Information, which is a charging document. When that document was filed, a judge would review the affidavit supporting the Information to determine whether there was probable cause to believe that a crime had been committed and that the person charged had committed it.

The new Information charged Michelle Engron Jones in two counts: Murder, and Neglect of a dependent as a Class B Felony. The maximum sentence at that time for murder, as charged, was sixty years in prison. The charging Information alleged that Michelle Engron Jones, on or between July 1, 1992 and August 31, 1992, did knowingly kill another human being, namely Brandon Sims, by striking at and against the person of Brandon Sims, thereby inflicting mortal injuries upon Brandon Sims, causing Brandon Sims to die. This formal language was necessary to follow the legal definition of murder. In essence, the State alleged that Jones had killed Brandon by beating him, causing his death. The State would also have to prove that Brandon died between July 1, 1992 and August 31, 1992.

Murder was the first count, or charge. The second charge was neglect. In count two, the State claimed that Michelle Jones had custody of Brandon Sims and that when she knowingly abandoned him, he died.

The original trial date for the two neglect charges had been days away. It was also election season. Judges in Indiana are elected by party affiliation and there was a great deal of pressure on all of them. The timing was not good, but the case had finally broken. Michelle Jones was not going to get away with killing this beautiful child, if Mike Crooke and I had anything to do with it.

The judge and defense counsel were furious. At first, it was implied that the timing of the filing of the murder charge was somehow political. In truth, it had nothing to do with politics and everything to do with evidence. We *finally* had the evidence. Jones and her lawyers had rolled the dice. For nearly two years, she could have pled guilty to neglect and received a short or even probated sentence. Now she faced up to a lifetime in prison for killing Brandon.

Michelle Jones was taken into custody. She was dispatched to the Marion County Jail.

CHAPTER SIXTEEN

MOTIONS, MOTIONS, MOTIONS

A hearing was held on the day that the new Information was filed, and defense counsel and the court were incensed. The timing of the charges disrupted the initial trial setting. There was one important new witness and a few who supported her testimony. And there were plenty of accusations of misconduct. These were directed at me. I guess it was to be expected. Mark Earnest, who had been Jones' lawyer since she was at Midtown Mental Health/Wishard, was joined by two other defense lawyers connected with but not employed by the public defender's office. They vehemently opposed the filing of new charges. They demanded a speedy trial. They raged against me and the prosecutor's office. All of these motions were legally proper. The animosity was confusing. But Michelle Jones had killed her son. In my book, murder was the correct charge.

Michelle Jones, as her lawyers now referred to her, omitting her maiden name, had been out on bond since her initial arrest for neglect. Despite admitting that she left her four-year-old child alone for a week, and that he had died, the court had released her on bail. From what witnesses told us, Michelle, or Malikia as she had renamed herself, used that time for partying, clubbing, planning, meeting men, and having a grand time. She moved to Gary, Indiana, then back to Indianapolis. Apparently, no worries, no regrets. During the same time, Kevin and Arlene were devastated. Even after the juvenile court proceedings, they refused to give up hope that Brandon was alive.

Two significant motions were filed by the defense. One was a motion to exclude all of Jones' statements because of Indiana's *corpus delicti* rule. *Corpus delicti* is Latin for "body of the crime." Normally, in a murder case, the body of the victim is proof of that person's death. That is the independent proof of a crime. Here, there was no body. There was no significant physical evidence, only a stained carpet when Michelle moved out of her apartment. We had no blood. No DNA. No physical evidence at all. But we had a missing child. We had her testimony that he was dead. We had to prove that a crime was committed before her incriminating statements to police and her friends would be admissible. It was going to be a challenge. Especially with a ticked off judge and three lawyers blasting away on the other side.

The other motion that the defense filed was "let to bail," which was a motion to permit Jones, now charged with murder, to remain free while the trial was pending. In most murder cases, the defendant is committed to jail prior to trial to ensure that she does not flee or harm anyone else.

In Indiana, if a defendant could prove that the charges against her were tentative with a paucity of proof, she could be released from jail and remain free before and during her murder trial. The legal standard required a defendant to prove that the evidence or "proof against her was not evident and that the evidence was not strong." It would be interesting to see what the defense team came up with.

Should Jones be released? She had been free since 1992 when she killed Brandon. She had appeared at every court date after she was released on bond for the neglect charges. I believed that it was likely that bail would be granted. In my book, she deserved to be incarcerated, but the judge would decide.

Judge Magnus-Stinson ordered that we make all witnesses available to the defense within twenty-four hours. She intended to hold a hearing to determine whether there was sufficient evidence for the case to go to trial. If the Court found there was insufficient evidence, she could dismiss the case, with prejudice. Judge Magnus-Stinson was not a happy camper. *Put up or shut up*, I thought to myself as I ducked out of the courtroom. There was work to be done.

The filing of murder charges was news. The fact of the murder charge was splashed over the front of all the local newspapers and was the lead story on many of the television news channels.

Jeff Modisett had been the Marion County prosecutor before Scott Newman was elected. Modisett was closely aligned with Evan Bayh, the democratic governor of Indiana. He was probably an acquaintance, if not friend, of Judge Magnus-Stinson. He had announced his bid to run for Indiana attorney general. He was the Democratic candidate and strongly favored to win the upcoming election. Modisett was quoted on the front page of the *Indianapolis Star* as saying that it was nearly impossible to convict a person of murder without the body. He echoed what many prosecutors and defense lawyers seemed to think of the case: it could not be won.

Great. I hope Scott Newman hasn't read the paper yet, I thought as I headed into the first day of the *corpus delicti* hearings. I was gratified to find that Cale Bradford joined me to oppose the motion. He had been in contact with Clarissa Dunlap and he was chief trial counsel. I was glad to have him.

I took a deep breath as I entered Judge Magnus-Stinson's courtroom. I looked at Bradford. He smiled confidently. Mike Crooke was also in the courtroom. He looked grim.

CHAPTER SEVENTEEN

THE *CORPUS DELICTI* HEARING

The hearing on *corpus delicti* included testimony on October 24, 25, 28, 29, 30 and November 4 and 6, 1996. The Court was thorough and allowed the defense to call and examine most of the State's witnesses. In addition, defense counsel called witnesses to support their motion to have Michelle Jones released on bail before the trial.

Although the defense feigned surprise when we added witnesses, testimony revealed that Jones' lawyers knew about and had spoken to every one of them. It made sense, of course. She knew who she had spoken with and what she had said. Only the State didn't know. But the defense made a major issue of the "added witnesses." I was impressed that the defense had been in contact with so many witnesses and was well prepared. They defended her fiercely.

Jones' lawyers were allowed to take sworn statements from Clarissa Dunlap and Saundra Holiday. Then they examined them in the courtroom as part of their motion hearing. There was no jury present; the judge was still annoyed with the "late" filing of the charges and so the examinations were brutal with scarce judicial intervention. Questions that would never have been allowed in the presence of a jury were permitted over my objections. The witnesses were subjected to more than the "thorough and sifting" cross-examination that the law permitted. They were taunted, argued with, challenged on religious issues, and sometimes brought to tears. Despite the onslaught, one by one, each witness testified to what they had seen, learned, or heard from Jones.

A key issue during the hearing was why Clarissa Dunlap decided to come forward at the late date that she did. Her testimony drove Cale Bradford from the courtroom. Clarissa Dunlap walked confidently into the courtroom and down the aisle to the witness chair near the judge. She was wearing an attractive black skirt-suit. She was tallish and attractive. She maintained exceptional eye contact and looked directly at the judge as she was being sworn. She settled comfortably into the witness chair. There was no sign that she had been dragged down to Indianapolis at the last moment, taken a noisy and lengthy bus ride, been deposed, and was now was being questioned again.

"I'm exhausted but she looks great," I whispered to Bradford. He agreed.

Clarissa Dunlap testified that Michelle Jones, who introduced herself as Malikia, had contacted Clarissa Dunlap's mother, who was a well-known Santeria priestess, for help. Apparently, this happened after Jones moved to Gary following her arrest on the neglect charges. Clarissa Dunlap's mother was known as Mama Yea-Yea.

In July of 1995, Jones came to Mama Yea-Yea's home to participate in a Misa, which is a religious service in the Santeria Vodun religion. There were several women who participated in the service. It consisted of prayer and calling upon one of the participant's (Aria) spirit guide, Josefina. During the service, Josefina warned Jones that she was "in trouble." Prayers and trances took place.

Aria, who was no longer speaking through Josefina, looked at Jones and said, "Brandon was killed, and it was not just an accident." She did not respond. After a few other events, she was asked to leave for a few minutes and then she returned to participate in closing prayers.

As the service was breaking up, Clarissa Dunlap spoke to Jones in Mama Yea-Yea's kitchen. She asked what had happened to Brandon. Her testimony was elicited by Steve Laudig, one of the defense lawyers.

"What did Michelle tell you?" Laudig asked.

"That she had been beaten and put in closets," Dunlap replied.

"She, being Michelle, had been beaten and put in a closet?" Laudig inquired to clarify the word tense issue.

"Yes. She had been beaten and put in a closet," Dunlap said flatly.

"Did she identify who had beaten her and put her in a closet?"

"She didn't. She never said to me a first and last name," Dunlap responded quickly as the lawyer stopped.

"Who did you understand it to be?"

"Her husband at the time."

"And did she say anything else?" Laudig continued.

"Yes."

"What was that?" Laudig wanted to know.

"He had beat her and put her in a closet, and when she got out of the closet, she ran out of the house and when she came back, Brandon was dead, and she buried him," Dunlap enunciated each word to emphasize what Jones told her.

"What?" I whispered to Bradford. "She wasn't married at the time. This is a new story."

He nodded, apparently mesmerized by the testimony.

But, as the testimony revealed, Jones later changed her story. In September of 1995, Clarissa Dunlap, whose nickname was Duny, prepared beef tongues in a ceremonial manner. She described the tongue, wrapping, and contents to a T. She testified that Jones was present as she prepared it. Dunlap wrapped the tongues and gave them to her.

"Michelle placed the tongue at Crown Hill?" I mouthed to Crooke. "Witness tampering?" It was certainly an attempt to dissuade someone, but it appeared to be the prosecuting attorneys and police, not a specific witness. "Clarissa Dunlap said *tongues*. Plural?" I asked Crooke. He nodded.

We'd only found one tongue. I wondered where the other one had been left.

Dunlap testified that the purpose for the tongues was to cause problems to the people who were talking and to the people involved with the court system. The name of the judge was not included with the tongue. Jones also gave Dunlap dirt from Scott Newman's home or office, photographs of Newman and his wife, and of Modisett and his birth date and other statistics. She wanted Clarissa Dunlap to do harm to these people.

Dunlap did several other "works" for and with Michelle Jones to try to prevent a trial. Jones had given Dunlap some additional information. She told Dunlap that she kept taking child support from Kevin Sims after Brandon was dead "because the baby's father owed me that."

She also told Dunlap more details about how she disposed of Brandon's body. Friends of the two told her that Jones had admitted to burning Brandon's body before she buried him.

Clarissa Dunlap testified that she continued to do things to assist Jones through the summer and fall of 1995. In November, she stopped doing work for Malikia.

"Did you do a work for her in November?" Laudig's tone was sarcastic as he pronounced the word *work*. He had begun to smirk.

"No. I stopped doing works in October," Dunlap responded evenly.

"That was the time of your last work for her?"

"Yes."

"You didn't do any work for her after October or November?"

Was Laudig going to repeat every answer? I asked myself.

"I didn't do any work for Malikia after October," she reiterated.

"Why?" he demanded.

"Because there were a lot of unusual things that were happening," Dunlap responded. Just the way she said it, I knew something was coming. And it was not going to be a plus for the State.

"What unusual things?" he dared her to respond.

"One, they found the beef tongue, sir." Dunlap said it as though Laudig already knew the answer.

"How do you know this?" he commanded.

"Because it was on the news or something. I don't remember exactly how I found out that they found it, so I cannot tell you exactly about that," she said.

Okay, I said to myself, *nothing too weird so far*. Well, there was a tongue, but I was sure the judge had been to Katz's or the Carnegie Deli in New York City. Nothing horribly shocking so far.

That was until Dunlap finished by saying, "I had unusual phenomena happening at my house, candles exploding, I heard babies screaming, things were flying across my house." She said this as if it were an everyday occurrence.

As Dunlap testified, Cale Bradford began to shrink down in his seat. He edged away from where I was sitting, apparently distancing himself from the witness and the case.

"What things?" asked Laudig, obviously enjoying himself.

"Well, in one particular instance, a glass just completely moved across the table, wham, and it just moved across the table and fell on the floor. One that was on my dresser just fell," she retorted.

"Yesterday, you said the following, according to the excerpt of your statement prepared by the prosecutor's office: 'candles were exploding, things were falling off the walls, sudden movement, wham, pow, crashing, strange sounds,'" Laudig read.

"Yes," Dunlap said matter-of-factly.

"What were the strange sounds?" Laudig asked.

"Babies screaming."

"Smells?"

"Yes. Burning smells. Yes, that's what I said," Dunlap repeated.

"And that was the last time you did any works for Michelle?" This was the third or fourth time he asked. I could have objected, but Dunlap gave him the same response every time.

"What do you mean, when those things started happening?" she asked.

"Right," he said.

"No. The last time I did work for Michelle was in October. Those events continued to happen for a while," Dunlap explained.

"How long is 'a while'?"

"Up until December that I know about."

I wondered how this testimony would affect Judge Magnus-Stinson. She would determine Clarissa Dunlap's credibility for purposes of the motion. I would worry later about how a jury might perceive this information. The questioning continued.

"How did you finally stop these things from happening in your house?" Laudig asked, sneering.

"Because I went into prayer and prayed and asked God to please forgive me if I had done anything wrong. To please forgive me if I had lied. To please forgive me for my ignorance about the situation. And please put Brandon's soul at some rest. And I promised that I would tell the truth if anyone ever asked me about the situation regarding Malikia and Brandon," Clarissa Dunlap answered seriously.

"But you didn't call the police in November of 1995, did you?" Laudig accused.

"No," she concluded.

None of this was *too* disturbing to me. I mean, a Santeria priestess for a star witness? Hey, Michelle Jones picked her, not me. Crooke looked at me accusingly. Neither of us had heard anything about this when we had interviewed her. But then again, we never asked her why she decided to speak with us. Bradford walked out of the courtroom. I guess it was too much for him. Crooke looked like he wanted to leave too.

Clarissa Dunlap continued to answer, clarifying and expanding on her testimony. She described a disintegrating relationship with Malikia. She testified that she observed Jones kicking a young child and knocking him down. Apparently, Steve Laudig already knew about the incident, or that's how it appeared from his questioning. He did not allow Dunlap to describe in detail what she had seen Jones do to the child, aside from kicking him and knocking him down.

Laudig changed course and tried to show that Clarissa Dunlap had a motive to come forward. Specifically, that she and Michelle Jones had both wanted the same man. Jealousy is one of the oldest motives known to mankind. It is the stuff of many Bible stories. Was that true? I wasn't convinced that Clarissa Dunlap was inspired by jealousy as Laudig accusingly examined her. But I wasn't the jury. Or, for that matter, Judge Magnus-Stinson.

Despite the interesting detours in questioning, Dunlap was very specific and unshakable about Jones' confession. I got to question her after the defense had spent hours asking her questions. She was obviously tired.

"Would you tell us, specifically, ma'am, whether or not you asked the defendant at that time whether she had beaten Brandon?" I asked.

"Do you want me to tell you the conversation?" she responded inquiringly.

"Yes."

"Okay. The conversation was to Michelle regarding her telling the truth about the situation with Brandon. And when I questioned her about it, she said, yes, I beat Brandon. I said 'what happened to the story about the closet' and she said 'my whole house was a closet.'"

"When you indicated she started telling you about beating Brandon, did she admit to you during that conversation that she had beaten him on more than one occasion?" I probed. "Yes."

"And specifically, what did she tell you she would do after beating Brandon?"

"She said that she would lock Brandon in his room with saucers of food and cups of water."

"And did she [Michelle] tell you what she had done immediately prior to leaving for several days and then coming back and finding Brandon dead, what did she tell you?" This was the key testimony.

"She had beat Brandon," Clarissa said quietly.

"And did she say what she did after beating him?"

"She left him in a room with some saucers of food and a cup of water." Apparently, that wasn't the entire answer. Clarissa Dunlap would elaborate. But I couldn't get the saucer of food out of my mind. Why would Brandon need a saucer of food and a cup of water?

The witness continued, "I asked Michelle, I asked Malikia, I said, 'Malikia, what did you do, did you beat Brandon to death and leave him?' And she said, 'I guess so.' I was upset and she was upset. And she said, 'I guess so.' Like that."

Dunlap told Judge Magnus-Stinson that Michelle Jones also told her that she intentionally misled the police as to the whereabouts of Brandon's body. She took them to the wrong spot.

Dunlap testified the other ceremonial works for and with Michelle Jones she'd done included a "hotbox" and piquets. For those ceremonies, my name and the judge's name were added to the others. There were five different ceremonies that Dunlap performed for Jones. Each was intended to harm or quiet the subject. Dunlap testified that she had spoken with Jones' lawyer, Mark Earnest, nearly a year before she had come forward and called Bradford. Earnest had been the one to provide her with the name of the judge to include in the hotbox. Jones had given her the names to put on the beef tongue list.

While I thought little of this (instead focusing on the flying glasses, babies crying, and the smell of burning), apparently Judge Magnus-Stinson took it far more seriously. At the end of Dunlap's testimony, the Court had some questions.

"You indicated that you did this hotbox, which was in what month?" the Court asked.

"I did that in October," Dunlap replied.

"And in addition to Prosecutor Newman and Mijiza (Saundra Holiday) and Jeff Modisett, my name was included?"

"Are you Jane Magnus-Stinson?" Dunlap asked innocently.

"I sure am," the judge replied.

It was one of those moments in court. How does one anticipate that kind of exchange in a murder case? If the judge was upset, her response did not show it. Her face revealed nothing.

"Well, yeah," was the witness's response.

"What does that entail?" the judge wanted to know. She was very serious.

"What do you mean?"

"Doing a hot box?" the judge clarified.

"Just to make them fight so they won't be able to get along with each other," Dunlap responded, for the first time somewhat defensively.

"Miss Marger Moore asked you something about *causing harm to people*, if any of your intention in performing these ceremonies. I mean, there's a big difference to me between making people not get along or not communicate well, and causing them harm. Were any of your ceremonies intended to cause physical harm to people?" Although she was demanding a response, the Court's tone was even, almost quizzical.

"Let me – I have to explain this to you. When Malikia, I was doing the stuff for Malikia, she had full knowledge of what the stuff was for. I cannot sit down and predict for sure if what I do at that time will cause a person physical, mental, or emotional, or spiritual damage. The work that I did for Malikia was to cause problems for the people. Now the manner in which the problems manifested, I had no way specifically of knowing what exactly was going to happen. It was no way that I could have said, 'okay, Scott Newman's dog is going to bite him in the morning.' I can't do that. All I can do is to do the work, make the request, that is it."

The judge looked flummoxed. Was she worried? Like a curse? Huh? Did she hear the important stuff that Clarissa Dunlap had divulged?

Clarissa Dunlap did not run in the same circles as Mahalia "Kadisha" Aamir, Saundra Holiday, or Michelle Jones' Indianapolis friends. She lived in the northern part of Indiana, a three-hour drive from Indianapolis. We wanted to show that she could only have known about the beating to death from Jones.

Throughout all the testimony, Michelle Jones sat impassively with her lawyers. There were moments when she was animated, but rarely. In those moments, I would see her lean over to Mark Earnest and through tight lips, say something. She looked down at the table most of the time. She did not make eye contact with any of the witnesses except for Saundra Holiday. She looked at her with a hard, unblinking stare.

The Court took a break. Crooke just gave me a look that would have stopped a charging elephant. He walked into the hallway without a word. He wasn't exactly terrifying, but I did not want to be the target of that look ever again.

I sat alone in the courtroom. I thought about Clarissa Dunlap's explanation and her analogy to Scott Newman's dog biting him. Did she somehow know that the elected prosecutor really did have a dog? It wasn't a well-known fact. Indeed, the only way I knew was from Scott Newman's holiday card that had a family portrait on the cover: Scott, his wife, and their adorable beagle. How did Clarissa Dunlap learn about the pup? Coincidence?

I had little time to ponder the testimony that had shaken Bradford and Crooke or to consider the mystical implications of dog bite references. There were other witnesses and each one provided a small bit of additional evidence of murder. I knew that the building blocks of a case were there. I just had to assemble them, if the Court let us move forward.

Cale Bradford never returned to the courtroom. We never discussed the impending trial again.

Defense counsel questioned Carol Kohlmann, the forensic serologist for the Indianapolis-Marion County Crime Lab, who had examined the carpet samples from Jones' and Brandon's apartment. The results were persuasive but not absolute.

The defense lawyers also questioned Donita Berlyn, the person at Eli Lilly who was responsible for keeping records about Jones' employment and benefits. She testified that Michelle Jones had insurance through Eli Lilly, beginning in 1990 for herself and Brandon. Because Eli Lilly is self-insured, all claims go through Eli Lilly and the records were in the custody of Eli Lilly. She worked at Eli Lilly from 1990 until January 1994, when she took a leave of absence for "educational purposes." She returned to work at Eli Lilly nine months later.

Ms. Berlyn testified that the first claims for Brandon's health coverage began on June 1, 1990. There were additional claims in June, July, and August of 1990. There were no claims for Brandon after that date, although there were several claims for Jones. There were no prescriptions, routine vaccinations, physicals, or any other care for Brandon. When Jones took a leave, she requested only single coverage. She did not cover Brandon. When she returned to work at Eli Lilly on September 12, 1994, she requested that her records be corrected to show no dependents.

The hearings dragged on, but because of the publicity, another witness contacted the Indianapolis Police Department. Her name was Carol Moody. She had information about the Georgetown apartment. Apparently, she had entered the apartment with Janet Norris, another witness whose testimony had been heard by Judge Magnus-Stinson.

Every day of hearings, Michelle Jones' attorneys filed and argued additional motions. Motions to exclude evidence. Motions to exclude witnesses. Throughout the process, I was denied the ability to review the juvenile court records. The defense had a preview of the hearing through that testimony. The court was going to protect her in every way. I was okay with that.

Kevin Sims was called into court for the hearing, as were most of the witnesses the State had named as potential witnesses at the trial. The defense lawyers were questioning nearly every trial witness so there would be no surprises at trial. Michelle Jones had the benefit of knowing what every witness would say at trial, if her attorneys asked the right questions during the hearing. This would be one of the most unsurprising trials ever had. That was if the judge allowed the case to go to trial.

CHAPTER EIGHTEEN

THE FOUR DAYS MICHELLE JONES WAS AWAY

I was learning more about the case and the witnesses. It was like a dress rehearsal for the trial. As a trial lawyer, I never had that opportunity before. The closest I had come to it was a mistrial, a horrible situation requiring that a case be retried because of some error of law that occurred during the trial. This was different.

As a mother, I had been stunned that another mother could leave her son alone in their apartment for days. I would have been worried every second, frazzled. The question of what Michelle Jones had been doing during that time was a significant one. But I had never really asked the witnesses about that. Crooke and I had been too focused on the length of time away, the return, and most importantly, what had occurred before she left Brandon alone. But the pretrial hearings allowed us to learn more.

As I listened to the testimony, I could not imagine the type of person that Michelle Jones had to be. *Heartless* was the only word I could use to express it. It was unimaginable. Several of the witnesses' testimony touched on those days away, but I was most struck by the testimony of Deborah Asante. She had no reason to lie. She was a lovely woman. Elegant, nearly regal. Deborah Asante seemed proud and maternal. I was again struck by the quality of friends Jones had — at the time she killed her son and afterwards. These women provided support, encouragement, opportunities.

While she had endured a difficult childhood, these women in her life were incredible.

Deborah Asante was the founding director of the Asante Children's Theatre. She and her company produced three plays a year, giving children from eight to eighteen the opportunity to learn about the theatre. It was a magnificent community enhancement.

Asante testified that she first met Michelle Jones in 1988 or '89 through the Mentor Mother's program. Asante was directing a play and Jones had been selected to be an actress in the production. From that first meeting and for years, she and Jones remained close.

Jones worked for Asante and the children's theatre as a production manager from 1991 until about 1994. Asante testified at the hearing about meeting Brandon at rehearsals and at the annual picnic. She told Judge Magnus-Stinson about her learning from Jones that Brandon had gone to live with his father's mother in Tennessee.

I asked her about the critical time frame. "Did you take any trips with Michelle Engron Jones during the summer of 1992?"

"Yes. We went to a theatre conference together," Asante responded.

"What was the role that Michelle Engron Jones was supposed to play at that conference?"

"Well, as production manager and as artistic director, we were both there to represent the company, and network, and learn, learn as much as we could about making the company a better theatre company."

"Where was that convention?" I said, hoping that another piece of the puzzle was falling in place for Judge Magnus-Stinson.

"It was in Detroit."

"And approximately when was that?" I needed to prove that Brandon had been killed between July and August 1992. That was what we had claimed in the charging Information.

"It was early July 1992. I think right after July 4th," Asante recalled.

"How long were you and the defendant gone for that convention?"

"I think about four days."

"Did you learn where Brandon was during the four days that you and the defendant were in Detroit?" I asked, eliciting from the witness another lie by the defendant.

"She said he was with a babysitter." Deborah Asante was shaking her head slightly and looking at Jones reproachfully.

Michelle Jones was "networking" and meeting people while Brandon Sims was home alone? I couldn't believe it. But it got worse. She told Asante that she met someone "nice" at the convention. While Brandon did what? Alone. *Are you kidding me?* I thought. *Her child, four years old, was home alone and she's meeting men?* I was astounded. I watched the judge's face. She revealed little. Michelle Jones looked at the defense table. No eye contact with Deborah Asante, her former mentor.

"Did Miss Jones ever tell you that she went to visit that man?"

"Yes." Asante nodded.

"Did she indicate when she'd gone to see him?"

"She might have told me on the way home that he had asked her to come visit," Asante replied.

Also startling was Asante's description of how Jones continued to volunteer after Brandon Sims died. Asante told the court that "Michelle was the best production manager I've ever had, before or since." In the two years after Brandon was killed, she continued to volunteer at Asante's Children's Theatre.

Asante described Michelle Jones the summer after Brandon died and for the next two years. "She was efficient. If she said she was going to do it, she would do it. She had an eye for detail. She was, she had energy that ... but this is ... you know, this is all ... well, she had good energy with the kids. She was, she would think of things that I didn't think of. She was good. She cared a lot about what everybody thought. She had a drive, you know."

I talked to Crooke in the hallway. He didn't seem surprised. I wondered if years of being in the homicide unit had hardened him that much. I was incredulous. I wanted to go home immediately and hug my children. I didn't want to believe that a person could be so pitiless.

When the hearing resumed, Asante explained that Jones was living with a mutual friend, Mahalia "Kadisha" Aamir during late 1993 and 1994. She testified to what Jones had disclosed about Brandon Sims. Asante and I were pretty aligned in our reaction to the story she told about abandoning Brandon. When asked about the details of the disclosure, she testified, "I had kind of lost it after that. I remember that Michelle said that she tried to bury him, and I don't remember much else because I just couldn't believe, I couldn't picture this happening, and I kind of just spaced, but I do remember Michelle saying that."

It was shortly after this conversation with Asante and Mahalia "Kadisha" Aamir that Jones admitted herself to Midtown. When she released herself, she never again spoke with Deborah Asante about Brandon. Never returned to Asante Children's Theatre. Asante only saw her a few times after that and before the hearing.

State witness after witness was examined by the defense and cross-examined by the State. Every critical witness was a strong, independent, accomplished African American woman. In addition to Deborah Asante, the testimony of LeTava Muhammad (Parker) was solidly persuasive. She had been one of Michelle Jones' closest friends, attended mosque with her, and provided daycare for Brandon for several months. LeTava had more contact with Brandon in the months before his death than anyone else we had been able to locate. Her testimony was damning.

CHAPTER NINETEEN

LETAVA MUHAMMAD (PARKER)

LeTava Muhammad had come forward as a result of the publicity surrounding the juvenile court proceeding. She had called Mike Crooke and he had followed up by taking her tape-recorded statement. Muhammad testified that she called the police because the only photograph of Brandon in the newspaper was of him in diapers. She wanted to offer photographs of Brandon that were more up to date with the last time she had seen the child. She thought that if the police were looking for Brandon, more recent photographs would be helpful.

I really didn't know why the defense had called her as a witness, other than to establish that she did not personally witness Michelle Jones beat Brandon to death. This line of questioning had become rote with many of the State's witnesses. During her questioning, she indicated that she met with Steve Laudig, who had given her a copy of the transcript of her statement given to the police.

Mark Earnest was examining Muhammad. The defense team had divided the witnesses among themselves and I had not yet determined whether there was a pattern, or if it was just a random process based on which attorney was available on the day the witness testified. Muhammad was confident but very quiet and unassuming.

LeTava Muhammad testified that she met Michelle Jones through the mosque that they both attended, sometime in 1991. The last time she saw Brandon was at her home two days after her son Alejandro's birthday party. The party was held on July 1, 1992.

Earnest asked whether the party had been a sleepover since Brandon remained at Muhammad's home for an additional two days. She explained that Jones promised to pick Brandon up after the birthday party. But without a telephone call or any other communication, she just left Brandon until she showed up, unannounced, two days later. After she took Brandon away on July 3, 1992, Muhammad never saw him again.

I asked her to describe her relationship with Michelle Jones.

"As I said, we met at a place of worship where we were both worshiping at the time, and we became friends, and eventually she severed our friendship, or severed the relationship for her own personal reasons. She wanted to move on in her life, and I can respect that, but that was our basic relationship. We both were married, we had things in common, we both were parents, our husbands spent time together, and we spent time together. We visited together. We did social things as well. We travel — even to date, we have a lot of the same interests. We are, we're active in a lot of the same community events, and so we had a lot of things in common."

Earnest asked Muhammad about the timing of Jones leaving the Nation of Islam. Apparently, the two had remained friends after Jones separated from Damon Jones and left the mosque. It was obvious that this was not the answer that Earnest hoped to elicit. However, it was what LeTava Muhammad testified about Brandon that was remarkable and sad.

She testified that Brandon spent a good deal of time at her home without his mother present. Brandon played with her children. But there was much more.

Mark Earnest asked, "And what types of things, if any, do you recall telling the police officers or the prosecutor about how Michelle behaved around Brandon, or treated Brandon, rather?"

She didn't hesitate. "Brandon was very crazy about his mom. I mean, she's his mother. And they had a relationship that was a, for the most part, a typical parent-son relationship. There became some difficulties around the time of the divorce proceedings, or when the divorce was coming into play. There was tension. It got to the point Brandon began to complain, or tell me things, and I'm sure he told other people things, that were going on at home. And Michelle was a pretty rational person. I mean, I don't mean to say that like outside of normal, but she was not unapproachable about anything. Any concerns I had with Brandon at all, but he began to tell me that she was leaving him home alone, or, or locking him in his room, or he was always hungry, or he was being punished by not being allowed to eat. And if I spoke with Michelle about any of these things, there would always be, of course, a logical explanation, or at the time they lived in apartments, and so if she went to take the trash out, assumingly she had to leave out of the building, to do so, and so I, it would always be, well, hon, she's not leaving when you see her leaving out. Those were concerns of his." Muhammad was sort of stumbling. Guilt mixed with loyalty?

Muhammad explained that she didn't take everything that Brandon said at face value. "And as a parent, if a child comes to you, it's almost hard to just take what they're saying. You have to try to interpret it from a parent's point of view, and then discuss it with an adult that would be involved. Brandon was very ... he, he got to the point where he was always hungry. I mean, it was a given at my home when he came to visit that I would just feed him. I didn't, I couldn't say exactly what was happening within the home, but the results of it were obvious.

"The results of it were becoming more and more obvious or apparent, and he, he did become withdrawn in the sense that he felt the need to sneak and ask me for things, and not that he tiptoes, but just talking to me in low tones, or always asking me for something to eat. Generally, the signs that I'm speaking of are not eating with the other children. Typically speaking, if we were all at a function and our children are here and it's a social occasion and we're feeding all the children, Brandon very likely would say, 'no, that's okay, my mom said I had food at home' or he didn't eat or things of that nature. Well, he may turn right around and come back and ask you for something."

Mark Earnest tried to lead her to the conclusion that Brandon's precocious puberty was the reason that he was always hungry. She did not agree. "It didn't make sense to me at that time simply because he was also saying that he wasn't allowed to eat, and that I did know. I knew myself that there were times that as a form of punishment he was not allowed to have his dinner or something of that nature, and from Michelle, as I stated, at that time." Muhammad had observed Jones withholding food from Brandon as punishment and discussed it with her. She added that she had seen Brandon being hit by Michelle Jones and also observed bruises on him.

LeTava Muhammad described an escalation of abuse. Brandon would admit to her, when alone with her, that his mom had caused the bruises, but when Jones was around, he would blame it on himself or other things. "I've never seen Michelle draw blood on Brandon, but I have seen her get very angry over something that I would say would be rather minor, and that those times I'm speaking about would have to be times when she did become stressed over going through a divorce." She continued. "We discussed these things, and that was during a time that I was, like I said, I babysat for him during that time.

"Michelle never hit Brandon in public. Her punishment for Brandon in public was to make him stand facing a wall or sit quietly near a wall, and that could go on as long as, till she told him he could move."

Mark Earnest asked whether this was a "timeout." Muhammad distinguished a "timeout" from Brandon's punishments. "No, this was standing facing a wall, not moving or anything. You just stand there facing a wall."

Muhammad was asked again about Jones' disappearances. She described another time when Jones failed to pick Brandon up at her home and left him there for days.

Earnest changed subjects and focused his questioning on Damon Jones. He implied Michelle Jones was shunned when she left the mosque and her husband filed for divorce.

Muhammed disagreed. "But as far as from the church, I would have to say no, because in all actuality, or from our religious aspect, that would not be anyone's place to do something of that nature or say anything about whether you, you know, were to marry or divorce."

Earnest also tried to suggest that it was Damon Jones who was abusive. But Brandon never told her that Damon Jones had done anything to him. Nor had Jones accused Damon of abusing her or Brandon.

Mark Earnest completed his questioning and I rose to my feet. My first questions to LeTava Muhammad were about the photographs she had provided. There were four of them, all taken at Alejandro's birthday party in July 1992. She described Brandon, and the photographs showed his height and a far more slender child than the pudgy toddler pictured in the father-and-son photograph.

Muhammad revealed during questioning that in the months between January and July 1992, while the Joneses' divorce was pending, Brandon was at her home four to five times a week. Michelle Jones was working at Eli Lilly and involved in a number of community activities. Muhammad recalled that Jones was involved with a theatre group. I asked her how long Jones continued to be involved in community activities.

"Those continued actually, actually until, I would say, pretty recently. Even after the last time I saw Brandon, Michelle was always very active in community activities. I saw her, always saw her at Kwanza festivals. She was active in the children's theatre, dance troupe. She did a lot of things that; she was just an active person, so this was not unlike her."

I wanted the judge to know how Jones treated Brandon before his death. Muhammad knew all of that. She testified that the bruising became worse, more frequent, during the divorce.

"In fact, you saw him with busted lips nearly all the time," I stated.

"I saw him with busted lips on at least more than one occasion. When I say busted lip, the skin on the lip being broken where blood had shown," Muhammad replied. "Michelle used a shoe to whip Brandon."

When Earnest objected to the term *whip*, Muhammad clarified that she had seen Jones hit Brandon repeatedly with a shoe.

"And, during the months, as it got towards the summer of 1992, on at least three or four occasions, you saw Michelle Engron Jones hitting Brandon with a shoe to the extent that you felt she had lost control?" I asked.

"To the extent that I felt that it was far too much. It was more than what the incident required," she said emphatically.

I asked where on Brandon's body she was hitting him with a shoe. She answered, "The hitting would be, initially it would probably start on, on the butt, or the buttocks … but if he squirmed, which, of course he did, being hit, she continued to spank him wherever it landed."

Brandon told Muhammad that he had been hit or beaten with a shoe when she was not present. And the hitting escalated as July 1992 approached.

"In addition to seeing bruises, busted lips, observing hitting, and knowing about his hunger, were there also occasions, ma'am, where you observed that Brandon had what appeared to be injuries to his head?" I queried.

She responded that she had seen Brandon with these injuries twice in the couple of months preceding July 1992. Brandon told Muhammad that his mother had injured him, unless she was present. Then he changed his story and denied that it was her who had hit him.

I asked Muhammad about her son's birthday party on July 1, 1992. She explained that she expected Jones to drop off Brandon for the party and come back to collect him a few hours later. She did not return for Brandon until two days later. And she had done the same thing three times before in the period between February and July 1992. No prior arrangements or discussion about leaving Brandon: she just didn't pick him up.

"That, and that was the standard. If he had been at my home for a couple of days, it was usually with no prior arrangement," the witness explained.

Jones and LeTava Muhammad had discussed Jones' divorce from Damon Jones. She never said that Damon was hitting her or Brandon. The problem, according to her, was that Damon wasn't paying enough attention to her. She felt neglected.

Through this testimony I kept thinking about Arlene Blevins, Brandon's paternal grandmother. She had raised him from the time he was seven months old until he was nearly three years old. She desperately wanted to be in Brandon's life. She wanted to help in any way possible. She was available to take him if he had become too much for Jones. And Jones had friends. Many good friends.

Muhammad explained that as Jones kept leaving Brandon, without explanation or prior agreement, and as the injuries and punishments escalated, she and her husband offered to keep Brandon. Jones refused.

"I offered to ... well, I asked her if she would allow Brandon to come and live with me and my husband and our children for a while until she got through her divorce and got back on her feet emotionally. It took a great toll on her, and she did tell me that, no, she had considered foster care for him but she didn't think that she would be doing anything of that nature at this time, and I took her for her word. I-I took her word for it."

The guilt in her voice was palpable. She was choking out these words.

LeTava Muhammad never saw Brandon Sims after July 3, 1992. Each time she ran into Jones, she asked to see Brandon or at least a photograph of him. Jones never showed her a photograph and never had Brandon with her.

I realized I had not gotten back to questions about what Earnest had called "timeouts." So, I asked her, "How long was the longest period that you observed this four-year-old child compelled to face the wall?"

She replied, "It could go anywhere from ten minutes to thirty-five minutes to even longer. However long we were having a conversation, or if she was doing something else."

I reminded Muhammad her about her statement, given to law enforcement, and she confirmed that at least once she was present when Michelle Jones made four-year-old Brandon stand in a corner, unmoving, for about two hours. During that time, she warned Brandon that if he moved, if he was "fidgety," as Muhammad described it, he would have to stand or stay in the corner longer.

I had no further questions.

The judge wanted to know when and how the relationship between Jones and LeTava Muhammad had been severed. The judge asked the witness, who responded, "Right after the birthday party. I continued to try to contact her over a couple of weeks, calling her at work, and with her not returning my calls. And when she did finally return my call, she told me that she wanted to put that part of her life behind her, and she thought it best that our relationship not continue." She testified that the conversation took place about three weeks after Alejandro's birthday party.

Michelle Jones wanted to "put that part of her life" behind her. I wondered if that included Brandon, who was obviously dead by the time she broke off her friendship with Muhammad. Easy to comprehend. How would she explain that Brandon was no longer living with her? Just change gears. Get divorced. Stop being a mother because you killed your son. And "put that part of her life behind her."

I tried to consider how I would try to present this testimony to a jury. The defense had already moved to prevent the jury from learning about the prior beatings, the insane discipline, and her not feeding the child. The rules of evidence prohibited the use of character evidence, including prior bad acts by a criminal defendant, such as those described by LeTava Muhammad.

Muhammad's testimony at the *corpus delicti* hearing could be excluded from the trial of the case for a number of legal reasons. Criminal defendants cannot be convicted because they have "bad character," meaning that they are not nice people or have done bad things in the past. In theory, using prior bad conduct in a criminal case would allow a jury to convict a defendant based upon what he did previously instead of for the crime charged.

For example, if a defendant was accused of cruelty to animals for drowning his dog, the prosecution could not introduce evidence that he had previously drowned his cat to convince the jury that he had done the same to his dog. This is because the prosecution would be using that prior bad act to try to prove that the defendant did it again, acting in accordance with his bad character.

But there are many exceptions to the rules prohibiting prior bad act testimony. If the man had been convicted of harming his cat, and that conviction was one of moral turpitude, it might be admissible. Also, if the man had drowned his cat by dangling her from a pier at the end of a rope, and the dog had been killed this same way, then the evidence might be admissible to show a plan. If he had killed his neighbor's cat and then the dog, and both had been eating his flowers, that might be admissible to show motive. Despite a multitude of exceptions to the rule precluding the use of this evidence, it was most often deemed inadmissible because of a catch-all rule. That rule directs that if the evidentiary value of the evidence in establishing the crime under consideration is outweighed by the prejudice that it would cause the defendant, then the evidence should be omitted from the trial.

The State would argue that the evidence was admissible to prove Michelle Jones' motive, intent, and knowledge. But there was little guarantee that Muhammad's testimony would ever be heard by the jury.

How does a young woman do the things to her child that Jones had done? Would a jury believe that she was not responsible because she'd had a tough childhood? How far does that take a woman as obviously intellectually gifted and talented as defendant Jones?

I considered who would make the best juror for this case. Would young African American women side with Jones? What if they had children of their own? Would men feel sorry for her? She was, after all, an experienced and accomplished actress. I had little time to focus on jury selection as we continued to have hearings nearly every day. This was not my only case; I had all of the arson cases for Marion County, another major murder trial, and other professional obligations.

Oh and I had young children myself. My oldest had just turned seven and the youngest was not yet four years old. In between witness preparation, hearings, and running out to fire scenes, I attempted to be a mother myself. I was beginning to suspect that the huge pot of macaroni and ground beef that I made every Sunday for the family was becoming a despised food. I promised myself that I would cook really good and diverse meals again once the trial was over. Takeout from Number Two Wok would be a thing of the past. Steve, my husband, was doing an incredible job picking the kids up after daycare and school each day, helping our oldest with her homework, going to their soccer games and other events in my absence. But the mere thought of his cooking scared all of us. Just not in his wheelhouse.

I wondered if Sgt. Crooke had a wife and kids. I had never discussed it with him but assumed that he did. He was quiet most of the time, but what's the saying? Still waters run deep or something like that. He came to court every day. He seemed to wear the same blazer. I wondered if he had several in the same dull gray tweed, worn and a bit wrinkled. He paid attention. He did very little talking and a great deal of listening. I avoided his "look" for the remainder of the hearings.

CHAPTER TWENTY

THE COURT RULES

On November 6, 1996, we all reconvened in Criminal Court Two. Michelle Jones was at the counsel table with her three lawyers. I sat at our table with only Mike Crooke. As the judge took the bench, I looked over at Michelle Jones. She was expressionless. She was dressed in a jail uniform, looking tiny in the oversized shirt and pants. She had been held in the Marion County Jail since her arrest on the murder charge.

Steve Laudig argued first for the defense. His oral argument supplemented the written brief the defense counsel had submitted to the Court. His argument focused on the fact that Clarissa Dunlap was a Santeria priestess who was jealous because her boyfriend had been stolen by Michelle Jones.

The State's response reminded the court of Arlene Blevins' testimony. Michelle Jones had told Arlene that she was not going to raise "a freak," referring to Brandon's precocious puberty and reminded the Court of the witnesses who described the harsh treatment and discipline she had imposed on this young child. We argued that Clarissa Dunlap did not know any of the other witnesses, yet her testimony was corroborated by several of them. While she was the only witness to confirm that Jones confessed to beating Brandon to death before leaving him alone for days in their apartment, other evidence supported her testimony.

In his rebuttal argument, Laudig urged the Court to disregard the testimony that linked the beating of Brandon Sims to his abandonment and subsequent death. Laudig, with his voice raised and his face flushed, expounded, "The State's witness, Saundra Holiday, can be accurately described as an unmedicated bipolar manic depressive who hears voices while in a car driving up to Chicago, and has a mystic communication with our client. Is that a credible witness? Okay. Now, Clarissa Dunlap, she's not mental, but much of her evidence was obtained immediately after going through a trance state with phantom babies running through walls of the hall." He continued with his sarcastic diatribe, ignoring that all these women had been chosen as friends and confidants by his client, not the State of Indiana.

The State responded by directing the Court to facts that had been proven during the hearings. Before the arguments on the *corpus delicti* motion and let to bail motions had been completed, all three of her lawyers had spent considerable time and words trying to convince the Court that the State could not and had not provided sufficient evidence to go to trial.

Michelle Jones' lawyers asked the Court to provide a written order containing what were called findings of facts and conclusions of law. In Indiana, a party is permitted to insist that the judge provide a written order ruling on certain matters. A written order facilitates an appeal, but also clarifies the issues for trial. Because a written ruling was required by law, the Court did not rule after the arguments were completed, instead taking the matter under advisement.

I hated the phrase "under advisement." It meant that we would not know how the Court would decide the issues for some period of time. I would have to exercise patience. And so would the defense, despite a fast approaching trial date.

Several days later, Margo Jones collected my mail from the Criminal Court Two prosecutors' mailbox and brought it to my office. There were two orders that she had retrieved.

She handed me the first order. It was titled order setting bail. This was not a good sign. Bail is usually not permitted when the charge is murder. But the defense had argued and presented testimony to support bail in this case. Michelle Jones had shown up for every hearing before we had charged her with murder and there was little reason to expect that she would flee now. The law provided bail in murder cases *only* where the defendant could establish that the State's proof was weak and the presumption in favor of the charge was minimal. The Court was permitting Michelle Jones to bail out again.

The Court also used this order to make some additional evidentiary rulings. The Court refused to allow the carpet samples and testimony concerning the preliminary findings of blood and subsequent findings of human proteins in the carpet taken from the Georgetown apartment in evidence. The jury would never know about that evidence.

Next, the Court discussed LeTava Muhammad's testimony about the beatings with a shoe, standing at the wall, bruises, busted lips, and other injuries. We had argued that the evidence was admissible to show Michelle Jones' intent. The Court refused to allow the evidence for that purpose unless the defendant "opened the door." Opening the door by one party can allow the other to introduce otherwise inadmissible evidence. If, during the trial, Jones' lawyers put on evidence or asked questions that led to an inquiry about her intent to kill Brandon, then the jury could learn of the prior abuse. The Court also disallowed the testimony that Brandon was deprived of food as punishment, to prove motive or knowledge with the same caution. The defense had to tread carefully lest it open the door to the presentation of this evidence. But the jury would probably never learn about the escalating violence against Brandon Sims at the hands of his mother.

I wondered if there would be a trial. On the other hand, why would the Court have ruled on these issues if she intended to dismiss the case?

The bail order included some factual and legal conclusions on the propriety of bail.

> The Court has concluded that the evidence elicited supports an inference that Brandon Sims was murdered. Having so concluded, the alleged admission to Clarissa Dunlap is admissible, and the Court must also consider it in evaluating the strength of the State's case on the murder charge.

The Court discussed Clarissa Dunlap and felt that she was not a very credible witness because of the jealousy, the alleged burglary of her former boyfriend and Michelle Jones' homes, and her perception that Jones' confession was somewhat equivocal. Because the Court was allowing Dunlap to testify, the jury would determine her credibility at trial.

The Court set bond at fifty thousand dollars, which had to be posted by a surety.

Well, Michelle Jones would have her freedom — for a while longer. The State had been precluded from using some very strong evidence of Jones' guilt. The carpet evidence was out. And the impact of LeTava Muhammad's testimony was nullified. Could I prove the case? I wasn't sure.

Margo handed me the second order from the Court. I've never in my life read the last chapter of a book first, but in this case, I immediately flipped to the last page of the ten-page order. It read: "The court therefore concludes that the State has met its minimal burden of proving a *corpus delicti* as to both Counts I and II, and Jones' confessions can be admitted." I put my head on my metal desk. I would be able to present the evidence to a jury. While I had to prove the murder by a much higher standard at trial, Brandon had his deserved chance to get justice. Proof beyond a reasonable doubt would be far more challenging than meeting the "minimal standard" the Court had found. Crooke and I were going to do our best.

In the nine pages before it reached its ultimate conclusion, the Court described the testimony of the witnesses and applied the law to those conclusions. Some of the Court's findings were helpful for our trial preparation. The Court found that the testimony and evidence supported an "inference that Jones knowingly left four-year-old Brandon alone while she went to Detroit for at least a four-day period. No person has seen Brandon alive since that time, which supports an inference that he died then. The brown spots found on the carpet in Brandon's room when Jones moved out supported an inference that Brandon was harmed in such a manner as to bleed there."

The Court never mentioned Clarissa Dunlap in this order. Nor did the Court comment on Saundra Holiday. That would be left to the jury. Presenting Clarissa Dunlap's testimony in a way that the jury would believe was up to me.

I had five full days before the trial would begin.

CHAPTER TWENTY-ONE

JUST BEFORE THE TRIAL

The defense, Sgt. Crooke, and I had spent so much time preparing for and then conducting the hearings in this case that exhaustion had set in. While I can't speak for the defense lawyers, though like me they had other cases, other responsibilities and hopefully a life aside from this case, Sgt. Crooke was responsible for supervising all the homicide detectives on his shift and more. He hadn't spoken a word in court other than when he testified, but he too had to be worn out. He had located, shuttled, and met with our witnesses. He had dedicated all the time we needed to prepare. He had been a trooper.

Shortly after the Court's orders were entered, Michelle Jones and her attorneys filed a waiver of trial by jury. This meant that the defendant wanted to give up her right to have the case heard by twelve jurors from the community. Instead, she wanted Judge Magnus-Stinson to hear the case. Well, she already had. The defense knew that the State, who also has an absolute right to a trial by jury, wouldn't waive a jury. We had all read the Court's orders. So the motion was an attempt to further bias the Court in the defense's favor and against the State. It was a legitimate tactic. I believed Judge Magnus-Stinson, despite her irritation with the timing of the murder charges, was a fair and knowledgeable judge. But this case had to be decided by the community. Is it really okay to beat your child, leave him alone, and then hide his body? Is that neglect or murder? A jury would tell us. It was obvious the State would not agree to such a waiver. We insisted on a jury trial.

On Monday morning, I entered Scott Newman's office with some news that may have altered the course of the case. He lambasted me. He could have been heard across the street at the Market. He shared his frustration with my performance at the hearings, the Santeria issues, and suggested that I was now afraid to try it. He pointed out that this was a high-profile case and he was the one who had to be re-elected. His comments were demeaning and more hostile than I had ever experienced. He blasted me with, "just get down to the courtroom and do your job." I just nodded my head and got onto the elevator.

Great way to start a trial, I thought, holding back tears. I was earning less than I had paid my secretary in my private practice in Florida. I am a native Floridian and had lived in Ft. Lauderdale before moving with my husband to his home state. I loved being a prosecutor, but I certainly was not in it for the money. I didn't think that I deserved to be berated either. But I had to get my mind back into the case.

When I reached the courtroom, the judge expected to avoid a trial. I announced that I was ready for trial. The judge insisted that I return "upstairs" to convince Newman. The judge thought that I was joking (I wasn't) when I told her that I would take my bodyguard with me. Crooke was armed. He would be approaching Newman. I'd let him take the lead.

After only a day's delay, the trial was set to begin. A large jury pool of seventy-five Marion County residents had been brought into the court room. Whenever a case has been in the news, a larger group of people has to be questioned about their ability to serve. That is because many people have seen the news or read an article about the case and have formed an opinion about the defendant's guilt or innocence. Defendants are entitled to jurors without fixed opinions, jurors bound by the presumption of innocence.

All of the jurors were brought into the courtroom and seated in the jury box, and the pews in the back of the courtroom. Each had completed a written questionnaire that the defense had prepared. The State had input into the questions or removal of questions and the Court had ultimately approved of the contents. The jurors had been instructed to complete them individually before they entered the courtroom. This would save a great deal of time and provide more accurate information about the jurors.

When jurors are questioned as a group, their answers tend to be briefer and more consistent with what the juror perceives the Court (or lawyer or his fellow jurors) wants to hear. Written questionnaires, reviewed individually, give us greater insight into that juror's thought process, notions, biases, and knowledge about the case. As I looked over the jury pool, there were a relatively large number of African Americans in the venire. That was unusual for Indianapolis. For some reason, I took it as a good sign. I wanted Michelle Jones to be judged by her peers, not by mine.

CHAPTER TWENTY-TWO

CALL YOUR FIRST WITNESS

Voir dire is what jury selection is called. It is the process of asking questions of prospective jurors and determining whether they can sit as the judges or finders of fact in a case. While this questioning is supposed to help seat a fair jury, no one, except perhaps the judge, wants a fair jury. Every side wants a jury more favorable to their side than the other side.

We started with seventy-five prospective jurors. Many of the venire had read or heard about the case. Several had already formed strong opinions about the guilt or innocence of Michelle Jones. (We weren't permitted to ask whether they were convinced of her guilt or innocence.) There were only five prospective jurors left when we completed the questioning and arrived at a jury composed of twelve people. We also selected two alternate jurors. The alternates are selected so that if a juror became ill, or unable to continue, there was another person who could fill the slot. Indiana required a unanimous verdict of twelve jurors.

The Court gave the jury some preliminary instructions. They were told not to read or listen to anything about the case. The jurors were warned not to form an opinion about Michelle Jones' guilt or innocence until all the evidence had been submitted. They were told the start and stopping time for each day of the trial, and about note taking. The judge seemed to enjoy communicating with the jury. She tried to put them at ease.

The jury was excused for the day. But we kept on working. Jurors frequently think that their time is being wasted when they are sent home early or ushered to the jury room. In fact, most of that time, the lawyers and judge are working. After the jury was selected, we spent the day working on jury instructions, which would control the trial and be read to the jury at the end of the trial. We needed to know what law the judge would apply before we started making our opening statements or presenting witnesses. It was a lengthy process.

The next day the jury arrived, settled in the jury box, and was given some additional instructions. Each side gave their opening statement. This meant that I started, because the State had the burden of proving the defendant's guilt. I slowly explained to the jury, maintaining eye contact with each member, what the evidence was going to prove (I hoped). After I finished, Jones' lawyers had the right to give an opening statement. They also had the right to wait to do their opening statement until after the State had presented all its evidence and rested. Defense counsel made an opening statement right after mine. It was a good choice, I thought.

The real trial was about to begin. Lt. Mark Rice was at counsel table because Crooke was making one more effort to find the body of Brandon Sims. Rice and I were alone at the prosecution's table, which was closest to the jury. Jones and her three lawyers, all dressed in professional-looking clothing, sat at her table. I thought she looked young. But she also looked resolute. She seemed confident but quiet. I had never heard her speak a single word.

Indy 500 fans listen for the words "gentlemen, start your engines." Race horses and their jockeys wait for the gunshot to start their race. For lawyers, it is the phrase "call your first witness" that begins the real trial of any criminal defendant. I listened as Judge Magnus-Stinson said those words. Then I stood and followed her instruction.

The first witness for the State was Dr. Ora Pescovitz, Brandon's physician for his precocious puberty. Usually, the first witness in any trial is supposed to be interesting, enlightening, and have a depth of knowledge about the case. But sometimes a witness's schedule dictates the order in which they are called to court. Dr. Pescovitz was only available at this time and would not be able to reschedule. So she would start our case.

Dr. Pescovitz told the jury where she had obtained her undergraduate and medical degrees, her training after medical school, and that she was a pediatric endocrinologist. She explained that endocrinology involved disorders of growth and puberty, as well as diabetes.

"My area of special research interest is in the area of precocious puberty and I've published extensively in this area, having published more than fifty articles on the topic."

I asked her whether she was "considered probably a nationally renowned expert in the field of precocious puberty."

"Without wanting to sound arrogant, I would say yes." This serious physician, wearing her white lab coat with her name and the name of the hospital embroidered on it, smiled a bit. "I'm the director of pediatric endocrinology at Riley Children's Hospital."

I knew that the jury, freshly minted as it was, had to be wondering what on Earth this woman was going to testify about in a murder trial. They seemed focused on her every word.

Dr. Pescovitz testified that she first met Brandon Sims on June 15, 1990. He had been diagnosed as having precocious puberty. He was two years and seven months old. Michelle Jones had brought him to his appointment. The physician conducted a vast assortment of tests after she examined Brandon, trying to pinpoint the cause of his disorder. The testing actually excluded some causes of his condition, such as a brain or testicular tumor, or a condition involving the adrenal glands. He was finally diagnosed with an extremely rare condition: **gonadotropin**-independent precocious puberty. Dr. Pescovitz shared these results with Jones in July 1990.

"What are the physical characteristics that one would have observed, a layperson, about Brandon as a two year old or a two and a half year old that would have been different from what one would have seen in a normal two year old?" I asked.

"Probably the most obvious thing to a layperson observer would be his large size. Children with precocious puberty end up having a pubertal growth spurt at a prematurely early stage. So they grow too fast for their chronological age," she explained.

"And is that in all areas of their development or only their physical development?" This was fascinating stuff. I hoped that the jury thought so as well.

"Their physical development is accelerated; their emotional development and intellectual development is age appropriate," she told the jury, looking in their direction. When she examined Brandon, his intellectual and emotional development were age appropriate.

The direct examination of Dr. Pescovitz continued as she described how, if left untreated, Brandon's condition would have affected him. We would later prove that Michelle Jones failed to obtain any treatment for Brandon, despite having excellent health insurance and the financial means to pay for any needed medications or care.

"When a child has precocious puberty, and specifically the type, the rather rare type that Brandon had, what would one anticipate in terms of the developmental stages of that illness or disease ... do we call it a disease or illness?"

"It's a condition. If left untreated, I suppose that's what you're after, if it's untreated. If left untreated, the long-term consequences of this condition, the most significant long-term consequences are that a child will continue to grow very rapidly during the childhood years, that child will end up having premature fusion of the growth plates, and then as an adult will be extremely short. There are some other manifestations of the disorder during the childhood years in that the child is producing an excess of the pubertal hormones and those may manifest in an increase in body odor, an increase in the secondary sexual characteristics that are associated with puberty."

When Dr. Pescovitz met with Michelle Jones, first for the evaluation and later to explain Brandon's test results, the physician told her about the ramifications of his condition and the need for treatment.

Jones brought Brandon in for visits on August 3 and 14, 1990. She also called and provided a family history that revealed no genetic link for the condition. Dr. Pescovitz recommended that Jones start Brandon on a therapy to lower his elevated testosterone levels. Although she prescribed therapy for Brandon's condition, Dr. Pescovitz never saw Brandon again and he was not treated at Riley Children's Hospital for his condition.

Defense had no questions for Dr. Pescovitz but reserved the right to recall her. I had omitted to ask her about medical records requests. I received the Court's permission to do so.

"Dr. Pescovitz, did any other physician, at any time, request copies of Brandon's medical records?" I asked.

"Not to my knowledge. We sent copies of our communication to his original referring physician," Dr. Pescovitz declared.

No one else, at any later time, requested her records or the testing that had been done to determine Brandon's diagnosis or to treat him. I hoped the jury understood.

We were done for the day. The jury was given the Court's standard warnings not to read the newspaper or listen to the news about the case or discuss the case with anyone or form any opinions about the case.

With the jury gone, the judge instructed the State to have a full day of witnesses ready to testify the next day. She intended to get this case to the jury as soon as possible.

One serious issue was the health of Mahalia "Kadisha" Aamir. Aamir was the person with whom Jones lived from Thanksgiving of 1993 until she went to Midtown at Wishard and for a few weeks after she was released from the hospital. It was Aamir to whom Jones first confessed to leaving Brandon alone. Aamir had been admitted to the hospital for a serious brain issue. It appeared she had a tumor and would not be able to attend the trial. This would be a significant blow to the case. Kadisha Aamir's credibility, which was to be judged by the jury, was essential. If she was unavailable, we could read her prior testimony to the jury, but it would not have the same impact. I was worried for Ms. Aamir, whom I respected and liked, and for our case.

Steve Laudig renewed his motion for a gag order. He said, in open court, with at least one reporter present, that we were "searching." Anyone with any knowledge of the case would assume what he meant was that we were searching for Brandon's body. I was annoyed he made such a comment with reporters still present in the courtroom. The judge seemed to share my annoyance. She denied the request again.

After I left the courtroom, I met Kevin Sims in my office. I planned on calling him the next day and wanted him to be prepared. As I talked to him, it dawned on me that he was still in denial.

"You know that Brandon is dead, don't you?" I asked this large black man who seemed like a gentle bear from a bedtime story. He immediately broke down, sobbing.

How had I become so disconnected with this father's feelings about his son? The guilt I felt in saying that sentence, with such a lack of empathy, was enormous. It took Kevin some time to regain his composure. I knew he kept on hoping that Brandon was alive. He had been in the juvenile court hearing and heard with his own ears Michelle Jones' admission that Brandon was dead. Yet he still hoped that he would be reunited with his son. Without Brandon's body, Kevin Sims would never give up hope.

CHAPTER TWENTY-THREE

BRANDON'S FATHER AND GRANDMOTHER TESTIFY

Kevin Sims was the first witness of the day. I wanted to be careful not to harm this man further by questioning him or subjecting him to the defense's cross-examination. It's always a balance. Trying to prove a case without inflicting further emotional damage. It was not an easy task. I knew the defense would focus on the fact that Kevin was in prison when Brandon was murdered. It was all they had, except that at seventeen he had impregnated Jones at fourteen.

I would let the jury know these "bad facts" so that they would not come as a surprise. As to his criminal history, Kevin's charge was nonviolent. It was his first offense.

"The State would call Kevin Sims, Your Honor," I announced.

The jury knew Kevin was Brandon's father. They watched the large man walk down the aisle to the witness stand. He sat down. His head was lowered, and he spoke in a soft voice.

After he was sworn to tell the truth, I asked Kevin about how he met Michelle Jones. He was a junior at Arsenal Tech High School and she was a freshman. They continued to be together when she became pregnant. He had been at the hospital for Brandon's delivery. His son was born on November 11, 1987.

Brandon's birth certificate was put into evidence. Kevin said that he had a relationship with Brandon. "From the moment he was born, I was there," he explained. He was the father. He had a car seat in his car for Brandon; he cared about his son's safety. Kevin told the jury that while he did not marry Jones, he went to court to legitimatize their child and agreed to pay child support. He was biologically and legally Brandon Sims' father.

The paternity judgement was placed into evidence. It was dated May 22, 1988, and showed that Michelle Christina Engron and Kevin Lamarr Sims were the parents of Brandon Lamarr Sims. She was given legal custody of Brandon, and Kevin was to have visitation with his son.

Kevin testified about bringing Brandon to live with him and Arlene Blevins.

"Why did he come to live with you?" I inquired.

"Because the defendant Engron or Miss Jones was placed into the Guardians Home, and at that time, they was wanting to put my child as a ward of the court. So, the counselor of the Guardians Home gave me and my mother the option to come and pick Brandon up to come and get him to keep from being a ward of the court." He was still speaking shyly but was beginning to open up.

"And did you want to do that?" I wanted the jury to know.

"Yes, we did," he answered without hesitation.

Kevin said that he had gotten Brandon from Jones. Brandon lived with Kevin and Arlene from the time that he was six or seven months old until he was three years old. Kevin identified some Walmart professional photographs of Brandon taken shortly after he came to live with Kevin and his mother. He also had a photograph of Brandon at about three and a half years old, with a woman's legs at a stove in the background. The child was not smiling, but instead staring into the camera. Brandon was dressed in a long-sleeved horizontal-striped shirt, pants, and sneakers. He did not look happy. The photo was marked and entered into evidence.

While Kevin was in jail, his mother, Arlene Blevins, took care of Brandon. She brought Brandon to visit Kevin and mailed photographs frequently. When Brandon was returned to Jones, Kevin tried to keep in contact with his son. He wrote to Jones, who apparently responded once, enclosing the photograph of Brandon in the kitchen with her at the sink. The jury was not permitted to learn the content of Kevin Sims' letter or her response.

Kevin was released from jail on September 11 or 14, 1992. He had tried to write letters to Brandon while he was incarcerated. I asked simple, short questions to which he replied.

"When you got out of prison did you make any contact or attempt to contact the defendant?"

"Yes, I tried to contact the defendant on her job."

"Where was she working?"

"At the time, when I was trying to contact her, she was working at Eli Lilly."

"Why did you try to contact her?"

"Because I wanted to see my son," he said.

Kevin made arrangements when he was released from prison to resume paying child support. The monthly support came directly from his paycheck. He had a job and was living with his mother. I asked Kevin to explain to the jury what attempts he made to see Brandon.

Steve Laudig objected. This was a pattern. When Kevin became comfortable and was trying to tell his story, Laudig would object. This time he objected asserting that Kevin's efforts to find his son were "irrelevant." The Court disagreed and permitted him to respond.

"Like I said, I tried to contact her on her job and she would always be late for a meeting or you would get her voicemail and you would leave messages."

I wanted to slow down Kevin's statements because he had begun to speak more rapidly. He was obviously getting upset. Laudig kept objecting to testimony about Kevin's increasingly insistent attempts to see Brandon.

"Let me slow you down," I said. "Did you actually ever speak with her, the defendant?"

"Yes, I did," he said.

"How many calls and voicemail messages had you left before you even got to speak to her in person?"

"I would say numerous amounts. I can't exactly recall the number." To me, his testimony rang true. He refused to embellish or exaggerate. He was telling it like it was. I wanted him to just tell the jury what he did.

Kevin explained that when he left voicemail messages they were just, "Please contact me. I would like to see Brandon." Michelle Jones never called him back. He testified that she knew the place where he was living with his mother. She never came by with Brandon. When she finally called Kevin back, she told him that she was late for a meeting and would call him back later. She never did. For months, Kevin kept trying to contact her to see his son.

"Did there come a time when you actually went in person to try to find the defendant to see your son?" I asked.

"Yes, I did. In spring of 1993, I went to Lilly's to try and see her in person. That's when I was informed that she was on an educational leave." He didn't know where she lived and so he didn't try to contact her at her home.

Brandon's father even contacted the Child Support Division to see whether they could reveal where his child support was being delivered. They would not provide that information. Finally, Kevin hired an attorney and "went to court." This was the juvenile court case so I could not ask questions about it.

My last questions to Kevin focused on whether he had ever seen Brandon after Jones regained custody from Arlene Blevins. He answered that he had not.

Steve Laudig cross-examined Kevin for the defense. He asked his questions in rapid-fire succession. He stood between Kevin and the jury so they could barely see Kevin's face. Laudig demanded to know whose legs were in the photograph of Brandon crying while wearing the striped shirt. Kevin said that he thought the legs were of Michelle Jones. She had sent him the photograph of Brandon while he was incarcerated. With a letter.

"You were eighteen years old when you first met Michelle?" spat Steven Laudig in Kevin's direction.

"No, I wasn't. I was around seventeen years old."

"You were almost eighteen though; isn't that true?" Laudig demanded.

Kevin continued to speak quietly and calmly. "I can't recall the exact date when me and Michelle met."

"She was barely fourteen, isn't that true?" asked Laudig.

"I don't know exactly," Kevin responded.

Then Laudig asked for Kevin's weight and height. Apparently, he wanted to compare it with Jones'. Laudig asked Kevin to describe her weight and height when they met. Kevin said, "She's probably about her same build now."

Really? Laudig wants to make this a rape case? There was no evidence at all that this relationship was anything except consensual. I could have objected but for what purpose? When I finally did object, Laudig backed off saying he had no further questions "along that line."

"Now why was Michelle sent to the Guardians Home?" Laudig asked.

"Because her mother put her out."

"And how old was she at the time?" Laudig demanded.

"I guess fifteen," Kevin replied.

Laudig asked about his prison sentence. Kevin had been convicted of a B Felony. The same felony Jones faced for neglect of a dependent causing death. The second count of the Information. Lawyers are not legally permitted to argue the length of potential sentences before the jury. Laudig wanted the jury to know how many years in prison Jones was facing if she was convicted.

"You spent three years in prison on a B Felony burglary, but you could have spent up to twenty years in prison, because that's the possible maximum sentence on a burglary, isn't it?"

"Yes, it was," Kevin said.

I didn't ask any more questions of Kevin. They had both been young when they'd had sex and she had gotten pregnant. But they were two kids. Kevin had loved her and I thought that came through to the jury. Kevin was no Einstein. I bet that Jones had forty points on him on any IQ test. But it was clear that Kevin loved Brandon and had done everything in his power to be a father, limited as that may have been.

The Court gave the jury a break. When we were at recess, the Court commented about the *slick* way that the twenty years for a B Felony had been brought to the jury's attention by Mr. Laudig. She didn't seem pleased. She had an odd look on her face. I must have had an inquiring look on my face because the Court said, "I'm smirking about the B Felony. It was very interesting during that last exchange. That's all I'm smirking about." I don't think Judge Magnus-Stinson was a fan of "slickness" in lawyering.

Sergeant Mike Crooke had become worried that morning because he recognized one of the jurors as someone he knew. He had not been in court during jury selection. Crooke immediately told me about it and I assured him that the juror had disclosed the relationship to the Court and counsel. But we wanted to be very careful about every step taken in this trial. During the break, I advised the Court and defense counsel that Sgt. Crooke knew the juror in question. The Court thanked Crooke for speaking up about it, but told him that everyone knew about it already.

The State called our next witness, Arlene Blevins. She was about my age, despite being a grandmother. She was a good-looking woman, conservatively but casually dressed. She stood tall and proud. She did not look at Michelle Jones as she walked up the aisle and was seated in the witness chair.

In Indiana, the judge gives the oath to each witness, not a clerk or lawyer as it is done in other states. The interaction between the Court and the witness as the oath is administered, in my mind, added solemnity. As Judge Magnus-Stinson asked Arlene whether her testimony would be the truth, the whole truth and nothing but the truth, their eye contact was unwavering.

She identified herself as Kevin Sims' mother and Brandon Sims' grandmother. Brandon was her first grandchild. She testified that she had a relationship with Brandon from the day he was born. I asked her to describe the relationship between Brandon and Kevin.

"Kevin loved Brandon and Brandon loved Kevin" was her brief and yet expressive response. She testified that when Brandon was born, Jones was living with her aunt. For the first six months of Brandon's life, Arlene saw him almost every week. Sometimes two to three times a week. But then Jones was taken away from her aunt. She was going to be placed in a teen group home. Brandon would have gone into foster care. Instead, Arlene and Kevin asked to have Brandon placed in the home they shared.

Brandon lived with her from the time he was seven months old until after his third birthday.

I asked her, "Can you tell us, ma'am, about Brandon as a child; was he timid, was he playful, what was he like?"

Mark Earnest objected, claiming that the response would be irrelevant. I thought it was important to know how much Brandon changed after living with Michelle Jones for less than a year. The Court overruled Earnest's objection. Arlene described Brandon.

"He was a fun little boy. You know, he loved music. He was always busy, and he had, he loved to play, he was a playful little kid. He was a joy to have." She was beaming with pride.

"Was he energetic?" I asked.

"Very."

"Did he have initiative?" I wanted to know.

"What do you mean?" she asked, not understanding my question.

"Was he able to do things for himself?" I rephrased the question.

"Pretty much so, yes." She told the jury how Brandon loved to play with balls. And he loved to dance.

"Did he get into things in the kitchen and climb up and around like toddlers do?"

I knew this was an important line of questioning, even if the jury would not know why until later. Defense counsel apparently anticipated the inferences that could be drawn from Brandon's ability to get food out of the refrigerator, open cabinets, and reach the sink. They vehemently objected to these questions. Defense counsel insisted upon arguing every objection at the bench. This meant that instead of making their objections from counsel table, where the jury would know what was going on, they whispered arguments to the judge, standing at the side of where she was seated and away from the witness. They didn't want the jury to know that they were trying to keep important testimony out of the trial.

The Court overruled their objection.

I asked Arlene, "Do you remember my question?" She just looked at me. Deer in the headlights. "I take it that's a no," I teased. "Brandon, as a toddler, when he was living with you, was he able to climb up on cabinets?" I rephrased.

"Yes."

"Get into things?"

"Yes."

"Open the refrigerator?"

"Yes."

She also recalled that Brandon was "potty trained" from the time he was about two years old. He was able to go to the bathroom himself or tell her that he needed to go.

"From the time he was potty trained, when he was about two, until he ultimately left your home, had he stopped wetting the bed at night?" I asked.

"He had stopped wetting the bed," she said these things with certainty. She knew this because Brandon would sleep with her.

Arlene said that she returned custody of Brandon to Jones at her request. "After Michelle became emancipated, you know, she wanted her baby back and I felt like I had to give him back to her." Jones had sole legal custody of Brandon, but she did not take him back immediately. By the time she took Brandon from Arlene, she was living with Damon Jones.

During the years Brandon lived with Arlene, she noticed that he was physically maturing at a very early age.

"He started developing pubic hairs and he was having like, you know, body odor like a teenager, you know, like young adults, puberty, going through puberty, and these kinds of things. Those were physical things that I noticed about him," she explained.

"At the time you were observing this, and while the defendant still, or you still had Brandon, was the defendant employed?"

"Yes. She worked at Eli Lilly."

"And do you know whether or not she had insurance through Eli Lilly that covered Brandon?" I asked, looking more at the jury than at the witness.

"Yes, she told me she did."

Arlene explained that Kevin had taken Brandon to the Well Baby Clinic for his physicals and shots. She returned Brandon to Jones because she felt legally and morally obligated to do so. Arlene told Jones that she wanted to see her grandson as much as possible. She expressed to Jones that she would take Brandon on weekends, or any time Jones needed her. She had worked for BryLane for seventeen years and Jones knew where to reach her, whether at work or at home.

It was also important that the jury know how Michelle Jones felt about her son's precocious puberty. "In the months after you gave Brandon back to the defendant and shortly thereafter, did you learn whether or not she had taken him to a specialist concerning his fast maturing?"

"Yes, she called me at work and told me what the doctor had told her. I asked her what was going on with Brandon and asked her what their treatment would be concerning that. She said that he had precocious puberty and they were going to give him medicine to slow it down. They couldn't stop it. But they could slow it down to some extent."

She was speaking too quietly. I was afraid that the jury would not be able to hear her answers. I slowly walked to the end of the jury box at the far end of the courtroom. I hoped that she would speak more loudly to be sure that I could hear her answers.

"Did Michelle express her reaction to his condition?" I asked loudly.

"At that time we talked about it and she said that *she did not want to raise a freak.*"

After that conversation, she called Jones many times in an effort to visit with Brandon, yet was only allowed to see him two or three times over the next year. Except for a single visit, no weekend visits were allowed. Eventually, Jones stopped answering Arlene's calls despite the many messages that she left.

"I called her on the job, left messages, you know, that I wanted to see him, spend time with him. She called me once after the last visit and told me that Brandon, when he came home, that he could not spend the weekend with me any longer because when he came home he acted a little strange, you know, like he was going back home, per se, so that I could not keep him over a weekend any longer anymore." Arlene was beginning to tear up as she described that phone call with the defendant.

Arlene testified that she offered all the time to keep Brandon. "I offered to keep him anytime." Even though Michelle would not respond to the telephone calls, Arlene left messages asking to see Brandon and offering Michelle assistance in babysitting Brandon.

The last time that Arlene spent the day with Brandon was during the summer of 1991. There was a family reunion and Jones allowed her to take Brandon for the day. Brandon was a little more than three years old.

After that, she saw Brandon as she drove by the mosque where she knew Jones worshipped. She kept trying to contact Jones so that she could visit with Brandon. She would call Jones' work number and leave voice messages; Jones never called her back.

Sometime later, Arlene and her sister were driving by the mosque and saw Brandon playing outside. He saw them and ran to the car and got in. They hugged. Jones came over to the car. Arlene asked her if she could visit with Brandon again. Jones said, "I'll get back with you." But she never got back with Arlene.

The last time that Arlene ever saw Brandon was shortly after his fourth birthday. He was at the mosque and she drove by and spoke with him. By now, she had even sent messages to Jones' husband about visiting Brandon. She continued to call and leave messages. There was no response. During 1991, 1992, and 1993, Arlene left two to three messages a week on Jones' Eli Lilly voicemail asking to see Brandon. Sometimes she called every day.

Then she tried to find where Jones lived, but Jones kept moving and could not be located. In winter of 1993, Arlene learned that Michelle and Damon Jones had divorced. She found out from Damon, Michelle's ex-husband.

Although she spoke with Michelle Jones' cousin and kept trying to track her down, Arlene never saw Brandon Sims again. And she never took him to Texas. Never took him to Tennessee. She was a broken woman. While explaining about her never-ending searches for her grandson, she was in tears.

Mark Earnest stepped over to cross-examine this broken-hearted witness. I had no idea why he would attempt to challenge her testimony, but he did.

He started gruffly. "Now your son is Kevin Sims?"

"Yes, he is."

"And Kevin met Michelle when they were at Arsenal Tech High School?"

"Yes, they did."

"And Kevin got Michelle pregnant when she was fourteen years old?"

"From my understanding, yes."

"And she had Brandon when she was fifteen years old?" he demanded.

"Yes."

"Kevin is a few years older than Michelle?"

"A couple of years, yes."

Arlene Blevins agreed that Jones had been going to school and had a part-time job when Arlene was caring for Brandon. Jones and Kevin continued to see each other until he went to prison. She described it as "they sputtered." Jones did not have a car and relied on Arlene to bring Brandon for visits while she was at Miller House. Earnest asked where else she had visited Jones and she told him the group home as well. She confirmed that she cared for Brandon from the time he was seven months old until he was three.

Mark Earnest turned his back to Arlene Blevins after his last question. With his rear to this witness, and without another word, he walked to his table. He never mentioned that he was sorry for her loss.

CHAPTER TWENTY-FOUR

MICHELLE'S FRIENDS BEGIN TO TESTIFY

The State's next witness was LeTava Muhammad. I had to be very careful when asking Muhammad questions because of the Court's order prohibiting the State from asking her about the prior abuse of Brandon by Michelle Jones.

Muhammad testified about meeting Jones at the mosque and described how they had become friends. She also explained that after a while she had befriended Brandon and became his sitter. Jones worked at Eli Lilly during the time that she and Muhammad were friends. She also participated in many after work activities including the theatre, a dance troupe, and other community events.

During Muhammad's testimony, the State introduced into evidence the divorce papers that Michelle Jones had filed. They were dated September 6, 1991. Jones was the one asking for a divorce. She and Damon Jones had been married less than one year. They had married on September 29, 1990. In her sworn Petition for Dissolution of Marriage, she attested that she and Damon had separated on July 7, 1991. The ground for divorce was that the marriage was irretrievably broken. She requested that the court reinstate her maiden name: Michelle Christina Suzanne Engron.

Muhammad testified that she became a regular sitter for Brandon around January of 1992. By then, Michelle and Damon were already separated.

"Could you describe what Brandon was like in early 1992?" I asked.

"What type of child he was? He was a four-year-old little boy. Very typical, very playful. He was a larger child than most four year olds, but he was a normal four-year-old little boy. He was loving. He was a child," she said.

I had warned her about the Court's ruling and asked that she not mention the prior abuse unless a defense lawyer asked her about it. I tried to compose questions that did not invite her to explain what she had seen and learned from Brandon.

"When you say he was larger, did you have a son at that time?" I asked.

"Yes."

"How old was your son?"

"Seven."

"And how tall was Brandon compared to your son?"

"He was the same height," she replied without hesitation.

"However, emotionally and psychologically, how did he compare to your seven year old?"

Her explanation was simple but thorough. "Brandon was the physical size of my seven-year-old son, but he behaved as a typical four-year-old little boy. So regardless to his size, he still behaved what would seem immature if you judged him off of size because you would mistake him for a little older than what he was."

Muhammad testified that Brandon slept over at her house regularly. He used the bathroom and was potty trained. He never wet the bed. She continued to care for Brandon until May 1992. After she stopped providing his daycare in May, she only saw Brandon during social visits with Michelle Jones. She made sure Jones knew that she was available to babysit for Brandon anytime.

On July 1, 1992, Jones dropped Brandon off at the Muhammad home for her son Alejandro's birthday party. Muhammad identified photographs she had taken of

Brandon at her son's party. In these photos, several children were pictured. She pointed to Brandon. Brandon had been a real, live child. I wanted the jury to realize that. The photographs helped.

Laudig interrupted my examination of Muhammad to point out that the State had enlarged the photographs. *Darn right we did*, I said to myself. I want the jury to see that little boy's innocent beautiful face.

I asked Muhammad when Jones picked Brandon up after the birthday party. She testified that Jones came to get him on July 3, 1992. She sadly confided to the jury that after that day, she never saw Brandon again.

However, Muhammad saw Michelle Jones at many social events in late 1992, 1993, and 1994. She never had Brandon with her. Muhammad always asked about Brandon. Jones habitually told her that Brandon was at a sitter's or with one relative or another. The last time Muhammad saw Jones at a social event, Jones said that Brandon was out of town but would be returning soon. When she asked if Brandon could come and visit with her family, Jones said sure. That never happened.

The cross-examination of Muhammad was brief. Laudig insinuated that she knew Damon Jones before she knew Michelle. She responded that she met both of them at the same time. He also asked whether Michelle Jones left their mosque. She replied that Jones decided to leave the mosque after she separated from Damon Jones.

I was trying to understand the defense. Was it poor Michelle, pregnant as a teen? A bad marriage? Was the idea to blame everyone but herself? I figured we would find out soon enough.

The Court was in recess while we discussed the physical condition of Kadisha Aamir. The bailiff interrupted the discussion approaching the judge with a note in his hand. The jury had a question. It was rare that jurors were permitted to ask questions, but Indiana law permitted it. Any jury question would be reviewed by the judge and counsel, then a decision would be made about the legality of asking or answering the question.

This question was a request for the height and weight of Brandon Sims when he attended the July 1, 1992, birthday party. I intended to return LeTava Muhammad to the witness stand to respond. The defense objected, saying that the photographs "spoke for themselves." The Court wanted the jury to know the answer. Unfortunately, when she retook the stand, she was hesitant to guess. She really didn't know the answer.

Kadisha Aamir was still hospitalized. She was in bad shape and I worried about her survival. Not because of the case, we had her sworn testimony and I knew we would be permitted to use it if necessary. My concern was for Kadisha and her family. This woman was a good friend to Michelle Jones, yet truthful. I hoped that she had many years ahead of her.

Aamir had convinced her doctor to allow her to testify; she was one strong woman. She would be transported by ambulance from the hospital to the courtroom and then returned to the hospital. I notified the Court that we could expect her at 1 p.m.

It was only about eleven o'clock. Before Aamir arrived, I'd hoped to examine Damon Jones and Mae Engron, Jones' former husband and mother respectively. Both had appeared at earlier hearings after great efforts on the State's part (and Sgt. Crooke and his colleagues). Neither wanted to cooperate. The Court had ordered them to return to be witnesses at the trial but neither showed up. They were not necessarily trying to protect Jones; they had their own problems. The Court could issue bench warrants and have them arrested and brought to court, or the defense could stipulate that their prior testimony could be read to the jury.

The defense did not want to stipulate, but we had done everything possible to haul them into court. Ultimately, and over the defense's objections, we read the prior testimony of these two witnesses into evidence. Mark Earnest had done most of the questioning of Jones' mother, Mae Engron. She confirmed that she had not seen or spoken with her daughter since 1986. She had never met Brandon. She never took Brandon to Tennessee or Texas.

The trial was moving quickly. Although the defense objected to much of the proffered testimony, it was going smoothly. It was baby steps. Every witness had a tiny role in the overall case. The case was circumstantial, since no one was present at the time immediately before or when Brandon died. The direct evidence of Jones' guilt was her own statements, lies, excuses, changed stories, and ultimately her confession to Clarissa Dunlap. It would be the cumulative effect of all of the evidence that would either convict or free her.

The next witness was Deborah Asante. Deborah Asante had a dramatic flair. She did, after all, found, direct and operate a children's theatre company. But it was just a flair. Nothing more. She was also expressive, well-spoken, and straightforward. She described her employment as storyteller and director of Asante Children's Theatre, which was frequently referred to as ACT. Asante had lived in Indianapolis for ten years and operated ACT for seven years.

"Did there come a time, during the course of your experience that you met the defendant, Michelle Engron Jones?" I started.

"Yes."

"Could you tell the jury when and where you met her?"

"We first met probably about eight years ago as part of the Mentor Mothers program. I was directing a play about teen pregnancy and Michelle was one of the young actresses involved."

"Could you describe to us whether you saw her again and what your relationship was or built into?" I apparently needed a break. My question was terrible. I hoped that she understood what I meant. It was my job to be clear and direct, not babbling.

"We met again at least probably three or four years later. 1990. Probably the end of 1990 and 1991," Asante replied.

I asked her about the circumstance of their reacquaintance and she responded, "She had come to a show and said that she was really impressed with the work we were doing and if she could help she would like to and she started working with us."

Asante told the jury that rehearsals took place from 5 to 7 p.m. on Mondays and Wednesdays, and most of the day on Saturdays. And the week before the performance, known as Hell Week, they rehearsed almost every day.

"What type of things did she do?" I continued.

"She was the production manager so she did a lot of stage managing and organizing some of the paperwork for the children, like applications, and she was my right hand," Asante said.

"During any of the rehearsals during that period of time of 1990 and 1991, did you ever see Brandon?"

"Yes, I saw Brandon when Michelle first started working with us and then at the annual picnic," she responded. She testified that it was at the picnic that she last saw Brandon. It was June 1992.

"When you say that you saw him when she first started working with you, how many times did she actually bring him with her?" I asked.

"One time to a rehearsal. And one time to the picnic. So I saw him twice."

Deborah Asante knew that Jones worked for Eli Lilly all the years that she was involved with the theatre. Jones continued acting as a production manager for Asante Children's Theatre until 1994.

I asked Asante to describe what Brandon looked like. "Cute little boy. He was tall for his age. I think he was about four years old."

"Tell us the types of things that you and Michelle did during the course of the latter portion of 1992 and '93," I inquired, changing the subject.

"We went to a conference together in July 1992. It was a black theatre network conference. Michelle was the production manager and it was a conference where you network, and there were workshops to better your skills as a theatre person, and so I always try to take advantage of those kinds of things. And especially ... Michelle's young and bright and I wanted to take her to something that would make her skills grow."

Asante now knew that four-year-old Brandon had been left at home alone during that conference. The meeting was held at an upscale hotel in Detroit. Jones drove them to Michigan in her car. They left on the Wednesday or Thursday of the second week of July 1992. They came back on Sunday night. I wanted the jury to know, in detail, what Michelle was doing while her young child, not even old enough for kindergarten, was alone in his room dying.

"During the course of the time that you were gone, ma'am, could you describe what you observed Miss Jones doing in Detroit?"

Mark Earnest jumped to his feet objecting. As I responded to his objection, he insisted and the Court permitted us to approach the bench. Asante was permitted to answer the question.

"Attending workshops and performances and networking."

"Were there social events?" I asked. Once again, before the witness could respond, Earnest asked to object at the bench. His objections were again overruled.

"It was all mixed together, social and business. It was a gathering," she answered.

"Now, as you rode up there together, did there come a time when you asked the defendant where Brandon was?"

"Yes. She said with the babysitter," Asante replied.

"On the way back from the conference or during the conference did you learn anything from the defendant about contacts she'd made?"

Mark Earnest objected. The Court again overruled the objection.

"Yes. She was excited because she met someone, and they had invited her to come to see them," she replied, remembering the conversation.

"When you say someone?"

"A man that was also involved in theatre. She was very excited because he seemed like an interesting person," Asante explained.

"What else did she tell you about her future plans?" I asked.

"That she was going to go visit him. She told me that he lived ... I think Georgia. I think Atlanta, but I'm not sure about that." Jones later told Asante that she had visited the man and it had been disappointing. Asante didn't recall much about the visit but thought that Jones had driven to see the man.

"During the remainder of 1992, and talking about 1992 up through about the fall of 1993, was there ever an occasion where you again inquired of the defendant about her son, Brandon?" This would be the first time the jury learned about Brandon being left home alone during the Detroit trip. I suspected that they had been waiting to find out why we had discussed the Detroit trip in such detail.

The jurors were very attentive throughout the trial. The composition of the jury was nearly fifty percent Caucasian and fifty percent African American, with a mix of men and women. One juror, an African American registered nurse, seemed to pay even more attention than the other jurors. I believed that winning her vote was critical to this prosecution. She was no shrinking violet.

I wanted Deborah Asante to tell the jury the excuses Jones had provided about Brandon's absence. "Well, she, I should say, she volunteered to me that Brandon was living with his grandmother on her father's side in Tennessee, I think. Someplace south. That she had let him go and live with the grandmother." Asante was slowly shaking her head as she told the jury about the conversation. I'm not sure she was aware she was doing it.

"And about when did she tell you that?" I questioned.

"I can't say the exact date. But sometime after the summer, summer 1992." Asante was looking at the jury. Telling them what she knew. It was as if I was not in the courtroom.

"And did you ever ask about him again or learn where he was?" I invited her to explain further.

"I would ask about him and she would say he was okay. But we didn't talk about it much because when she told me that he was with the grandparent, I think that I looked like I disapproved and so I thought there was an awkward moment between me and Michelle when she told me so. I thought that she never talked about Brandon because she thought I disapproved of that arrangement. So that's why I thought she didn't talk about it," Asante replied.

Jones continued to serve as a production manager at ACT. Just before Thanksgiving of 1993, she began living with Kadisha Aamir, a friend of Asante's. Asante had known Aamir for several years. Aamir's children were involved in the theatre. Although she was living with Aamir, she was still working at Eli Lilly.

In the first week of January 1994, Aamir called Asante and asked her to come to her home. I asked Asante to describe what she observed when she arrived.

"Michelle was upset, I could tell. She was on the couch and everything. It was very tense or, you know, energy. Because I knew, Kadisha said it was about the baby and I should come." She looked weary.

She told the jury that the three women were in Aamir's living room as the conversation continued.

"Can you tell us, please, what the defendant told you in that conversation in January of 1994?" I urged.

"That Brandon was dead. That she had left Brandon and come back, and he was dead." The words seemed to be rushing from Asante.

"What else did she tell you about Brandon's death?" I urged her to continue.

"That she left him alone in the apartment and gone away, I'm not even sure what trip it was, and come back and he was dead," Deborah Asante started. "She said that she put him in a box and taken him and tried to bury him, or buried him. And that she had driven someplace, and she didn't remember. But it's cloudy to me because at that point I kind of lost it myself. I didn't focus in on it because this was unbelievable to me."

"Did she tell you how she transported Brandon's body?"

"I just remember she said she put him in a box in the car and that she drove," Asante replied.

I tried asking her some of the details of the conversation, but her memory was sketchy. Then, I continued, "Did she tell you where she had left him?"

"I think she said she didn't remember either because she was crying at that point. And like I said, I kind ... because I couldn't believe it, I couldn't picture Michelle doing this, I couldn't believe it. So, I kind of went out of it myself at that point after she said he was dead. And I remember her saying 'the box.' And I couldn't picture it. But she was crying and saying she didn't remember where because I think Kadisha was asking her. Kadisha was calmer than I was at that point and I think Kadisha was asking her more questions to try to find out where Brandon was." Deborah Asante was crying, but quietly remembering.

"We suggested that she turn herself in maybe to a mental hospital because she was under duress and she did. She said she would," she added. Asante visited Jones at Midtown.

But they never discussed Brandon. Asante saw Jones after she left Midtown but it was not the same.

She explained, "Michelle came back but it was awkward for both of us. I didn't know what to say to her. I felt for her, but I couldn't forgive her. And I think that she felt it. I wanted to help her, but I didn't know how. And so it was very awkward. And she came back one time and then she never came back."

Defense counsel did not ask Deborah Asante any questions, but the jury had a few. The Court asked the questions the jury had of Deborah Asante.

"You said the defendant drove the alleged victim's body. Whose car did she drive?"

Deborah Asante answered, "I assume her car. But I don't know."

"How long before you left for Detroit did the defendant know of the trip?"

"Probably about a month. She had about a month's advance notice of the Detroit trip."

It was time for lunch. I wondered if the jury would digest the significance of Deborah Asante's testimony. Crooke and I ate at the Market. He seemed to think it was going well. It was hard to tell. I was beginning to think of him as Columbo, one of my favorite television show characters. Unlike Columbo, played by Peter Faulk, he wasn't a talker. But the dress, hair, and intelligence were there. I just couldn't figure out what he was thinking, and he never said.

CHAPTER TWENTY-FIVE

A DRAMATIC AFTERNOON

When the jury returned from lunch and confirmed under questioning by the Court that they had not heard or spoken anything about the case, the State called Mahalia "Kadisha" Aamir to the witness stand. Aamir was sitting in a wheelchair and had a bandage around her head. She told the jury that she had come from Methodist Hospital and would return there after her testimony. She also told the jury that her sobriquet was Kadisha.

Aamir testified that she had lived in Indianapolis for thirty-eight years. She had "birthed five and raised seven" children.

I wanted to ask her the important questions before she became too exhausted. But I had to educate the jury about her relationship with Jones first. Kadisha testified they met through Asante's Children's Theatre because two of her children were in the cast. Kadisha was also on the board of ACT.

"Do you know when it was that you first noticed Michelle Engron Jones involved with the Children's Theatre?"

"June of '92."

"And was there a particular function that you were in in June of 1992?"

"We were at the annual cast picnic after the season was over with," Aamir recollected.

"And how were you introduced to the defendant?"

"She had ... I was standing talking to Deborah Asante, Michelle was watching Brandon, her son Brandon. When Michelle came back, she introduced us."

"And did you have a chance to see and speak with Brandon?"

"Yes."

"Aside from that one meeting with Brandon in June of 1992, did you ever see him again?"

"Yes, on my way leaving the picnic."

"Was that the same day?"

"The same day."

"Aside from those two times that you saw Brandon both on the same date, did you see Brandon again?"

"No."

"Did you see the defendant again?"

"Yes."

"And could you tell us how you saw her?"

"The season was over with for Asante's Children's Theatre. I seen her on a social basis," Aamir explained.

"And how long did you continue to see her socially?"

"Quite often from that summer on until she asked could she stay with me."

Aamir was speaking softly but with authority. Every juror's eyes were fixed on her. Mine too.

"During the period of time between June of 1992 and when she came to stay with you, did you ever have a conversation with the defendant about her son Brandon?"

"Yes. The first conversation that I had with her was in November of '93 when she moved in with me. And between Thanksgiving and Christmas, I asked her how was her son doing and she told me that he was okay, and that he was with his father and grandmother."

"Did you ask her any further questions?"

"Well, I asked her; she said that the father was married and that they were raising Brandon, and I asked her how did she feel him calling another woman mommy and something related to Christmas, and she said, no, that that didn't bother her," Aamir reported.

Michelle Jones was still working at Eli Lilly and was also still active with ACT and a dance troupe called Fire. Saundra Holiday, who was also called Mijiza, was the director of the Fire dance troupe.

I questioned Kadisha Aamir about whether she had been contacted by anyone after her conversation with Jones about where Brandon was living, concerning his whereabouts.

"Brandon's father and grandmother contacted me in December 1993," she recalled.

"As a result of those contacts, did you have any conversation with the defendant?"

"Yes," Aamir responded.

"Could you describe the conversation and what the defendant told you?" I asked.

"I asked her, I mentioned to her that I had talked to Brandon's father and his grandmother and they wanted to know where Brandon was at. And she told me that Brandon was dead," Aamir responded quickly.

She questioned Jones about Brandon's death. "I asked her, 'when they find Brandon, will they find his bones broken and his skull smashed in?' and she said no. And I asked her, 'where is he, what happened?' and she told me that she went out of town and when she came back, Brandon was dead. She said that she stayed out of town for a week."

"Did she tell you *where* she left Brandon alone?" It dawned on me that the jury had not been told much about Michelle and Brandon's living arrangements. They would not know about the blood but they needed to know the two shared a two-bedroom apartment.

"In her apartment."

Aamir explained that Jones told her she left Brandon at the apartment alone for a week while she went out of town during the summer with Deborah Asante and Mijiza. (I hoped that the jury remembered that Mijiza was Saundra

Holiday's nickname.) By this time, the courtroom was still and completely silent. The jurors were sitting forward in their seats and Judge Magnus-Stinson, who was always attentive, was taking copious notes.

"Did she go into any further details about what happened to Brandon or what she found when she came back?" I queried.

"She said that when she got back he was in his room and she checked him, and he was dead."

"Did you inquire about whether or not she attempted to obtain any assistance?" I probed.

"She said that she was afraid and really didn't know what to do. And she stayed in the apartment a day or so and then she came home one night, and she just picked him up, wrapped him in a blanket and put him in her car."

"Did she tell you what she did with Brandon's body, in terms of after she put it in the car?"

"She said that she drove around for a while. She couldn't really remember how long she drove. She was on the interstate. She came to a wooded area, bushes, and she stopped and took him out of the car and laid him down."

Aamir had an incredible memory. While she testified, she looked at Michelle Jones. The look was maternal rather than antagonistic.

After Jones described what had happened to Brandon, Aamir took her to Midtown Mental Health. She stayed with Jones after they entered Midtown and was present when Jones spoke with a woman who Aamir described as small-framed with gray hair. I knew that this was Toni Goffredo, the State's next witness. Aamir testified that Jones told the person at Midtown essentially the same things as she told her and Deborah Asante.

I asked whether she had visited and spoken over the telephone with Michelle while she was at Midtown. Aamir confirmed that she had spoken with and visited

Michelle while she was in the hospital. She described those conversations.

"We talked about his death. She spoke about a lawyer, that she said someone had helped her obtain a lawyer. And we talked about her health."

"So she advised you that she obtained a lawyer while she was still at Wishard?" I asked incredulously.

"Yes. She obtained a lawyer while she was in the hosptial," Aamir replied.

Aamir's response was not what I had expected: why would someone having a breakdown contact a lawyer? Anyway, there was another bench conference and the defense objected to the line of questioning that I had begun. All three lawyers were arguing and insinuating. The Court had been patient.

I protested, "Judge, once again we have two lawyers with one witness each making objections. I'm not sure who's on this—"

Steve Laudig cut me off, saying, "There's no jury here."

The Court apparently had finally had enough. This multi-lawyer attack on me personally and the State's case had been constant since we filed the murder charge. Actually, it had started before we filed the murder charge.

"It isn't a point of whether there's a jury here or not, it's tag-teaming. *And if you guys can't handle Diane one on one, then that's your problem.* But it's one lawyer per witness, that's the rule," Judge Magnus-Stinson said.

Okay, I confess I appreciated the Court's comment. After months of personal attacks, hearings, and just plain being exhausted with little assistance from anyone in my office, it was nice to have the Court reprimand them. None of that had to do with the prosecution of Michelle Jones. She said nothing and I doubted she had asked her attorneys to act that way. She wanted to avoid prosecution and certainly conviction, but she didn't direct how her attorneys acted in court. It was on them.

And it wasn't just the multiple lawyers objecting, arguing, and interjecting, it was the defense as a whole. Every witness had been treated as if they were an enemy of the defendant. Nothing was further from the truth. Some of them had been close and loyal friends and still wanted to protect her from her own criminal conduct.

After Michelle Jones left Midtown, she lived with Kadisha Aamir and her family. She quit her job at Eli Lilly and was planning to return to school full-time. She lived with the Aamir family until the end of March 1994. Never did there come a time, after she had gone to Midtown, that she denied that Brandon was dead.

How many women, I wondered, *would have allowed Michelle Jones to return to their home, when they had children living there, knowing what Michelle had admitted to doing?* Kadisha Aamir was far more forgiving than most. Did she and her husband worry while Jones was there? Did they make sure that one of them was home with the children at all times? Or did they believe she was not a threat to their children? I had never discussed this with Aamir but wished that I had.

I had no further questions. Attorneys for Michelle Jones had no questions of Aamir. But the jury had one and the Court decided to ask it.

"Did she, I assume this is referring to Ms. Jones, did Ms. Jones mention if anyone helped her dump the body?" the judge asked.

"No," Aamir responded.

Whenever the jury asked a question, it gave some insight into their thinking. A question about another person helping move the body had to relate to the prior question about Brandon's weight and height. Was there a juror who doubted that Jones could hoist the body of her son after he had died? It seemed off the wall. Still, I wanted to satisfy the juror's curiosity.

Mrs. Aamir seemed very tired and was shrinking into the wheelchair. I needed to send her back to Methodist Hospital as soon as I could.

"Ma'am, did the defendant indicate to you whether she was alone or with someone else at the time she returned and found Brandon dead?" I asked.

"She mentioned that she was alone," she confirmed. I hoped this answer satisfied the inquisitive juror.

We all watched as one of the bailiffs slowly and carefully rolled Mrs. Aamir from the courtroom.

Bernice Starks was the next witness. She was Michelle Jones' aunt and Mae Engron's sister. She testified that Jones and Brandon had lived with her for a very short time before Brandon went to live with his paternal grandmother, Arlene Blevins. The last time that Ms. Starks had seen Brandon was when he was about two years old. She visited with him at Arlene Blevins' home. She had not seen him after that visit. The defense had no questions for Ms. Starks.

One of Michelle Jones' great aunts, Mary Chapman, was our next witness. She too had been introduced to Brandon when he was still in diapers. She guessed that he was about two years old, but he wasn't walking. She never saw him except for that one time. She never had custody of Brandon.

Another great aunt, Helen Starks, provided the same testimony as the other family members. The defense had no questions for Mary Chapman or Helen Starks.

The defense had invoked the rule of sequestration at the beginning of the trial. The Court granted this routine motion that prohibited a witness from telling anyone outside of the courtroom what they had said in court. The purpose of the rule was to keep witnesses from trying to tailor their testimony to seem concordant. Usually, if two witnesses had finished testifying, they could speak with each other but because of the animosity in this case, we had instructed all our witnesses that they were not to discuss their testimony with another witness, even if they both had finished testifying. This had become awkward because many of the witnesses were family members or close friends. As they left the courtroom they were not allowed to even greet each other.

Our paralegal, Margo Jones, remained in the courtroom to help coordinate the witnesses. The afternoon's witnesses were sitting outside the courtroom on a long wooden bench. Of course, Sgt. Crooke was also in the courtroom with me. Although he didn't say much, it was good to know he was there. This guy had tenaciously worked this case when many other detectives would have given up or been satisfied with the neglect charges.

Toni Goffredo was called into the courtroom. She introduced herself to the jury and explained that she worked at Midtown. She was an intake technician. Her job was to meet with people who came to the facility to assess whether they should be seen by a mental health professional. Goffredo explained that Michelle Jones had come to Midtown with a friend. Goffredo interviewed the defendant while her friend stayed with her.

"Specifically, what did she tell you she did in regard to her son?"

Jones' story, at least the part about leaving Brandon home alone, had been consistent.

"She told me, somewhere between a year and a year and a half prior, being with her son in the place that she lived for a matter of weeks, and that she believed that she had not been taking care of him." Goffredo sounded very nervous.

"Did she tell you specifically anything about a trip that she had taken?" I asked, trying to direct her testimony to the important disclosures.

"Yes. Subsequent to that time period I'm talking about, she said she had left her premises for about a week."

"Did she say who she left at her apartment?"

"Yes. Her son," Goffredo replied. This was like pulling teeth. She just was not very forthcoming.

"Did she tell you whether he was alone?" I asked.

"She didn't say that specifically; I had assumed he was alone," Goffredo surmised.

Laudig sprang from his chair and objected to her "assuming anything." He was right. I hadn't asked her to speculate or assume. The Court sustained his objection and instructed the jury to disregard her assumption. *Let's try this again*, I thought.

"During the conversation, did the defendant ever name or suggest that any other person had been home with her son?"

"No," she stated. Back to dentistry.

"Did she tell you what happened after she returned from this trip?" I asked.

"She said when she returned she found her son there and that he was dead," Goffredo finished.

"Did she tell you what she did with her son's body after she returned?"

"She said that she took her son's body and got in a car with it. She told me she had driven around to someplace off an interstate and somewhere off that interstate had placed her son's body and covered it somewhat with dirt."

Goffredo did not know whose car Jones had driven, whether she had called 911, or how she knew Brandon was dead. Goffredo explained that she had contacted law enforcement because she was a mandated reporter, obligated by law to do so. She had no further contact with Michelle Jones after the single interview.

I was surprised when Steve Laudig said he had a few questions for Goffredo. Neither he nor the other two defense lawyers had asked a single question all afternoon. Goffredo hurt his client's case the least. Maybe he was getting cramps in his legs. Laudig was concise. Goffredo worked at the crisis unit of Midtown. The purpose of the center, she testified, was to assist people when they walk in to the center or the emergency room or wards at Wishard, and then intervene in that crisis.

"Michelle gave you permission to call the police, didn't she?"

"Yes."

"She was only there for medical treatment, wasn't she?"

"As far as I know," she replied.

No one had additional questions for Ms. Goffredo. The Court asked the jury if they had questions. There were none.

I was getting the idea that the defense was just waiting to attack Saundra "Mijiza" Holiday and Clarissa Dunlap. Clarissa Dunlap was the only witness to establish that Jones had beaten Brandon, causing his death. Other witnesses provided circumstantial evidence of the murder, but Clarissa Dunlap delivered the confession. The animosity with Holiday was confusing to me, I just didn't get it. Anyway, the defense's game plan eluded me. As a prosecutor, it is always a good idea to know what the defense has up their sleeve and how they intend to persuade the jury. But in this case, I hadn't a clue. Jones' lawyers were certainly not discussing strategy with me.

The trial was continuing at breakneck speed. We were more than halfway through the State's case and we had only used two days. So far so good. I thought that I saw Cale Bradford stick his head into the courtroom during Mrs. Aamir's testimony. I was so focused on her words that I really didn't pay much attention to the back of the courtroom.

Our most credible witnesses had already testified. We had to convince the jury that Brandon could not be with Michelle Jones' family or friends. We had the legal burden to prove that Brandon was dead. And that Michelle Jones had killed him. We'd spent all our time so far establishing Brandon's death. There had also been testimony about her neglect, but not a lot about her culpability in killing him. That testimony was about to begin.

While Margo went to fetch our next witness, Susan Burke argued an objection to his testimony. Our next witness was an expert on flies. Yep, the kind that one swats, if one is lucky. Burke argued, again, since this had already been raised and overruled by the Court, the jury did not need an expert to tell them about flies.

"The jurors have experience with flies. We've all dealt with them at picnics, that we know we're taught from an early age on don't leave waste around because it will draw flies. I think that it's highly prejudicial to allow that kind of testimony in this case when it's not at all related to the flies observed in this case. I think that Miss Norris testified that she smelled a urine smell and that she did not notice anything else out of the ordinary. Therefore, this testimony serves only to raise an inference which is highly prejudicial to the defendant and in no way aids the jurors."

The Court disagreed, concluding that the witness's experience at crime scenes would assist the jury. She excluded his training on flies and pigs. Honestly, I didn't remember the pigs, but the Court apparently remembered his prior testimony and report included remarks about flies around pigs.

The State called John Brooks, an employee of the Indianapolis-Marion County Forensic Services Agency. Very few cities or counties had their own crime lab. We were very fortunate we did. The lab had a great deal of sophisticated equipment and well-trained and educated staff. Most importantly, the Marion County Prosecutor's Office obtained results much faster than most jurisdictions. Other agencies, who relied on the state crime lab or FBI forensics, ended up waiting months or years for test results.

In this case, we were not relying on Brooks for test results; it was his experience that we wanted him to share with the jury. Brooks testified that his job was to go to crime scenes and assist investigators from any of the police and law enforcement agencies in Marion County. He had worked in the field for about twenty years for the Marion County's Sheriff Department. That was before he joined the crime lab. He had been to about a thousand crime scenes involving crimes against persons.

I began my questioning, intending to get to the flies as quickly as possible. While I knew the jury wouldn't immediately understand the basis for the testimony, that would come next. I began to inquire.

"What are your job responsibilities once you go to the scene of a crime against a person?" I asked.

Brooks was nerdy, overweight and wearing the gray overalls-type jumpsuit assigned to crime scene techs. "Our primary job is to document through mainly photography, sketching if necessary, and the retrieval and proper packaging of evidence so that it can be analyzed." He had obviously memorized his job description. He testified in Court frequently. He said that he was a trained observer of crime scenes.

I continued, "And during the course of your experience, have you ever dealt with flies?"

"Yes, I have. Flies, as we all know, are predominate in the warmer months. The fly infestations that I've been involved in are responding to organic material," he said.

"Now when we are talking about flies at a crime scene, I know there are a couple flies around the house that I might swat away, what volume or number of flies have you observed at a scene that involved something decaying?" I asked.

He was thoughtful. "If it's an open area, probably several hundred. If it's an enclosed area, it could be literally in the thousands."

"What types of things, in your experience, attract that volume or intensity of flies?"

Brooks answered that it was decaying organic materials. I asked him to be more specific. "This could be garbage, decaying flesh, blood." Brooks looked at the jury as someone at the lab had obviously trained him.

"And have you in fact seen that number of flies attracted to decaying flesh and blood?" I inquired.

"Yes, ma'am, I have."

"Have you had experience at crime scenes where there was urine?"

"Yes, ma'am, I have. I have never seen that volume of flies at those scenes." Brooks had no dog in this fight. He was just sharing his experience.

I showed Brooks a photograph that he had taken when he had gone to the Georgetown apartment. He had been there to remove the carpet samples the jury would never hear about. He had taken a photo of the front of the building showing the window in Brandon's room. Once he identified that photograph, I had no further questions.

Susan Burke asked Brooks some questions about his testimony. She had him reiterate that flies are attracted to garbage and that many flies might descend on garbage. She also asked him whether flies were attracted to feces. He agreed that flies were attracted to feces. They were also attracted to blood.

Trial lawyers know that the first and last witness of every day are the most important. When the jurors arrive, they want to be intrigued. They hope that there will be important evidence presented. Similarly, before the jury leaves for the day, trial lawyers want to give them a witness whose testimony they will think about overnight. And sometimes, as a prosecutor, you just call whomever the detective or your staff has rounded up in time for court. We had a witness today that I thought would be thought provoking overnight. She was the records custodian for Eli Lilly. Although her information was pretty dry, it was also critical to the State's case. Well, at least I thought it was.

Donita Berlyn was the witness. After she was sworn, Berlyn explained that she was a paralegal in the human resources division of Eli Lilly. She was responsible for maintaining the records. I asked her about the records she had brought with her to the trial.

"I've brought with me healthcare election forms. I've brought with me tax exemptions selections. And I've brought with me a personal history folder." Berlyn could not have been duller. I hoped that the jurors were not too tired to listen.

I continued, walking to the end of the jury box so that the jurors would all be able to hear Berlyn. "Did you determine whether or not Michelle Engron Jones was an employee of Eli Lilly and Company?"

"Yes, she was. The records reflect that she was employed as a summer co-op student on or about May of 1989. She was hired as a full-time employee on or about May of 1990 and remained an active employee until she left on a leave of absence on January 24, 1994," she read in a monotone from the voluminous documents she was holding.

"What was the basis for her leave of absence?"

"She'd indicated the reason for the requested leave was educational leave. She had applied for the leave about a month earlier. She returned full time to Eli Lilly on September 12, 1994."

"During the time of Ms. Jones' employment at Eli Lilly, did she receive benefits, or did she have health insurance coverage?" I asked.

"Yes, she did. When she joined Eli Lilly, she elected family coverage in May of 1990 and she had selected as dependents, her husband at the time, Damon L. Jones, and her son, Brandon Sims."

Berlyn further explained that because Eli Lilly was self-insured, they did not purchase insurance from a company; instead they set up a fund to pay for their employees' healthcare claims. Employees would fill out a healthcare claim form and submit it to the health plan. When Eli Lilly received the form, they would mail a check to the employee for reimbursement. Eli Lilly maintained all the records for their employees. Berlyn brought all of the records regarding Michelle Engron Jones.

"Did your search of the records reveal that claims had been made for the provision of healthcare to Brandon Sims?"

"Yes."

"And on what dates were the services purportedly provided, at least those that were paid for by Eli Lilly?" I asked.

"Our records reflect claims for five occasions or visits for Brandon Sims," she replied. "The first date was June 1, 1990; second date was June 15, 1990; the third date of service was July 11, 1990; the fourth date of service was August 3, 1990; and the fifth date of service was August 31, 1990." Berlyn had obviously familiarized herself with the records because she recounted this information smoothly. The claims all related to IU Medical Center or Riley Children's Hospital.

"Now, if I understood your prior testimony, did Brandon continue to be covered under the Eli Lilly insurance throughout the period up to 1994?" I queried.

"Yes," Berlyn replied.

"During that entire period, aside from the care that you've told us about during the summer of 1990, were there ever any other health claims for Brandon Sims?"

"We have no record of any additional claims being filed with the Lilly Health Plan," she said flatly. She also stated that Eli Lilly had a prescription drug plan under which mother and son were covered. She elaborated, "We could find no record of pharmacies filed on behalf, for pharmacy claims on behalf of Brandon Sims."

In contrast, during that time, Michelle Jones was covered both by insurance and pharmacy benefits, and she used them. She also had an Eli Lilly provided life insurance policy. When she first became a full-time employee, she designated her beneficiaries.

"On September 25, 1990, the records reflect that Michelle designated Damon Jones, her husband at the time, and Brandon Sims, her son, as the beneficiaries of her life insurance proceeds."

"When she returned to work in September of 1994, was the defendant again asked to select the type of coverage that she wanted on her insurance?"

"Yes, she was," Berlyn voiced.

"At that time did she select single or dependent coverage?"

"At that time, she selected single coverage." Berlyn looked up from the documents as she read the answer.

"At that time, was she again asked to name beneficiaries for her life insurance policy?" I inquired.

"Yes, she was."

"Please tell the jury who she named as beneficiaries."

"The records reflect that Kadisha Aamir was selected as the primary beneficiary." She mispronounced Kadisha's names. There were no contingency beneficiaries on her life insurance.

"Miss Berlyn, were funeral expenses provided under the life insurance policy, the Eli Lilly life insurance policy?"

"Yes. But they were never claimed by the defendant."

When we moved to introduce the actual Eli Lilly records, the defense objected. We reminded the Court that the defense had received these records in discovery. The Court asked Mark Earnest why the records could not come in. He responded that he had not yet reviewed them. The Court insisted on a stipulation that the documents were admissible and would later be admitted.

The jury was excused. It was nearly Thanksgiving and I planned to cook for our extended family. My kids loved the holidays and I loved spending it with them. I thought about Brandon.

All of us remained in the courtroom long past the time that the jury was excused. There was work to be completed.

We continued to decide what to do about Damon Jones. He and his attorney could not be found. Crooke sent his partner to look for Damon at his last known address, but he was not there. Damon's attorney had not returned the Court's telephone call.

I had been on my feet questioning witnesses all day. I couldn't wait to take my shoes off. In fact, I had slipped them off as soon as the jury left the courtroom. I don't know if the judge could see my bare toes. I wondered if, after the hours in court, she had slid hers off too.

Despite starting the case with the judge furious at me and the State, it seemed that the testimony was convincing her, if only a bit. At least she was overruling some of the many defense objections. I advised the Court that we would be done with all of our witnesses by late in the afternoon of the next day, November 21, 1996.

CHAPTER TWENTY-SIX

MAKE OR BREAK IT: CLARISSA DUNLAP TESTIFIES

Our first witness of the day would be Clarissa Dunlap. The defense knew she would be called this morning and I felt certain they were fully prepared to cross-examine her. The extent of that cross-examination was critical. If the witness had been a priest, no court would allow an attorney to mock the clothes that he wore or his beliefs and rituals. What judge would allow a lawyer to discuss whether a witness believed that a virgin had given birth? What court would consider allowing an attorney to laugh at the giving of wine and wafer? Imagine: "You don't really mean it when you say 'this is the body' or 'this is the blood.'"

Clarissa Dunlap had faith in her religion and its ceremonies. She was a religious leader, a spiritual leader. The fact that her religion was not mainstream in the United States was irrelevant.

The State believed that Michelle Jones' lawyers intended to attack Dunlap's credibility by showing she was different. Her religion was different. Before the jury was brought into the courtroom, I argued that her Santeria Vodun religion and the ceremonies attached to it should be off limits as a means of impeaching her. The arguments became heated.

"In regard to witness Clarissa Dunlap, the State moves that she not be asked what her religion is or anything concerning her religion. Your Honor, in reading the Indiana Constitution, four of the rights in its bill of rights are various rights of religion. Here, to use the religion, Voodoo or Santeria Vodun, as a means of impeaching Clarissa Dunlap's credibility is a violation of her constitutional rights. It would be no different than allowing defense counsel to ask a Jewish witness why she did not believe in Christ to impeach her credibility before the jury. Santeria is recognized by the United States Supreme Court as a legitimate practiced religion. It has hundreds of thousands if not millions of followers worldwide. And the rituals that Clarissa Dunlap described, in which Michelle Jones actively and readily participated, are religious ceremonies. So we ask that there be no mention of Clarissa Dunlap's religious beliefs or practices."

Susan Burke responded for Michelle Jones, who was a Santeria Vodun participant, a National of Islam religious follower (at least while married to Damon Jones), and apparently sometimes a Christian. "First of all, one thing that's very significant in this case is that part of the revelations that this witness makes came through a trance-like state that was part of this religion's practice. I think that in order to determine the validity of that, just as in any, if someone, for example, if you go with a more mainstream religion, if someone had a revelation of something in a prayer, dream, of whatever, that would be proper to bring out. I think that the fact that so much of this came through the religious practices and this led to information that was testified to and led to specific allegations against Miss Jones that to allow us not to at least explore that ... I think it's certainly proper in limine any sort of disparaging remarks about the religion, to use the religion itself, the fact that someone belongs to a religion as a means to impeach them, we have no problem with that. But I think that in terms of exploring what the practices were, what happened when the revelation was made, other issues like that are certainly relevant to the case and are certainly very important when the jury comes to determine what the credibility of the statements are," Burke concluded.

"If I might respond. The only trance-like state testified to in a very lengthy and detailed examination of Clarissa Dunlap, and you'll find it at page 100 of her testimony, was the Misa in July. The conversations that the State intends to elicit, and there are three of them exclusively, one was a telephone conversation which was unrelated to any religious state or activity or celebration where during the telephone call an alleged statement was made by the defendant regarding beating, abandoning, and then returning to Brandon and what was done with his body. That was in November. The second conversation, also totally unrelated to a ceremony except for a traditional holiday, being Thanksgiving, that at that point, and again not in the course of any religious ceremony, was another conversation that took place at Inowa's house. And you'll recall that's the one with the 'I guess so.' The only other conversation the State intends to introduce is one that took place in October, again unrelated to any religious ceremony, and I believe this one was also a telephone call. And that conversation was about misleading the police. All of these conversations took place months after the Misa which is the only 'trance' that existed. Your Honor, the only purpose to introduce evidence concerning that religious ceremony at all is to prejudice the jury against this witness. There can be no other reason," I finished.

The Court asked all of Michelle's lawyers, "Can you at this point in time, any of the three of you, think of a basis other than prejudice to introduce this evidence?"

Mark Earnest argued, "It's fundamental to create a foundation or a context on the relationship. They were not friends that went to high school. They were not college roommates. They met because of the Esu religion. That's the context and basis of the relationship in the beginning. She was a Voodoo priestess or whatever you want to call it, a priestess, self-proclaimed, and she at that time was an alleged practitioner. That is the basis of the relationship. So you cannot just have her on the stand and did Michelle say this without telling the jury about how did this relationship form, under what basis is the background of this relationship. That's a very practical and necessary reason having nothing to do with prejudice."

The Court accepted the defense argument. "And I agree with that. I'm going to deny the State's motion. But I will say this. There was an issue raised during the course of her testimony earlier about what her religion prohibited her from saying. And I upheld her right to follow her religion. So there are ways to get the facts out without having her violate her religious principles. And I don't want questions asked in such a way that might violate her religious principles," the Court ruled.

I continued to argue that preparing a cow's tongue, performing the Misa, all of these were irrelevant, but if they were brought out by the defense, the State intended to have the witness describe Michelle Jones' desire to harm the people that were prosecuting her and looking for her son. I asked the Court to instruct the jury that religious beliefs or ceremonies could not be used by the jury to impeach a witness's credibility. I wanted the jury to know that before the defense lawyers raised the issue.

The Court agreed to consider the State's request. But if an instruction was given to the jury, it would be after all the evidence, not before the defense questioned Clarissa Dunlap.

I thought about the photographs and stories I had read about firewalkers. Some barefoot person stepping onto a bed of red hot embers, walking a length of them to reach the cool earth. I felt like that was me as I announced Clarissa Dunlap as our next witness.

Clarissa Dunlap was again dressed in a conservative dark skirt and blazer with a starched white shirt underneath. Her hair was pulled back and tidy. She wore makeup that was minimal and well done. She walked confidently to the witness chair.

I looked over at Mike Crooke. He looked up at me without the slightest trace of emotion. He would kill me at poker.

"My name is Clarissa Jennifer Ann Dunlap Thurman," she said, spelling each name for the court reporter. I started by asking about her background. She testified that she had lived in Gary, Indiana, for twenty-nine years. She had a college education. She was a licensed practical nurse.

We moved to discussing the witness's relationship with the defendant. Clarissa Dunlap met Michelle Jones in July 1995. I asked her to point to the person she knew as Malikia. She pointed directly at Jones as she sat at the defendant's table.

"And where did you meet her?"

"At my mother's house," Dunlap replied.

"Between July 1995 and later in that year, could you describe to us the type of relationship you had with the defendant?"

"A friendly relationship." She looked in the direction of the defense table neutrally.

"And were the two of you involved from your social relationship with the same religion?" I wanted to get to the religious issues early and thoroughly.

"Yes."

"And to your knowledge did the two of you share your views and beliefs in that religion?" I asked.

"Yes."

"And was the defendant seeking spiritual advice from others in reference to that religion?"

"Yes," Dunlap said.

"During the course of time that you knew Michelle Engron Jones, did there come a time, and specifically in November 1995, when the two of you had a discussion?"

"Yes," she confirmed.

"Was it in person or by phone?" I inquired.

"It was by phone. She called me in Gary. She was calling from her apartment complex wherever she was, on Wallace."

"Now, in regard to this telephone conversation, could you tell us the subject of the conversation."

"Yes, Brandon Sims."

"Did you know who Brandon was?"

"Yes."

"Who was he?"

"He was her deceased baby," Dunlap replied quietly.

"In regard to the conversation, ma'am, could you please tell us whether or not the conversation involved how Brandon died?" I probed. I wanted the jury to be aware that an important matter was about to be discussed.

"Yes," she said.

I stopped for a few seconds and looked at her. I hoped that the silence drew the jury's attention. "Please tell us specifically what the defendant told you in that telephone conversation about how Brandon died."

"She stated to me that she had beaten Brandon, put him in the bedroom with cups of water and saucers of food, and then left," Dunlap said clearly.

"Did she tell you how long she was gone?"

"About two or three days."

"Did she indicate how long after the beating it was before she left?" I asked.

"She left then."

I asked if she had ever met or spoken with LeTava Muhammad. She said she had not. I asked her if she had met or spoken with Deborah Asante. She gave the same negative response. She had never met, known or spoken with Mahalia "Kadisha" Aamir, Toni Goffredo, or Robbie Flippin either.

"After the defendant told you that she had beaten and then left Brandon, did you ask her any of the details that she observed upon her return?" I tested.

"She stated to me that Brandon was dead," she said flatly.

"Did she tell you what she did with Brandon's body?" I queried.

"Yes, she did. She wrapped Brandon in a blanket and took him out of the apartment and put him in her car." She continued. "She took him to a site and buried him. She did not tell me where." Jones had not told how long it had taken her to drive to the site.

Dunlap testified that she met Michelle again during the month of November 1995 in Indianapolis at Inowa's home. Inowa is also called Valerie Hickman. I asked her to describe that meeting and what was said.

"During that meeting, did you ask the defendant a point-blank question about Brandon?" I questioned.

"I asked, 'Malikia, what did you do, Malikia, beat Brandon to death and then leave?'" Dunlap said.

"And in response to your question as to whether she had beaten him to death and left, what did the defendant say?"

"'I guess so.'" Clarissa Dunlap repeated Michelle Jones' words with a firm certainty. They came out as a confession more than an equivocal statement.

I wanted to preclude questioning or arguments that these communications were somehow dreamed or imagined, which I believed the defense would imply. So I asked, "At the time of the conversation that you just told the jury about, the two conversations, involving the beating of Brandon to death, at those conversations were they during the course of a religious ceremony?"

She didn't hesitate. "No, they were not."

I wanted the jury to completely understand the context of these conversations. "Were they during the course of religious services of any type?"

"No."

"Were they during the course of any religious actions or activities?"

"No."

"Were they during the course of your social relationship in speaking with a friend?"

"It was in the course of a social relationship," she confirmed.

"Now, after the defendant told you the things that you described to the jury, did that have an effect on your relationship with her?" I asked.

"Yes, it did," she admitted.

"You learned about these things in November of 1995; did you immediately contact law enforcement?" I was not gentle in asking this question.

"No, I did not."

"Did you speak to others about what you had learned from the defendant?"

"Yes, I spoke to other members, higher up, in my faith."

"At some point in time, you did come forward to law enforcement, is that correct?" I summarized.

"Yes, I did," she agreed.

"Now, did you and the defendant share any friends in common?" I inquired.

"Yes, we did." Clarissa Dunlap explained that Michelle Jones had introduced herself as Malikia. That is the name by which she was known, and the witness called her. I wanted to get into the "boyfriend" issue as well.

"At some point during that period of time, let's talk about July of 1995, who was the defendant dating?"

"Babatunde," Dunlap pronounced.

"And did there come a time when she started dating someone else, do you know?" This was getting into a subject that may have still been raw. I really didn't know. So I wanted to ask carefully.

"Yes, she was dating two different people," she responded. I asked her to explain. "One was Babatunde

and there was another guy in Chicago, in jail or something."
This was not getting to the man that they allegedly shared,
so I got right to the point.

"Did there come a time when you began dating someone
by the name of Mohammad Abubakr?" She answered
that she had. She started dating him on April 6, 1996, she
recalled. Her relationship with Abubakr ended near the end
of August 1996.

"Whose idea was it to stop the relationship?" I asked
sympathetically.

"His."

"When you and Mohammad broke up, did that have any
emotional effect on you?" Duh.

"Yes, it did. I was hurt."

"Do you know, after he broke up with you, who
Mohammad began to date?" I looked at the jury. *They got
it*, I thought.

"I don't know. I heard about several women. But the
one I understood he went back to was Jodi." No mention of
Michelle Jones. As I continued to question Clarissa Dunlap,
she denied that the break up with Mohammad was what
caused her to become estranged from Jones.

"Was the lack of closeness based upon your relationship
with Mohammad or based on the revelations of November
1995?"

"It had nothing to do with Mohammad. It had all to do
with what had gone on with that baby," she said emphatically.

"In addition to the two conversations that you've
described, did you ever have a conversation with the
defendant about where Brandon's body had been put or
placed by her?" This was my final line of questions and the
defense objected repeatedly. The Court recessed. With the
jury excused, the issue was argued. The Court ruled that
Dunlap could respond.

The Court also read two questions that the jurors had
submitted. They wanted to know if the defendant had given

Dunlap the timeframe of Brandon's death. The second question was asking about which religion we had been discussing.

When the jury returned to the courtroom, I hoped to answer their questions and have a response to my last question. The witness recalled the last question.

"Malikia indicated to me that the police, she went with the police to a spot and that she did not let them know where Brandon was because she was scared."

I made a record that the only reason that I was asking the next questions was based upon the Court's ruling and the question that had been tendered. Then I asked Dunlap about her religion.

"What is the religion that you and the defendant were involved with during the time frame that you described knowing her?" I began.

"Santeria Efa Yoruba," she responded.

"And are you and have you been an active follower and participant of that religion?"

"Yes, I have. For twenty-four years."

"And are you designated as a leader of that religion?"

"Yes, I am." She looked squarely at the jury as she said this. Just a statement of fact.

"In regard to your religion: did you ever have conversations with the defendant about her beliefs in that religion?" If the defense wanted to challenge believers of the religion, they would taint their client as well. She too had, at least for a time, been a believer.

"No, I didn't," Dunlap said frankly. What I found fascinating was that she wasn't seeming to embellish or exaggerate or trying to assert knowledge beyond what she had been told.

"Were you asked by the defendant at any time to take any actions on her behalf?"

"Yes."

"And the actions that the defendant asked you to take, did they involve the possibility of harming people?"

"Yes," she said guiltily.

"And did you, at the defendant's request, take those actions?" I looked at Michelle Jones as I asked.

"Yes, I did." In answering these questions, Dunlap's voice became softer and softer. The judge asked her to speak louder.

"In regard to the actions that you took at the defendant's request, did they involve other purposes aside from the ones that you've described?" I inquired.

"The purpose of the things that were done was to confuse the people involved in the case, to… It was intended to harm or confuse the people involved in the case," she stated.

"In at least one of the matters that you did at the defendant's request, did you specify who it was intended to affect?" The defense had obtained a court ruling that this was admissible. While I objected strenuously to this evidence, if it was going to come out, I wanted to bring it out during my examination of the witness.

"Yes, it was specific."

"Tell us the names that you recall from the list."

I would have never gone into this information. It diluted the real issues, whether Michelle Jones had beaten and then abandoned her four year old for nearly a week. But her lawyers intended to ask about this. The State needed to get out ahead of their questioning.

Before getting to the names, I wanted to lay a better foundation. Laudig objected to every question. The defendant's attorneys always had a right, even an obligation, to object. But he was interrupting before I had finished the questions. That part was intentional.

"Were you, yourself, at the time that you were doing these actions, involved in any way in the criminal justice system here in Marion County?"

"No."

"Did you know anyone here?" I asked.

"No."

"Who provided you with the names of the people placed on these lists?" I persisted.

"Malikia."

"Could you tell us her other name?"

"Michelle Christine Susan Engron Jones," Dunlap responded.

"All right. Again, who were the names or some of the names that you recall who were on those lists?"

"Some of the names that I can recall is Scott Newman, Cale Bradford, Jane Magnus-Stinson."

The jury probably knew that Scott Newman, my boss, was the elected Marion County Prosecutor. They may not have known Cale Bradford, Scott Newman's chief trial counsel. But they certainly knew that Jane Magnus-Stinson was the judge who was trying this case.

"Do you know who that is now?" My inartful and grammatically obtuse question was apparently understood by Dunlap because she continued.

"I know who it is now. Kevin Sims, somebody named Blevins, Mike Crooke, lieutenant I can't think of his name, your name, Diane Marger Moore," Dunlap said with almost professional ease. She was articulate.

"Were there additional names that you cannot recall right now?"

"Yes."

"Did you have conversations with the defendant concerning her beliefs of the effects of those actions that you were taking?" Sometimes, as a lawyer, the desire to sound professional results in a failure to speak plain English.

"Absolutely."

This series of questions resulted in a new onslaught of objections, bench conferences, and defense ire.

"Did you have conversations with the defendant regarding her beliefs as to the effects of the actions that you were taking on her behalf?"

"Yes."

"And what did she express to you?"

This was a question that Michelle Jones' counsel did not want answered for the jury. Laudig had already objected to this several times. This time he objected, insisting that I ask the time of the communication. These interruptions were succeeding. I lost my place. And asked another question, but Laudig decided to argue his case to the jury. Despite all the bench conferences that he'd insisted upon, now he wanted to "object" in a loud and easy to understand manner. This was risky. It was called a speaking objection, intended to persuade the jury regardless of the outcome of the objection.

"In regard to the acts that you performed for her, there was a list that you've described?" I persisted.

Steve Laudig, standing called out, "Your Honor, that mischaracterized this testimony. 'On behalf of her, for her' implies that our client directed that and that is not the evidence, as the State well knows."

The State shot back, "*That is the evidence.* And we object to this argument before the jury."

The Court responded, "I already indicated, Mr. Laudig, that's appropriate for cross-examination." The judge directed the witness that she could answer, adding, "I don't even know if the question was completed."

Okay, I thought. *Take a breath. Regain your footing. Start again.*

Clarissa Dunlap remembered my question, although I had forgotten it. Before I asked another, she responded. "Ma'am, there were several lists made with several names."

"What was your reason for doing those things?"

"Because Malikia at the time stated that she needed some help. She needed help," Dunlap said.

I asked her how many people in the world practice Santeria. Laudig objected and the Court did not allow the answer. The State had no further questions for Clarissa Dunlap. I walked back to the State's table and Mike Crooke. He almost, kinda, maybe had a very tiny upturn of his lips. One could not call it a smile. Perhaps he wanted me to know that we had survived. But cross-examination was about to begin.

Before they could ask Clarissa Dunlap any questions, the bailiff approached the Court. The jurors had questions. I resumed asking the witness questions.

"In terms of the religion that you said that you shared with the defendant, could you tell us if there's a more commonly known name for that?"

"Santeria? Yes, that's the most common name," Dunlap said, addressing the jury.

"And those actions that you took, the ones that you were describing, can you be more specific about the types of things that you did?"

Laudig objected, claiming that the question was "not very clear." The judge overruled his objection without waiting for me to respond.

"I did several things. For me to be specific I would—I made lists of names, I said prayers, I made things," Clarissa Dunlap replied.

"In doing the things that you said that you did, did you follow those religious prescriptions?"

"Yes."

I thought that covered the jurors' questions, so I returned to a few that I thought I had omitted. Dunlap testified that the defendant never said whether she was alone or with someone when she beat Brandon. Nor did she say if she was alone when she returned home after being away.

Steven Laudig would now be able to question Clarissa Dunlap. I didn't know how the jury would take to his bombastic and sarcastic manner of bullying a witness. Time would tell. He started out at a trot.

"Michelle did not insist you take any actions with regard to the making of lists, did she?" he demanded.

"That's incorrect," Dunlap said evenly but with emphasis.

"She didn't ask you to do anything with regard to lists."

"That's incorrect," she repeated.

"What's incorrect about it?" he spat.

"That Malikia did ask for assistance."

"But she didn't ask you to make lists, did she?"

"Malikia asked for assistance," Dunlap said again.

Laudig thought he could make her back down. So he asked it again, in a slightly different way. "And you decided what assistance, what form, that assistance would take, isn't that true?" he insisted.

"No," Dunlap responded.

"Did your religious beliefs lead you to conclude what assistance, what form that assistance would take?" His tone had moderated slightly.

"Yes."

"So, again, Michelle didn't ask you to do specific things, she just asked for general help; isn't that true?" he asked again, apparently hoping for a different answer.

"That is not true, sir," Dunlap reiterated.

"Now you previously testified that the assistance that you provided was just to create problems with regard to communication; you'd never mentioned the word harm before in any of your testimony, have you?" he insisted.

"I have not mentioned it to you, no." She glared.

"How many times have you prepared to testify here today with the prosecutor?" he demanded.

"I haven't prepared anything," Dunlap said indignantly.

"You've spoken with the prosecutor many times before testifying here today, haven't you?"

"Yes, I have. But they did not prepare me," she insisted.

"Well, you reviewed what your testimony would be, didn't you?" he claimed.

"I did not review anything."

"Did they review for you what your testimony would be?" He was now standing closer to her.

"Sir, I have no idea what they did." She was unruffled. But Laudig was getting red faced with anger. I wondered if he took blood pressure medication.

"But you were present at the meeting," he claimed.

There hadn't been a meeting. Because she lived in Gary, we had not met to discuss her testimony after the pretrial hearings.

"Sir, again, I will state to you I have no idea what the prosecutors did," she reaffirmed. "I did speak to them just like I spoke to you."

"Now Michelle has left your religion; isn't that true?" he professed, trying to distance his client from Santeria.

"I have no idea what Michelle has done." Dunlap maintained constant eye contact with Laudig. She would not back down, but she would apparently not speculate either.

"And isn't that a basis for us to conclude that you have a bias against her?" he demanded, nearly grinning at the jurors who were focused on Dunlap.

"Sir, again I will state to you, I have no idea what Malikia has done. She hasn't returned anything. So as far as we know, she's still an avid practitioner," Dunlap countered.

Laudig was being bested by this witness who refused to be taunted or manipulated. He was nasty as he hissed, "You know that is not true, don't you?"

"Sir, again I'll tell you I have not—"

I interrupted her with an objection. Laudig was being argumentative. I thought that he was annoying the jury. The Court sustained the objection and the lawyer continued.

"Now let's talk about Mohammad Abubakr. He was your boyfriend at one time, he was Michelle's boyfriend at another time; you know that to be true, don't you?"

"Yes."

"And isn't it true that he left you for Michelle; you know that to be true, don't you?" He was again accusatory pointing his finger and sneering at her.

"No, I don't." She had retained her composure, although it was clear she was getting irritated.

"Now, you have in the past broken into both Mr. Mohammad Abubakr's home and my client's home in an attempt to burglarize it, isn't that true?" he accused.

"No, that is not true," she replied.

Laudig sneered. "Why did you *break into* their houses?"

Clarissa Dunlap was getting frustrated. "First of all, Mr. Abubakr doesn't have a house, so I never broke into his house."

She was not allowed to finish her answer as Laudig said, "Okay, you're right. You broke into his mother's house, didn't you?"

"No, I did not," she said.

"You broke into a residence of his though, didn't you?" Laudig continued.

"Sir, I used a key."

"But you used a key without permission, isn't that true?"

"Absolutely incorrect," she said with finality.

"Well, you got into my client's house without permission though, didn't you? You admitted that previously when you testified, didn't you?" Now it was Laudig who was frustrated.

"Yes, I went in without her knowledge on that day," Dunlap admitted.

"Without her knowledge and without her permission," Laudig stated.

"Well, sir, to be perfectly honest, there was an open invitation because she was a member of my religious beliefs that people could freely go and come as they so choose," she responded.

Laudig insisted that Dunlap had broken into Jones' home to take some of Jones' clothing to perform a ceremony over them; she denied this.

"Isn't it true that you disliked my client because your former boyfriend chose her over you?" Laudig argued.

"No. Actually, Malikia is fine." Again, the witness's tone was even.

"And isn't it true that you dislike your former boyfriend Mohammad." I didn't know how this was relevant, but I did not want to interrupt the interrogation.

"No, I don't dislike Mohammad," she answered.

"Isn't it true that you have performed ceremonies to show your bias against my client, of urinating in a cup and threw it on her door so that your boyfriend wouldn't go through that door. Didn't you perform that ceremony?" Laudig bellowed.

I looked at Crooke who was sitting next to me, but further away from the jury than me. I had to look away because I was beginning to laugh at the absurdity of the question. He gave me a *keep it together* look and in a few seconds, I was able to obey. Even as I was looking away, I listened to Dunlap's response.

Ever so calmly, she responded, "Sir, that is not true."

Laudig kept asking questions about the alleged urine incident. Finally, he asked, "What did you do?"

Over my objection, she replied. "First of all, that was at the request of his aunt because she stated to me that Malikia had used charm magic on Mohammad and that they did not want, Mohammad's mother and his aunt did not want Malikia to have that type of control over Mohammad anymore," she explained.

"So that's why you did what you did. What is it that you did in response to this request for help?" Laudig asked.

"I took urine and water, holy water, and salt and put it down in front of the house." Clarissa Dunlap was pretty darn forthcoming. At least that was my take on her testimony.

"Whose house?" Laudig demanded.

"Well, it was in front of two houses. His aunt's and Malikia's," she explained.

"And that's because you were trying to work magic on her, true?" He had regained that sarcastic sneering tone.

"Absolutely not."

"Who were you trying to work magic on?"

"What that is for, sir, is to dispel any type of magic or craft that has been set out for someone," she explained.

Laudig was going nowhere, so he moved to another topic. "Would you please tell us your Santeria name?" he asked.

"Sure. Iyalocha Iyakeke Adunni Abeba Osunwe Oshuntoki Orishatola." She wrote out the spelling of her names for the court reporter.

"Now returning to your entry into Michelle's residence; that occurred in August?"

"I guess so, yeah."

"And in October?" he asked.

"I beg your pardon?" Dunlap questioned.

"And didn't you also enter in October?"

"I've only gone into Michelle's house one time, sir." Laudig said Dunlap had entered Mohammad's house on October 26, the same day she had entered Jones' house. She denied it and responded, "I've been into Mr. Abubakr's mom's house several times."

Laudig persisted. "One time without permission or knowledge?"

"Sir, I've been in that house several times when his mom wasn't there, when there was no one there but me because I had permission to do so because Mohammad and I were dating."

"And Mohammad's mother's name is?"

"Mother Tahirah," Dunlap said.

"Is she an adherent to your faith?" Laudig asked.

"Yes."

"And isn't it true that after you broke into my client's residence, she reported you to the police?"

"I have no idea if she did or she didn't."

Laudig insisted. "But you at some time came to know that there was a police report and that you had been reported for burglary, isn't that true?"

I objected but the Court overruled the objection. Dunlap would answer.

"Again, I don't know if she made a report or not," she replied.

"But you came to know that there was a report?" Laudig chided.

"No, I did not come to know anything because I didn't see the report and I didn't see the police."

"Isn't it true that shortly after you burglarized my client's apartment or residence and you knew that you had been reported that you came forward to the police with this story about the November conversation where she allegedly made some admissions to you?" Laudig said dramatically in *ah ha* fashion.

"No."

After argument, defense counsel was permitted to introduce police printouts showing that Michelle Jones had reported a burglary. The defendant's statements to the police were redacted by the placement of a white card over the printing. The printout showed that clothing belonging to Mohammad had been taken. Copies of the reports were provided to each juror. After they were reviewed, Laudig continued.

"You went into Michelle's house in late August 1996, correct?"

"Yes."

"And this alleged conversation that you had regarding Brandon with Miss Jones that was in November of 1995, is that correct?"

"There were conversations in 1995, yes."

"The one that you testified to where she allegedly told you something about Brandon's death?"

"Well, she told me something about Brandon's death twice in November, sir, can you be more specific?" Dunlap replied.

"You had met her in July of 1995, is that what your testimony was?"

"I believe that was the month, sir."

"And in February of 1995, you began seeing Mohammad Abubakr?"

"No, I didn't."

"When did you begin seeing him?"

"Mohammad and I started dating April the 12, 1996," she corrected.

"But you met him in February of 1996?"

"Right."

"And he left Michelle to go to you; isn't that true?" Laudig changed the order of the affairs. If the man left Jones to be with Dunlap, why would she have been jealous of Jones?

"I don't know where he came from. As far as I know, he came from his mother's house," she said.

"So, a conversation took place where, this alleged conversation with Michelle, in November '95, you begin seeing Mohammad in April?" Laudig repeated.

"Which alleged conversation?" Dunlap asked.

"The one with regard to the hitting. Now are you clear?" This was getting more intense.

"No. You need to be more specific, sir."

"When did Mohammad leave you?" he asked.

"Mohammad and I broke up July the 13th, I believe, or the 31st, 1996."

"Your entry into his residence and Michelle's residence occurred in late August?" Laudig asked for perhaps the third time. She never specifically answered his question. She reiterated that she had been in Mohammad's house several times that year. Even in July and August of that year.

"Then on or about the twentieth of September, you made an anonymous call to the Indianapolis Police Department or the Marion County Prosecutor's Office with regard to this matter, didn't you?" Laudig said caustically.

"On or about, yes, I did."

"In your direct examination, you said you performed rituals on Michelle's behalf, is that a fair summary of your testimony?" Defense counsel showed the witness numerous quotes from her pretrial testimony when she referred to the rituals as works. She agreed that "works" is a lay word for people who perform ceremonial assignments.

Laudig asked Dunlap about her response at that hearing where she described one of the works as Esu's task. "I believe I told you he was supposed to go out and cause harm or confusion with Mr. Newman and a couple other people," Dunlap replied.

"Who is Esu?" Laudig demanded.

"He is an African deity."

"Do you remember your answer as being the following: 'To go out and fight for Malikia and to fight with Scott Newman and Mijiza so that they would have problems with communication and they wouldn't be able to talk to each other to block their roles so that they would not have any luck in regard to prosecuting Malikia' — do you remember that as being your answer?" he continued.

"Yes."

"You didn't use the word 'harm' them on that date, did you?"

"I said fight, sir."

"You didn't say harmed," he insisted.

"I said fight, sir," she repeated.

Laudig was moving from topic to topic and then circling back. He raised a copy of the transcript of Dunlap's testimony from the *corpus delicti* hearing. Instead of asking about a specific question, Laudig repetitively asked Dunlap, "Do you know the next question?"

After she repeatedly responded that she did not recall the next question, Laudig would look at her incredulously as if every witness memorizes their prior testimony including every question that was asked. He was taking some of the questions and answers out of context.

"But on the other three works, Michelle was not present; do you remember that question?" Laudig asked in a rapid return to Jones' participation in trying to cause harm to the investigators and prosecutors.

Dunlap agreed that Jones wasn't present. Laudig quoted Clarissa Dunlap as saying that she did them to help Jones. Laudig scowled. "You did this on your own, referring to these works that you performed?"

"I did them solo. I did them by myself, yes. I did," she agreed.

"So, you did them on your own, right?" Laudig repeated what he thought was a great answer. This was a mistake. Getting a good answer from a difficult witness is tough. Never ask it again or the witness may explain, as Dunlap did.

"Excuse me, sir. Are you trying to say was I assisted in the work or did I do them because it was just a thing for me to do? I did the work by myself. But I did them at the request of Malikia," she clarified.

"You said you did them on your own," Laudig argued.

"I did them on my own. I did them by myself. Maybe I should have stated it better," she explained. When Laudig asked her if she wanted to change anything else from her prior testimony, I objected. The Court permitted him to continue.

"Is there anything else from your testimony that you'd like to change?" he demanded.

"Sir, if you…"

Counsel for the defendant demanded that the Court instruct Clarissa Dunlap to just answer yes or no. The Court did so.

"No."

"You committed a burglary for which you've never been investigated, charged, arrested or jailed." He was arguing to the jury and nearly ignoring her answers.

"No." She swore.

Laudig asked the question in parts again. She denied each of them.

"You've not spent a day in jail for that burglary!" Laudig roared.

"Sir, I did not commit a burglary."

"So, you've received a benefit from the prosecutor's office and the police department—"

"I haven't received any—

"—for not being prosecuted for a burglary that you've admitted, isn't that true?"

"Sir, one, I never admitted to a burglary; two, they have not given me anything or promised me a single solitary thing. Not even a glass of water."

Steve Laudig had no further questions. The Court asked if I had redirect. It was a tough decision. While the defense had landed some blows, Clarissa Dunlap's testimony was standing. I considered leaving it alone but decided that I needed to ask a few more questions.

"In that statement that counsel talked about, the sworn testimony, it was very lengthy, was it not?" I held up the thick transcript.

"Yes."

"Several hours?"

"Yes."

"Ma'am, did you say at page 154, were you asked this question? Question: 'Did she inquire of you as to whether harm could be done to those individuals who you were doing works about?' Do you remember that question?" I asked.

"Yes."

"And your answer was yes?" I continued.

"Yes," she acknowledged.

"Ma'am, were you asked the question, 'And did she want you to do harm to those individuals?' Do you remember that question?" I asked.

"Yes."

"And your answer was?"

"Yes."

Laudig was angry. He jumped from his chair and before he reached the center of the courtroom, he spat, "And that's because you are a Voodoo priestess and do harm to people, isn't that true? And you're doing harm by lying here today; isn't that true?"

"That's not true, sir," Dunlap said calmly.

I stupidly objected to Laudig's question. The Court agreed that it was compound and he was permitted to ask it again in smaller bites.

"You're a Voodoo priestess, correct?" he angrily exclaimed.

"No."

He sneered. "What are you?"

"I'm a Santeria priestess," she replied. *Good grief*, I thought. This was the risk of asking additional questions on redirect examination, if the judge will allow the opposing lawyers to ask additional questions as well.

"And I would understand that to be a Voodoo priestess," he claimed.

"No, you would not, that's not true. There's two separate religions," Dunlap replied.

"You've done harm to other people at other times; isn't that true?" Laudig roared.

"No," she denied his assertion.

"And you seek to do harm by lying here today in your testimony about Michelle. Isn't that true?"

Again, the Court overruled my objection. She could respond.

"Sir, I seek to do Malikia no harm. Harm her for what? She hasn't done anything to me."

Clarissa Dunlap was exhausted. She was allowed to leave the courtroom. Apparently, the jurors had no questions. I returned to counsel table and asked Crooke what he thought. He said he supposed that she held up pretty well under the circumstances. That was high praise from Crooke. I wanted to think about Clarissa Dunlap's testimony, but didn't have time. In fact, the Court didn't even take a break.

"Ms. Marger Moore, you may call you next witness!" the Court called.

CHAPTER TWENTY-SEVEN

FLIES, HUNDREDS OF FLIES

Our next witness was Janet Norris. She was a slender and well-dressed Caucasian woman. She walked slowly and looked nervously around the courtroom. Her eyes settled on Michelle Jones. She looked startled. She was also very soft spoken as the Court administered the oath and asked her to spell her names.

Under my questioning, Ms. Norris explained that she was a property manager for the Georgetown apartments from 1990 until 1993 or early 1994. She described her responsibilities as an apartment manager, which included leasing apartments, collecting rent, posting, and resident relationships. She added, "Pretty much everything that you do in the office, following complaints, inspections, move-ins, move-outs."

"When someone came to Georgetown Apartments while you managed it, what procedural process did you go through to determine whether or not they would be leased an apartment?" I started.

"First, they'd have to fill an application out. We'd have to verify employment, credit history, previous and present loan history, just different background checks on them," Norris replied.

"After completing that information, if someone was granted a lease, did they actually have additional paperwork to perform?" I wondered.

"Yes. They had to do a move-in inspection, sign a lease, and do—"

Mark Earnest objected. Apparently, he didn't want me to lay the foundation for the admission of Georgetown Apartments' documents. The Court told me to skip the foundation, unless there was an objection. While this would save time, it would diminish the perceived official nature of the documents.

Foundation, in the legal sense, is a requirement that before a witness can testify about a document, for example, the lawyer asking the questions must show the Court that the document is admissible under some exception to the hearsay rules, most frequently as a business record, and that the requirements for an exception are met.

For a business record to be admissible, the document(s) must be kept in the normal course of the business, made at or near the time shown on the document, by a person with knowledge of the matter contained in the document. A foundation must be laid for some opinion testimony as well, but that was not an issue here.

I intended to introduce into evidence and then show the jury Michelle Jones' lease application, lease, and the move-in and move-out inspection sheets after jumping through the foundational hoops. Because the defense had waived the need for me to establish the legal ground for using these materials, the numbered documents were in evidence.

The first document that Ms. Norris identified was a diagram showing the apartment complex and the location of every apartment. It identified the roads and driveways and showed how the apartments adjoined these areas and the parking lots. The drawing also illustrated areas that were devoid of apartments or streets, including common areas and fields.

Norris also identified several other documents in the file for the apartment Jones had leased. She verified that the Georgetown Apartments were in Marion County, Indiana.

This was essential to our case. In order to be prosecuted in Marion County for the crimes of murder and neglect, the killing and abandonment had to occur in the county. Frequently, jurors looked quizzically at me when I asked such an obvious question, but it was one of the "elements" or facts that the State had to prove in every case.

Michelle Jones rented the apartment located at 3655 Alexandria Court, Apartment B. She had a one-year lease beginning on May 1, 1992, and expiring on April 30, 1993. Norris described the apartment that the defendant leased.

"It was a two bedroom and one bath garden apartment."

"What do you mean by garden apartment?" I asked.

"It's a one level. Her apartment was on the bottom floor," she said.

"In those apartments, ma'am, and you described it as garden, could you describe aside from the interior what was the layout or format of the building?"

"Yes, I could," Norris responded.

Jones' lawyer objected to the questioning. Without waiting for me to respond, the Court overruled the objection.

"As you walked through, you could see the front door; it's the main entrance into the community as far as the building common hallway. You'd have to go down two or three stairs. You had an apartment on the left and an apartment on the right. Then you have to go upstairs to your third and fourth apartment. Michelle lived in the apartment on the right-hand side. Each had a common hallway."

"And in the common hallway there were a total of how many apartments?"

"Four apartments." Ms. Norris was showing the jury the layout using a floorplan that the State had enlarged and placed on an easel within easy eyesight of the jurors. "The back of her apartment faced ... it had a back patio area, she had a back patio window. It had a sliding glass door out to the patio," Norris related.

"As to the front of the building," I asked, "and specifically the apartment that Michelle Engron Jones leased, could you describe the windows that looked out the front of the building?"

"Sure. You just have the one window, which would have been the front bedroom window that faced the front of Alexandria Court. It was probably less than ten feet from the sidewalk and street. The window itself," she specified.

I showed her photographs of the front and back of the building that had been blown up and placed on an easel. There was also a diagram of the inside of the apartment and the photograph that Brooks from the crime lab had identified as the room from which he had removed the carpet.

"Miss Norris, can you tell the jury or show them how far from the ground the window came up in the interior of the apartment?" I asked.

"Yes, it was probably waist or maybe mid-stomach area," she replied.

"Perhaps you could come down here?" I asked her to step down from the elevated witness chair and walk to the floor area in front of the jury.

"I'd say the window ledge came up to about right there," she said, pointing to slightly below her waist and showing the jury what she meant. She returned to her seat.

"After the lease was signed, was there any requirement in regard to a move-in inspection?" I inquired, moving back to the apartment's file.

"We do have a move-in inspection that we give them at the time of move-in. You have to go through and do an inspection on each room to make sure there's no damages done. We ask the resident to write down anything that needs to be done so that we can send maintenance people over. And then they return this to us and we give them a copy of it." Norris had the move-in sheet in her hand as she spoke.

"Prior to even allowing a tenant to complete the move-in inspection, did you or your staff inspect the apartments to make sure, as best you could, certain conditions?"

"We would have our maintenance supervisor do that."

This area of questioning was important to my bit-by-bit evidence building. I wanted to take it slowly and step by step. If a juror missed some of this, it might undermine the entire prosecution.

Janet Norris described the procedure that was used to complete the move-in sheet. She or one of her leasing agents would go with the tenant to the apartment before they moved in. Room by room, the resident/tenant would mark the sheet with any observed problems. The sheet showed each room, including the living room, dining area, kitchen, hallway, bedroom one, bedroom two, and the bathroom.

Michelle Jones completed the sheet as to each room. She was meticulous.

"And did Michelle Engron Jones complete this form?" I asked.

"This would have been done by Michelle," Norris confirmed.

"Now, in a subcategory on that sheet, does it request whether there's some problem with various areas within each of those rooms?"

"Yes, there is."

"And could you describe the breakdown to the jury?" I asked, handing Norris the sheet that Jones had completed.

She read. "Sure. In the living room, there was some outlets that needed covers on them. And the closet doors were sticking. And in the dining area, it shows that the closet door was off track. In the kitchen, it states that there's supposed to be lights on the range hood, there was no lights. And that the refrigerator wasn't stable." The move-in inspection had obviously been taken seriously by the defendant. She noted minor issues that I surely would have overlooked.

"What things are listed, for example, in regard to the bedroom on the form itself?" I prodded.

"It shows wall outlets, ceiling lights, floors, windows, doors, closets. And it stated in bedroom one, in Brandon's bedroom, there's no outlet cover on the sockets."

"Were there any other notations made as to any other problem in Brandon's room on that move-in inspection?"

"No," Norris replied.

"At the time that the defendant came to sign the lease at your apartment, was anyone with her?" I queried.

"I believe her son was with her. I cannot say that; I don't know for sure," Norris said.

I asked her to step down. I requested that she show the jury some additional items on the blown-up diagram of the building in which Michelle and Brandon had lived.

"Was there an apartment directly over Michelle Jones' apartment, the defendant's apartment, in that building?" I handed Norris a pointer.

"Yes, there was."

"Do you know who the tenant was occupying it at that time?"

"I do believe it was Gloria Messer," she recalled.

"In regard to that apartment, ma'am, did you have observations of the defendant over the months between May and when she ultimately left the apartments?"

"The only time that I really seen Michelle was during rent time if she would bring the rent off, or drop it off in the rent box, either way."

"Could you describe what her appearance was?"

The jury had seen Michelle Jones each day in court, but they needed to picture her back when Brandon was alive and shortly after he was killed.

"Michelle was very well dressed. She had a very good job. She was very different compared to some of the other residents who lived there. Very chic just the way she dressed and carried herself," Janet Norris declared.

"Now, did there come a time where you noticed something unusual in regard to Michelle Jones' apartment?" I asked. Janet Norris had returned to her seat.

"Yes, I did," she responded.

I waited a few seconds for the jury to know that the next questions were important. I did not look over at them but noticed that Judge Magnus-Stinson did.

"Could you tell us, as part of your responsibilities as manager, what you did, if anything, in regard to walking the area?"

I hoped that the jury would follow her words on the diagram. This would help them better understand the layout of the buildings and the apartment.

"We would walk the grounds two or three times a week just to pretty much do a trash pickup and just to check the property out because we had so many problems going on there," she answered.

"When you say we, how many times a week did you walk the property?"

"I probably walked it probably three times a week."

"And in addition to your three walks, did any other individuals at your direction do the same thing?"

"Yes, they did."

"How would you walk around the complex?" I inquired.

"We would go down the main strip, which was Bunker, walk all the way through, do the walk across to Alexandria, and walk straight back down." At my request, she stepped down and showed the jury the path she took on the diagram. I also encouraged her to show the jury the location of the office on the diagram and how she had walked the route she had described.

"We'd walk all the way down Bunker through here. We'd cross to the laundry room and check out the pool area and walk back through this way." She demonstrated.

"Where's the pool area?" I asked, wanting the jury to know that this was an upscale apartment complex with amenities. "Now, although it doesn't show, are there any sidewalks in this community?"

"Yes," she pointed, "they're right here."

"And how close were the sidewalks to the windows in the buildings, specifically 3655?" I asked.

"As far as I am from this," she said, showing the distance between her and the easel, about five or six feet I guessed.

"Let me direct your attention to midsummer of 1992. Did you at that time notice anything *unusual?*"

"We were doing a trash pickup and we happened to walk by Michelle's apartment and there was hundreds of flies in the window," she said. Her expression reflected the revulsion she felt in seeing the insects.

"Now, the window you're referring to, is that the one that you, that is included in the photograph?"

"Yes."

"When you say you saw the flies, can you give us any better description for example of the density?" I asked as Mark Earnest interrupted with an objection. Again, the Court overruled it before I said a word in response.

"The window was covered with flies. I mean, there was hundreds of flies." She said with disgust.

"Now you've been in the residential leasing business for some time. Is that correct?" I began.

"That's correct."

"And had you ever seen that volume or density of flies in a window ever before?"

"No, I haven't," she said firmly.

"Have there been occasions during the course of your experience where people have left trash in their apartments and actually abandoned them?"

"Yes, I have."

"And have you gone in to check on those?"

"Yes, we have," Norris affirmed.

"In any of those instances, were there ever this density or *volume* of flies?" I asked.

"Not like this," she replied.

"When you saw the flies, did you do anything as a result of that?" I wanted to know.

"I did enter the apartment. I went through the apartment. We thought maybe she might have skipped on us and left trash or something in there, so we entered the apartment. Went through, went to the front bedroom window. There was no trash." She was becoming emotional.

"When you went into the apartment, was there anything unusual about the front door?" I moved away from the flies to calm her.

"No."

"Did it appear in the correct position?"

"Yes."

"The lock. Was it locked or unlocked?" I inquired.

"It was locked."

Janet Norris answered my questions as I asked about every room. The living room was not in disarray, no trash and fairly clean. There was no trash in any of the other rooms either. Norris moved to the front bedroom where she had seen the flies.

Before entering the bedroom, she looked at the door to the room. There was nothing unusual about it. There were no locks or padlocks on the door. The door handle on the bedroom door and all the doors in the apartment were at hand level. Norris demonstrated for the jury.

"As you went into that bedroom where you had seen the flies, could you describe the furnishings or any items that you found in and around there?" I continued.

"It was a kid's bedroom. I could tell because there were toys on the floor and clothes, but the bedroom was not disturbed in anyway," Norris noted.

"Now, what was the focus of your inspection of the apartment?" I queried.

"Just to find out if there was any trash in there that was causing the flies, to see if the resident had skipped on us."

"Was there any trash in that bedroom?"

"No. It just had a smell like urine. It was a very strong smell of urine," she finished.

"Did you find some other source in the room for flies?" I kept probing.

"We just kind of looked around and didn't find any trash."

"Were there flies in any room other than the child's room?" I asked.

"Not to my knowledge, no."

I asked whether there were chairs like kitchen chairs in the apartment. Norris said that there was a dinette set with chairs. She also said that there was a refrigerator in the apartment. During midsummer of 1992 when she entered the apartment, the refrigerator and electric seemed to be functioning properly.

"As a result of seeing the hundreds of flies, did you do anything?" I inquired.

"Went back to the office, contacted Michelle at Lilly's," she replied. Ms. Norris explained that she had the work telephone number in the leasing file.

"Tell us what you asked her and what she responded."

"I spoke with Michelle, I told her that we were doing a grounds pickup and we noticed that there were hundreds of flies in her apartment; we entered the apartment just to check it out to see if there was trash or she had skipped and that we noticed there was a really bad smell in the apartment, and she told me it was from her son peeing to bed and that she would take care of it," Norris recollected.

When asked, Norris also testified that during the summer, and up to that time, she had never seen flies in the apartment or Brandon's window. The impact of Norris' testimony was visible on the jurors' faces.

The business records had been admitted, and Norris went over them with the jurors. On the lease application, Jones listed two occupants of the apartment: herself and

Brandon Sims. She wrote that Brandon was her son, age four. Her emergency contact on that application was LeTava Parker, shown as "babysitter." It also included information about the defendant's automobile. It was a 1987 Chevrolet Cavalier.

The move-in sheet was neat, and the comments were printed in a clear and legible hand. It was the second document. Also shown to the jury were the defendant's driver's license, Eli Lilly identification cards, and some other identification. As Norris paged through the file, it was clear that there were additional documents in the folder.

I asked Norris if she had done a complete inspection of the apartment when she entered because of the flies. She did not. She just did a general walk through of the apartment.

Michelle Jones continued to live in the apartment where Brandon died for nearly six months. I just couldn't imagine it. She was still dancing with the troupe, working at Lilly's, and producing children's plays. And she was dating. I considered whether she brought dates home to that apartment. I imagined that some of the jurors were wondering the same things, but there was no way to know.

Norris confirmed Jones moved out on January 1, 1993. There were still three months left on her lease.

"At the time of her move-out, did you personally conduct an inspection of that apartment?"

"Yes, I did."

"Did you document that inspection in some particular way?" I questioned.

"The only way I did was on the security deposit return voucher," she said, showing me a piece of paper that had been marked as an exhibit. Norris said that she conducted the inspection and the document contained her writing.

"Upon your inspection, did you make a notation concerning the condition of the child's bedroom, the one that you'd seen the flies in?"

"Yes, I did."

"Could you tell us what you observed in that room?" I asked.

Mark Earnest again objected, and a bench conference interrupted the question and response. The Court overruled the objection and told Ms. Norris that she could answer.

"I had stated that the apartment was in good shape and clear but had brown stuff all over the floor. The bedroom floor," Norris responded.

"Which bedroom?" I inquired.

"The small bedroom floor."

"Was that the room where the flies were?"

"Yes, it was." She sighed.

"Did you attempt to determine what the brown stuff all over the floor was?" I queried.

"No, I did not," Ms. Norris confirmed.

The various exhibits were passed to the jury. We made copies for each juror so that they could take their time to read and review them. I watched the jurors and saw that each of them seemed to carefully review every page of the documents. When the last juror looked up from the papers, I asked the Court for permission to resume my examination of the witness.

"Ms. Norris, in regards specifically to the child's room, the room that you saw, is that room designated on the inspection sheet?"

"Yes."

"To your knowledge, ma'am, at the time that the defendant moved into that apartment, was there any brown staining on the carpeting?"

"Not to my knowledge," she answered. "And I would say that when she did the inspection she would have stated that because she would have been charged when she moved out."

Earnest objected to the last part of the answer as "speculative." The Court struck that part of her answer.

There are many ways to get information to the jury. I asked the question differently.

"Does the move-in inspection reflect any brown stuff at that time on the floor in the bedrooms?" I returned to the issue.

"No, it does not," the apartment manager replied.

When asked to describe the brown stain on the floor, Norris said that it was just a brown stain "all over the floor." She clarified that when she referred to the floor she meant the carpet.

I thought that I had asked all the questions that were needed but I returned to the State's table to speak with Crooke. He told me that I needed to ask another question. I followed his instincts. "Excuse me for jumping around a little bit. At the time in midsummer of '92 when you saw the hundreds of flies, were they on the inside or outside or both on the window?"

"They were on the inside," she declared.

"Were there any flies on the outside?"

"That I can't state," she said thoughtfully, but then continued, "but no, not like this. You would have noticed it."

"The window that you've described in the child's bedroom, did it have a closure on it?"

"Yes."

"Now the window itself, could you tell us how it opened and closed?"

Norris explained, gesturing. She bent both elbows and then straightened that as if she were pushing upward, palms forward.

"Did you lift the whole window or was it a half window or how did that work?"

"It was a half window to be lifted."

"Could you tell us how the window closed or what fastening device there was?"

"It had a lock in the middle of the window that you turned, and it would have gone into like a round lock socket." She was gesturing again.

"Were there any other locks on the windows?"

"No," Norris stated in her neutral tone.

The State had no further questions for Janet Norris. I slowly walked to our table, looking at Michelle Jones as she sat whispering into Mark Earnest's ear. Janet Norris was completely objective. She had no reason to fabricate. I briefly pondered what the cross-examination would entail. It was short.

"Miss Norris, you indicated that this was sometime in the summer of '92 that you saw some flies?" Mark Earnest asked her.

"Yes." She was continuing to answer only what she was asked. She had done that through her direct examination as well.

"And they were in the window?"

"Yes."

"The inside all by the window?"

"Yes."

Earnest continued, "So you went inside, and you looked around to investigate?"

"Yes."

"There weren't any flies by the closet door?"

"Not that I noticed, no," she answered.

"No flies by the bed?"

"Not that I noticed. There were just humming around the window area."

"And when you entered that room, you smelled this strong pungent odor that you felt was urine?" he insisted.

"Urine, yes."

"And it was strong?"

"Very strong."

"And then later on, you phoned Miss Jones and she indicated to you that her son had urinated the bed?"

"Correct."

"Now, you did this inspection, this move-out on January the first?" It was more of a statement than a question.

"Yes."

"Of 1993?" Earnest prompted.

"'93," the witness agreed.

"And you're not sure when you saw the flies, but it was sometime in the summer?"

"It was midsummer, yes," she corrected.

"Midsummer. So, the inspection was five, six, seven months later?" he suggested.

"Correct."

Earnest had been fairly gentle with the witness, encouraging her to agree with his questions. However, his voice became harsher as he asked, or told, her, "You spoke to a police officer, Lt. Rice, on October 23rd of this year, 1996?"

"Yes," she was unruffled.

"And he asked you some questions?"

"Yes, he did," she agreed.

"And he asked you some questions about when you went into the apartment?"

"Yes."

"Specifically asked you if there was any food on the floor or anything like that?" he persisted.

"And I could not give him any recollection if there was or wasn't. I just noticed toys," Norris offered.

"In fact, you said 'I can't recall'?"

"Yes."

"And you still can't recall?"

"No, I cannot."

"But there is a possibility there might have been?" he encouraged her.

"A possibility, yes, but nothing to draw flies like this, put it that way," she bluntly retorted.

He was sarcastic as he concluded, "In your opinion?"

"Yes."

Earnest said that he had no further questions for Ms. Norris.

There is an important rule to be remembered in every case. If the cross-examination has not hurt your case, do not ask any additional questions. It is a tough rule, because by nature, many lawyers want to have the last word. But that impulse has to be controlled. This is because your next questions may remind the defense of questions they should have asked. You may get a bad answer that diminishes the testimony you've elicited already.

There are a multitude of reasons to say, as I did, "No further questions, Your Honor."

CHAPTER TWENTY- EIGHT

THE UPSTAIRS NEIGHBOR

"The State calls Gloria Messer."

The jury had been accustomed to my center-of-the-courtroom announcements as each of our witnesses was about to enter the courtroom.

Ms. Messer was younger than the other witnesses we'd called so far. She wore elegant clothing that was not expensive but was well-pulled together. She looked at Michelle Jones as she walked to the witness stand. The Court administered the oath.

The witness corrected the record: her name was Glorianne Messer. I asked her several preliminary questions. She testified that she worked for IUPUI (Indiana University — Purdue University Indianapolis) and had been employed by the university for twelve years. She was a VA representative and senior records clerk.

In May of 1992, Glorianne Messer lived at the Georgetown Apartments in Indianapolis.

"And what was your address there?" I asked, although I suspected that the jury remembered that she was the upstairs neighbor identified by Janet Norris.

"3655 Alexandria Court, Apartment D," Messer responded.

"Now, where was Apartment D?" I asked.

"On the second floor," she said.

As I continued to ask Ms. Messer to describe where her apartment was located, Laudig stood.

"We would be willing to stipulate that this was Michelle Jones' upstairs neighbor if that would help us move along," he announced. *Gee, thanks, Steve. Try to ingratiate yourself with the jury much?* Of course, I said this to myself. The Court asked if the State accepted the stipulation. The State did. The Court instructed the jury, "The parties have stipulated, which means that it's a conclusive fact, that Miss Messer was Miss Jones' upstairs neighbor during 1992."

I resumed my spot in front of the jury box where I questioned witnesses. "Were you aware when the defendant moved into the apartment downstairs?"

"Not exactly. I knew that the apartment under me had been vacant for a while and then I noticed curtains were up. But I didn't really know who was there."

"Did there come a time when you noticed a person or people coming and going to that apartment?" I inquired.

"Yes."

"And who was it that was coming and going?"

"Mrs. Jones and her little boy," Messer replied.

"Did you know the age or the name of the little boy?" I resumed.

"No. I knew it was probably under five years old, but I never heard a name."

"Now, during the first several months of the tenancy, how often would you see the defendant?" I was looking in the direction of Michelle Jones as she sat at counsel table.

"Oh, maybe once or twice a week. Maybe once or twice on the weekends," Messer said with authority.

"Did there come a point in time, ma'am, when you no longer saw the little boy?" I directed her to the crux of her testimony.

"Yes."

"And when was that in 1992?"

"All I remember is it was hot weather," she replied.

"Did your apartment have a window that overlooked any area of the building?"

"My bedroom window."

"And what did it overlook?"

"Where the people that resided in my unit parked, and also the pool was right across."

"During the time that the defendant lived underneath you, did you observe her out in that parking area at any time?"

"Yes, when she and her little one would get in the car or when she would wash her car." Ms. Messer was well spoken.

"Can you describe for us, after you stopped seeing the little boy, whether you observed the defendant doing anything in regard to her car in the parking lot?"

"Washing her car," Glorianne offered.

"When you say 'washing her car,' could you describe to the jury whether this was inside or outside or both?" I wanted the details for the jury to consider.

"Both."

"How often did you see her doing that while it was still hot out?"

"Oh, I'd say every ten days or two weeks." Her reply was casual.

"And did she continue to do what you described, inside and outside?" I inquired.

"As far as I can remember," she responded.

"Now, from your apartment, were you able to hear downstairs?" I asked.

"From the bathroom I could," she informed the jury.

"Did you ever hear the little boy?"

"No," she said.

"Did you ever hear his voice or anything else?" I lingered on the subject.

"Concerning him?" she asked me.

"Yes," I responded.

"No. I never heard him," she admitted.

I asked Messer whether she had vacationed during that summer. She said that she may have taken a weekend, Friday to Sunday, but never any longer than that.

"Ma'am, when you parked your car, did you go past the window or near the window to the downstairs apartment to that bedroom?" I asked.

Steven Laudig objected because the question was not specific enough as to time frame. The Court sustained the objection and I tried to rephrase my question.

I asked Ms. Messer to show the jury where she parked on the diagram of the complex. She did and explained, "I would park sometimes right in front of our building, which we would all park at a diagonal. But other times I would park next to the pool, depending on how the parking was right in front of the units. Sometimes people didn't always park diagonally, and it was hard to park in there. So rather than bother with that, I would just park in front of the pool where nobody parked hardly at all," she rambled.

"During the summer of 1992, did you ever hear sounds coming from the downstairs apartment as you were in the parking lot?"

"No."

"Did you ever hear beating at the window?" I asked intently.

"No," Messer responded almost sorrowfully.

I had no other questions for Ms. Messer. Neither did the lawyers for Michelle Jones. I noticed that both Earnest and Laudig had objected during the witness' testimony. Apparently, the Court hadn't caught it, or decided to ignore it as well.

The Court took a lunch break. As we had been doing, Crooke and I raced to the Market (an actual market that was across the brick-paved road in front of the Marion County Government Center) to grab takeout. There were vendors and food places and arts and crafts in the Market. I had the same lunch every day of trial. Sesame bagel, toasted, light butter, and a slice of swiss cheese. Crooke had a more varied diet than I. We grabbed our food and returned to my office to discuss the afternoon's witnesses.

CHAPTER TWENTY-NINE

SGT. CROOKE TO THE STAND

When Court resumed after lunch, we wasted nearly two hours arguing over the reading of Damon Jones' prior testimony to the jury. The defense objected to every word, despite our having worked toward an agreement. The Court told us to call another witness and we would return to the Damon Jones issue later. One of the jurors had a doctor's appointment and the Court had agreed that he could go to the appointment and then return. In the meantime, the jury would take a break until the juror returned. She also soothed another juror who had vacation plans. "Don't worry, Mrs. Machette, you're going to be on that plane on Tuesday."

Sergeant Michael Crooke was called to the stand. It was not unusual for the State to call the investigating officer as its last witness. He would have heard all of the other witnesses' testimony because he was allowed to remain in the courtroom. He could then fill in any holes in the evidence that had been presented earlier in the trial. Detectives were experienced witnesses, comfortable in the courtroom.

Crooke was sworn in. The jurors had been introduced to Crooke during voir dire, but because he wore his plainclothes "uniform," they may not have realized his role in the case.

I needed to qualify Crooke as a witness. The process takes patience. It's easy to rush through an officer's background, but it's important. I took the time I needed, knowing that we could recall him tomorrow if we didn't finish in time. I asked Crooke where he worked, his assignment (unit supervisor in the Homicide and Robbery branch) and the length of time that he had worked for IPD. He testified that he had been with IPD for twenty-seven years, fifteen of those in Homicide Robbery.

Crooke told the jury about his training and experience. He spent his first seven years on the force in a patrol car. Then he worked as a crime prevention officer, went to detective school in 1980, then burglary and larceny detective and in vice. He described some of the in-service trainings that he had attended through IPD and at various colleges and universities. He also attended trainings through the International Association of Homicide Investigators, of which he was a member.

Crooke described the history of his investigation. He recounted how he first learned about the death of Brandon Sims. He described what he was told by the patrol officer, his visit to the hospital, and his later return to interview Michelle Jones at Midtown. Crooke spoke loud enough for the jury to hear without being overly loud or forceful. He was a schlub, à la Columbo, on the stand, as he was in other places. But he was smart, detailed, and very careful. He had his report in front of him and I made sure that the jury knew what he was looking at and why.

I asked him to describe his conversation with Michelle Jones at Midtown. Defense counsel raised and reserved the objections that had been expressed during the pretrial hearings. Reserving an objection meant that the argument that had been made during the earlier hearings did not have to be repeated during the trial. The Court overruled the objections again and permitted Crooke to share the details of his interview with her.

"Having been advised briefly of the scenario from Miss Goffredo, I asked her her name and solicited information regarding her child, date of birth of the child, father's name." Crooke was talking cop language and I wanted him to be more conversational.

"Now in terms of the information that you asked, were you able to understand and speak with the defendant without a problem?"

"Yes."

"Did she appear to understand your questions?"

"Yes."

"In regard to your questions concerning the father of the child, what specifically did she tell you?" I inquired.

"That Kevin Sims was the father."

"In terms of the information, at some point did you get to a discussion of what had actually happened to this child of hers?" Straight to the point.

"Yes."

"Could you tell us what she told you in that regard?" I cajoled.

"That she had left her child alone for a period of approximately one week," he said.

I interrupted because I wanted to be sure that the jury could hear and digest the entire story. As human beings, we do not hear every word spoken to us. Instead we hear in little starts and stops. A long narrative may not be fully understood by listeners, even jurors who are being very attentive. So short questions and answers deliver the most comprehensible testimony. I was trying to keep my questions precise. I had no concerns about the length of Crooke's answers. He was a man of few words.

"When she told you she had left Brandon alone, did she tell you where she had left him alone?"

"At 3655 Alexandria, the apartment there." Crooke pointed to the enlarged photograph of the building. He knew where I was going. I hoped he hopped on board allowing the examination to flow.

"Did you ask her questions concerning where she had gone?" I inquired.

"No," he said flatly.

"Did she tell you anything else about having left him there?" I prodded.

"That he was alone and unattended."

"Did the defendant tell you anything about what happened or what she observed when she returned?"

"That she returned and found him deceased," Crooke replied.

"Did she indicate to you how she knew Brandon was dead?" I asked.

"No."

Although the timing was not good, the Court interrupted the questioning to allow the juror to go to his doctor's appointment. Crooke stepped down from the witness stand and returned to his seat next to me. The Court announced that it would be in recess and the jurors filed out and into the jury room. The juror with the doctor's appointment would only be absent for an hour or so. No testimony could be received without all of the jurors and alternate jurors present. While the jury waited, we resumed discussion about the testimony of Damon Jones. Damon had not appeared in court despite being ordered to do so, but his testimony had been preserved from the pretrial hearings. Part of that transcript would be read to the jury.

When all of the jurors were available, we interrupted the testimony of Sgt. Crooke to read some of Damon Jones' testimony to the jury. I had the transcript in my hand and the jury knew that I was reading. I indicated that it was the testimony of an unavailable witness, Damon Jones. I read the jury the transcript where Damon was administered the oath. Then I continued:

Direct Examination by Mark Earnest: "Mr. Jones, do you have any personal knowledge of what, if anything, happened with Brandon Sims between the dates of July 1, 1992 and August 31, 1992?"

Damon Jones: "No, sir."

Cross Examination by Diane Marger Moore: "Did I understand your testimony, sir, to be that you were never in contact or alone with Brandon after you separated from your former wife?"

"That's correct."

"All right. Let me show you what's been marked as State's Exhibit 4, which purports to be a certified copy of the petition for dissolution of marriage. Could you look at this, sir? Do you recognize the signature on the second page of State's Exhibit 4?"

"Yes. It's Michelle's."

"Okay. And by that do you mean the defendant, Michelle Engron Jones?"

"Yes."

"And during the time that you were together, sir, that is, married to Michelle Engron Jones, you were aware that she had sole and exclusive custody of her son, Brandon?"

"Yes."

"There came a time, sir, long after you separated, a couple of years later, when you again met Arlene Blevins, Brandon's grandmother?"

"Right."

"Now this time frame, somewhere late in '92 or '93, can you be more specific when you next saw Miss Blevins, do you know?"

"I was out, um, may have been in summer, I think of '92 or '93, selling different products that I had at the time and she drove up to me on the street."

"At the time that you saw Mrs. Blevins, was she looking for Brandon?"

"Yes."

That was the end of the transcript of Damon Jones.

Mike Crooke resumed his seat on the witness stand. The judge reminded him that he had been sworn. I was permitted to recommence my questioning.

"After telling you what she found when she returned, did she tell you anything else?"

"That subsequently she had placed the child in her car, which she did say was a 1987 blue Chevy Cavalier, and that she had driven to police headquarters and was going to take the child there and report it, but basically because of religious beliefs at that time, elected apparently not to, and then subsequently returned to her vehicle and drove on the interstate and subsequently placed the child along the interstate."

I asked, "Did she tell you where on the interstate?"

"The description at that time was just basically, I think, I-65, somewhere north," Crooke repeated.

"Did she tell you whether she believed she could show you the exact spot where Brandon's body was?" I was turned around and looked at the defendant as she sat nonplused at counsel's table.

"Yes."

I asked Crooke some additional questions about Michelle Jones' awareness and competency at the time he met with her. He said that she gave Brandon's correct date of birth, age, where she had left him alone, and that she had left him between July and August of 1992. She had disclosed that Kevin Sims had been in jail. She described how she wrapped Brandon's body in a blanket when she carried it to her car.

"Did you ever again have an interview with the defendant?" I asked.

"No," Crooke answered succinctly.

"Did you make any arrangements or discuss anything during or at the end of that interview?"

"Yes."

"And what was that?"

"To pick her up and drive her to the location where she could point out possibly where the body was at," Crooke replied.

"Did you make an attempt to do that at the time that you had previously arranged?"

"Yes."

"What date was it that you had arranged to go back to the hospital?"

Michelle Jones knew where she had dumped Brandon's body, but refused to lead police to recover it. I was sure of it. And that knowledge gnawed at me. I believed that it would similarly confound the jury.

"On that day did you go anywhere?" I continued.

"Yes," he responded.

"With whom?" I asked.

"Lt. Mark Rice."

"Was anyone else with you?"

"No."

Crooke described driving northbound on Interstate 65 to the Attica/Frankfort exit. The purpose of their trip was to try to locate Brandon's body.

"Over the course of years between January of 1994 and the present, do you know how many people have looked on various areas of I-65 for Brandon's body?" I inquired.

Over objection, Crooke responded that between twenty and thirty people had searched for Brandon's body, involving about seventy man-hours. There had been at least four to five days of searching, including the use of cadaver dogs, search and rescue personnel from the Hendricks County Sheriff's Department, as well as the use of an infrared detection system through the Indiana State Police helicopter unit. The areas searched were based on what Michelle Jones had told Crooke during their January 1994 meeting.

"Now, in regard to your further investigation or additional things, sir, did you search for any other information concerning Brandon?"

"Yes. Well, to establish that the child existed, I obtained a certified copy of his birth certificate."

I interrupted. "How old would Brandon have been two weeks ago Monday?"

"Nine," Crooke informed the jury.

"Did you attempt to find out any information about whether he had ever been enrolled in school?"

"Yes."

"And what information did you learn?"

"There was no record of him being enrolled in an Indianapolis public school."

"Did you learn anything about whether or not a missing person's report had ever been filed?"

"There was none filed." Crooke then explained what a missing person's report requires and includes.

"Did you try to determine whether or not there were any medical records for Brandon after the summer of 1992?"

"Yes."

"And what were the results of your investigation?"

"I located no records," he responded.

"Were you responsible for any other evidence gathering in this case?" The extent of the investigation was important. Crooke had been thorough, and this was essential to proving that Brandon was dead. Modisett said that we couldn't prove death without a body. I wanted to prove him wrong. At the very least, Brandon deserved that.

Crooke detailed his investigation. He described obtaining records at the Georgetown apartment complex, locating some of the witnesses and interviewing witnesses.

I had no further questions. Time for the cross-examination. But the defense had objected and claimed that I had asked questions which encompassed the juvenile court proceedings. The Court asked Crooke some questions with the jurors outside the courtroom before ruling on the defense motion. The Court concluded that the objection would be overruled.

Earnest had the right to cross-examination Crooke. He began, "Detective Crooke, the first time that you went out to the psychiatric unit at Wishard Hospital, were you able to speak with Michelle Jones?"

"No," Crooke conceded.

"Why was that?"

"She was being attended to," Crooke explained.

"The information you obtained from her in terms of what she did with the body was that she took the body and she placed it somewhere off of an embankment off of Interstate 65; is that correct?" Earnest pressed.

"Yes."

"The first time that you had an opportunity to search for this body would have been in January of 1994?"

"Yes."

"And that would have been almost a year and a half or so, depending on when, from the summer of 1992?" Earnest calculated.

"Yes."

"Now, and you've been to that area, I-65, haven't you?"

"Yes, sir," Crooke said.

"Parts of I-65. And there are trees, and this is off of a grass embankment right off the highway; is that correct?"

"Yes."

"And it's exposed to the outdoors and to the elements; is that correct?"

"Yes, sir."

Finally, Earnest got to his point. Crooke was being as candid as any police officer with whom I had ever worked.

"Now, I don't like to ask this question any more than you're probably going to like to answer it, but in your opinion, after having been there and considering the fact that it may have been a year and a half, if not longer, do you think it's possible that the reason that the body isn't there is due to natural reasons and things of that nature?"

Crooke didn't hesitate. "Yes."

I had no other questions for Crooke.

I approached the middle of the courtroom. "Your Honor, the State of Indiana rests."

CHAPTER THIRTY

THE DEFENSE PRESENTS EVIDENCE

The jury was excused. In most criminal cases, the defense will argue what is referred to as a motion for directed verdict or judgment on the evidence. It is an argument to the Court that there was insufficient evidence of a crime, or a particular element of a crime to allow the jury to consider the case. There are certainly other motions that can be argued but this is the most common. It is important for criminal defense attorneys to make these motions in order to protect their clients' appellate rights.

Susan Burke argued the defense motions. I responded. In order for the Court to rule, the judge replayed the tape-recorded testimony of Clarissa Dunlap. The Court focused on Clarissa Dunlap's testimony where she "asked the defendant what did you do, Malikia, beat Brandon to death and leave him?" Burke reminded the judge that Jones' answer, as recollected by Clarissa Dunlap, was "I guess so." All motions were denied.

The defense advised the Court that they had a witness available to begin their case. They also told the Court that one of their witnesses, Valerie Hickman, was not available until the morning. The Court had already refused to allow the State to call Ms. Hickman as a witness for the prosecution because she was not disclosed far enough in advance of trial. I couldn't believe that the defense would call her but was pleased. I hoped that the Court would allow her to be called.

The State has an obligation to be fair and not surprise the defense with information they had not been provided before trial. I responded to the defense announcement about Ms. Hickman. I reminded the Court that the State had been prevented from calling Hickman. I also wanted the defense to be forewarned, that if they did call Hickman, I expected her to recount, on cross-examination, a conversation she'd had with Michelle Jones. During that conversation, the defendant admitted that her beating of Brandon "went too far."

"We believe that Ms. Hickman will testify that Michelle's admission was in the context of 'what happened and how did Brandon die?'" I cautioned the Court. Having this additional witness would be great for the prosecution.

Whether Hickman would testify was really up to the defense. The Court agreed to permit her to testify if the defendant called her as a witness. The State could cross-examine her.

The jury returned to the courtroom.

"The defense calls Tahirah Abubakr to the witness stand," announced Susan Burke.

This witness was the mother of Mohammad Abubakr, the alleged boyfriend of both Clarissa Dunlap and Michelle Jones, and an occupant of the apartment allegedly burgled by Clarissa Dunlap.

I listened as Mrs. Abubakr described her two jobs. She worked with Community Sentence of Indianapolis for four hours, and Women's and Community Service, a national organization. She programed for senior citizens. She also acted as a liaison to a Job Corps operation for young women.

Burke continued, "And do you know Michelle Engron Jones?"

"Yes, I do."

"And could you tell us how long you've known Michelle Engron Jones?" Burke asked.

"I've known Michelle approximately three years."

"And how would you describe the nature of your relationship?"

"I would say my relationship with Michelle is more parental in that we are friends and that relationship is a parental kind of relationship," Mrs. Abubakr replied.

"Now, do you also know a person by the name of Clarissa Dunlap, or Duny?"

"I know her as Duny, yes."

"And how long have you known Duny?"

"Since February of this year," Mrs. Abubakr said.

"And do you have any acquaintances in common with Duny?" Burke inquired.

"Only through the connection of our religious practice," Abubakr said.

"So you are both members of the same church?" Burke suggested.

"Yes."

"Now, in that church community, are you aware of whether or not Miss Dunlap or Duny had a reputation as to her truthfulness in that group?" Burke asked.

The State objected and requested permission to ask questions prior to arguing the objection. The Court allowed this.

I asked the witness, "Ma'am, you've never lived in Gary?"

"No, I have not." The tone of her response made clear that she did not like me, although we had never met.

"You're not familiar with people with whom Miss Dunlap works as a nurse?"

"No," she snapped.

"You don't know her friends and family in that community?" I questioned the basis for any opinion that Abubakr might be permitted to present.

"I only know her mother," she replied.

"And you've only known her or anybody, and you called them acquaintances, for less than a few months?" I pressed.

"Since February of this year."

I argued that the defendant had not provided a sufficient foundation to present the opinion testimony. A party is entitled to prove that a witness has either a good or bad reputation in the community for truthfulness. But the witness has to have first-hand knowledge of the community opinion. This was where Burke was heading.

Burke argued that community is an expansive term in the law and that the time that Mrs. Abubakr had known Duny was sufficient for her to know Duny's reputation for truthfulness in the community of their church. She did not specify which church they shared.

The Court concluded, "I think the objection goes more to weight than admissibility." And permitted the witness to answer.

The weight of evidence is the amount of credence that a juror might assign to some specific information. Admissibility is a determination for the court. In this instance, the issue was whether the witness had sufficient knowledge about what the community thought about Duny's truthfulness to share it with the jury. The Court found that she did.

Burke resumed questioning the witness. "Are you aware of whether or not she had any reputation for truthfulness in that church community?"

"Yes, I am."

"Do you know whether that reputation was as a truthful person or as an untruthful person?" Burke asked.

"I would say untruthful," Abubakr opined.

"On August 25, 1996, if you remember, did Clarissa Dunlap, or Duny, have permission to enter your home?"

"No, she did not," Mrs. Abubakr said.

"Was your home broken into on that date?"

"Yes, it was."

"Do you have any personal knowledge of any items that were taken at that time?" Burke asked.

"Yes."

"And what items would those be?"

"Those items was belonging to my son. His personal items, necklace and clothing items," Abubakr replied.

"Now, was anything, on that date when your home was broken into, was anything left in your home?"

"There was a three-page letter."

Her answer surprised me. I knew nothing about the contents of the letter.

"And did that three-page letter, did it have a signature on it?" Burke continued.

"Yes, it did."

The State had taken a sworn statement from Abubakr before the trial. She denied she had seen the letter. She testified that she learned about a letter from Mohammad or Jones. But at trial, she testified that the letter was signed by Duny and that she had seen Duny's signature in the past.

"Let's see this letter," I muttered under my breath.

Mrs. Abubakr could not produce the letter. She said that the police had taken the letter when she had reported the burglary to the police.

Burke introduced the print-out police report showing that this witness had reported the incident to the police. The narrative section of the report included the following:

> Victim states that her son's ex-girlfriend, Jennifer Dunlap, was the only person that knew where the key was to the house. She stated she entered the house without her permission, went downstairs, and took an undetermined amount of cassette tapes and personal clothing of her son, Mohammad. Victim states she will prosecute Jennifer Dunlap. Jennifer had left a note signed by her and left it downstairs in the basement. The note was sent to the property branch as evidence.

The report was passed to the jurors to review. Then Burke continued her examination of Mrs. Abubakr. "Do you know whether Jennifer Dunlap and Clarissa Dunlap are the same or different people?"

"I have no idea. I know the woman as Duny. I have heard Clarissa. The rest of it I don't know," the witness responded. She also told the jury that Mohammad was her son and that he was living with her at the time of the break in.

Burke wanted to ask the witness whether Duny was jealous of the defendant. Although she asked enough questions that the jury surely got the point, the Court disallowed the testimony over my objections.

It was the State's turn to cross-examine the witness.

"Ma'am, you knew Duny's, the person you call Duny, writing because she'd been involved with your son?"

Mrs. Abubakr's hostility was evident. "I knew her writing because I had seen her writing," she retorted.

"She, in fact, had been dating your son, had she not?" I asked.

"That is true. But I know the writings from documents of things, because she would always take notes at meetings, that's how I know her writing."

"But you also know that she had dated your son?"

"I do not deny that," she responded bluntly.

"During the time that your son and Duny were dating, she came to your home on more than one occasion?" I asked.

"Yes, that is true."

"As a matter of fact, whenever they were together here in Indianapolis, they were at your home?"

"Yes, that is true."

"On the occasion reported here," I said, referring to the police report that the defense put into evidence, "there was no damage to any door or any window?" I reiterated. "Duny let herself in with a key?"

"Well, when we filed the charges—" Abubakr began.

"Did she let herself in with a key?"

"Yes, she let herself in with the key," she mimicked. "She was unauthorized to be in my house," she insisted.

"In regard to the police report, ma'am, at the time, you did, in fact, tell the officer that you were willing to prosecute, right?" I asked.

"Yes."

"Detective Hayes did call you, didn't he?"

"No, ma'am." She shook her head.

"Ma'am, you were contacted on several occasions by law enforcement and you did not follow up," I stated more than asked.

"I was not contacted," she insisted.

"Did you follow up, ma'am?"

"No, I had not followed up, if that's what you're asking me!" she snapped.

"In fact, from the date of that, whatever it was," I was waving the report, "until defense counsel brought you in, you never, at any point, contacted anyone from law enforcement to provide them with further information, did you?" I demanded.

"No, ma'am," she said resignedly.

"In regard to your knowledge of Duny, and I did, in fact, ask you those questions when we met at my office — and at that time, ma'am, I asked you whether you knew her well and you said, no, that you did not." I had her statement in my hand.

"I don't know that I said that. I'm still saying I didn't know her well in terms of social contacts. I knew her within the context of the community," she said.

I read from a page of her statement, "Ma'am, what you said was 'I wouldn't say well because my only contact with her it was through limited numbers of meetings.'"

She agreed. "Yes."

"So, when you told the jury that you'd only known her for a period of months, and even within those months, ma'am, you really only saw her when your son brought her home or at meetings?" I insisted.

"No, that's not true," she denied.

I had no further questions and neither did Burke after we stipulated that Dunlap's full name was Clarissa Jennifer Dunlap.

That was the end of the day for the jury. They were excused to go home after being cautioned again not to read or listen to any news about the case. There were reporters in the courtroom for most of the trial, the newspapers continued to report on the case and it made the evening news most nights. No one wanted to have to try the case over again.

CHAPTER THIRTY-ONE

PREPARING FOR CLOSING ARGUMENTS

While every stage of a criminal trial may be important, working on jury instructions is one of the top contenders. Usually the Court gives what are known as "standard" instructions, which direct the jury how to deliberate, select a foreperson, and handle the verdict form. Included in the routine instructions are ones about reasonable doubt and the burden of proof. But in every case, there are additional instructions that each side urges the Court to give the jury. This is a time-consuming process because the discussion must be taken down by the court reporter in case there are appellate issues raised by the Court's failure to give a required instruction or giving an illegal, out of date, or improper instruction.

A court may instruct the jury to consider "lesser included offenses." These are less serious crimes that can be proven with the same evidence as a more serious one. Sometimes the defendant, through counsel, insists on an instruction on lesser included offenses, and sometimes the defendant rolls the dice that he'll be acquitted of the more serious charge and doesn't want to give the jury the option to return a "compromise" verdict. Prosecutors who are concerned about the strength of their proof may also request these instructions. All these issues are considered at what is called the charge conference.

Before the trial started, both sides had submitted instructions that they wanted to be given to the jury for the Court to consider. The Court had reviewed some of them with counsel, during recesses. But this Friday morning, we would hash out the instructions, so that all counsel could know what the Court's instructions would be and use them during closing arguments.

The State had to prove every element of the crimes, prove proper venue, and extinguish all reasonable doubt in the jurors in order to sustain a conviction. The defense had only to convince a juror, one juror, that there was reasonable doubt as to whether the defendant had committed the crimes charged. In Indiana, a jury verdict had to be unanimous. Not so in other states. But in Indiana, every juror had to find that the State had proven its case beyond a reasonable doubt. If even one juror found reasonable doubt, a mistrial would have to be declared. A mistrial meant that the case would have to be retried. If the mistrial was due to some form of misconduct by the State, then the case could be mistried with prejudice. No second chance to convict the defendant.

In this case, after much argument on both sides as to many of the instructions, the Court decided to give an instruction on the lesser offense of reckless homicide. Also, verdict forms were prepared for the jury. One was for murder, one for reckless homicide, and one for neglect of a dependent as a Class B Felony. On each verdict form, the word *verdict* appeared in the center of the page. Then the two possible verdicts as to each charge. The verdict form for the murder charge included:

VERDICT
"WE, THE JURY, FIND THE DEFENDANT, MICHELLE ENGRON JONES, **GUILTY** OF MURDER, A FELONY, AS CHARGED IN COUNT I."

FOREPERSON

DATED:_____

****OR****

"WE, THE JURY, FIND THE DEFENDANT, MICHELLE ENGRON JONES, **NOT GUILTY** OF MURDER, A FELONY, AS CHARGED IN COUNT I."

_____
FOREPERSON
DATED:_____

The other verdict forms were similar. After a few hours of work, the instructions were set.

All that remained of the trial was for the defense to call its last witness, closing arguments, and jury instructions. The Court had promised the jurors that the trial would be completed today.

The defense had not told me the name of their last witness, although I was hoping that they would call Valerie Hickman. We all took a break before the jury was recalled to the courtroom.

"The defense calls Detective Crooke," Earnest announced. He only had a few questions for the witness. Earnest asked the detective how the defendant was taken into custody. Crooke told the jury that she surrendered herself. Then he asked about statements that the defendant had made to him.

"Yesterday, you testified concerning her statement, which you took while she was in the psychiatric hospital?"

"Yes, sir."

"And she told you that she had placed the body of Brandon Sims alongside the highway; is that correct?" Earnest said in a companionable tone.

"Yes," Crooke agreed.

"And what else did she tell you she did after she took the body down to the side of the highway?" Earnest asked. "Did she tell you anything else that she did after she took Brandon Sims' body down to the side of the highway?"

"Yes," Crooke replied.

"What else did she tell you?" Earnest prodded.

"She indicated she remained with the body until daylight hours," Crooke responded.

I had never heard this before. I suspected that this additional information had been disclosed in the juvenile court hearing. How else would Earnest have known about it? She had never disclosed when she buried the body, so "remaining with the body" could have meant a few minutes or several hours. I looked at the jury. They did not seem impressed.

Those were all of Earnest's questions. Did I really want to ask Crooke anything further? I failed to follow my own steadfast rule.

"Did the defendant try to place Brandon's body in a secluded place where he would not be found?" I asked. Crooke, an honest man, said that the defendant had not told him that or he did not recall her telling him that.

My cross-examination had not helped the State's case. I should have asked nothing.

A juror wanted to know: "When the body was by the road, did the defendant leave the body wrapped in the blanked used during transport?" The judge asked Crooke the juror's question. He said he did not know.

The defense had no further questions for Crooke. It also had no additional witnesses. I guessed that Valerie Hickman confirmed to defense counsel what she had told me. Jones' admission that she "went too far" in beating Brandon would have been another serious blow to the defense.

I would never find out.

The defense rested.

The State had the right to call rebuttal witnesses in criminal trials. Rebuttal testimony is limited to contradicting evidence that the defense presented. Again, lawyers struggle with the need for the last word in the trial.

"The State of Indiana has no rebuttal, Your Honor."

The Court excused the jury. We reviewed the jury instructions one more time. The defense argued motions for judgment on the evidence. The motions were denied.

CHAPTER THIRTY-TWO

THE VERDICT

The State gave the first closing argument and the last. I gave a heartfelt closing. I believe that the defense's closing was equally heartfelt.

For the State, I reminded the jury of each bit of evidence; arguing, for example, that if Brandon had been alive and hungry for the days that he was left alone, he could have gotten food from the refrigerator. I reminded the jury that Arlene Blevins had testified that even at two years old, Brandon could open the fridge and climb up on the counter. If he was thirsty, he could have gotten water from the sink or even from the toilet if he was really thirsty. I looked at the registered nurse who was on the jury, and reminded her (and all of them) that if Brandon had not been beaten, he could have readily survived for four days without food, so long as he had water. There was running water in the apartment that Brandon knew how to reach.

I also described how, if Brandon was alone in his room, he would have looked out the window. Someone would have seen him. He could have called out to Ms. Messer. He could even have walked out the front door. He didn't.

My argument was not written down. It was impromptu. I wanted the jury to see the crime as I saw it. What mother would forget, in only a year and a half, where she had dumped her only child's body? What mother buries her son along a highway? What about the flies and the brown stain on the carpet? Didn't all of this confirm what the defendant told Clarissa Dunlap? I asked them to consider it all.

I read the jury instructions that listed the elements of the two charged crimes. I discussed every element of each crime with the jury. I explained the State's interpretation of what evidence supported each of the elements of each charge.

The defense attacked Clarissa Dunlap and her version of what the defendant told her. They worked hard to persuade the jurors that in order to convict Michelle Jones, they had to believe Clarissa Dunlap, a Santeria priestess, burglar, and scorned woman. They described the investigation as flawed and biased. It was a passionate plea for acquittal. They too reviewed the elements of each offense, reaching the conclusion that there was reasonable doubt. A lot of reasonable doubt. The defense lawyers urged the jury to conclude that the State had not proven their case.

After the emotional plea by defense counsel, I tried to convince the jury with an unemotional analysis of the case. I looked at Michelle Jones at the defense table. I walked up to her, wanting the jury to look with me.

"This woman murdered her own four-year-old child. 'I ain't gonna raise no freak,' Michelle Engron Jones told Arlene Blevins. And she didn't.

"Michelle had options. She was not stranded with a child she was incapable of raising. Arlene Blevins wanted to raise Brandon. LeTava Parker Muhammad offered to take him and raise him. Michelle Engron Jones was surrounded by the love and friendship of several strong, maternal women, all of whom would have helped her raise Brandon. A beautiful child."

My voice was quieter. "Instead of protecting Brandon, raising him, or even sharing him with the other women who loved him, Michelle beat him so badly that he would die from his injuries. Then she left him *alone*. Did he linger, starving to death? Imagine that child, *alone* in his room, terrified, in pain, starving, the little plates of food that Michelle claimed to have left him gone. Why did she leave him food on a plate when he could open the refrigerator or climb up on the cabinets to get food? The only reason is because she beat him so badly that he couldn't get food or water. She beat him to death. He would die from the injuries that she (I was pointing at Michelle) inflicted. You must convict her of murder and for abandoning that precious child, of neglect as a Class B Felony."

The Court read the final instructions to the jury. She also gave the jury a written copy of the instructions to take to the jury room with them. After the jury settled into the jury room, the bailiff gave them three verdict forms and all of the evidence. It was up to those twelve people, the jury, to decide whether Michelle Jones had knowingly murdered Brandon.

We were permitted to leave the courthouse while the jury deliberated. There was no way of knowing how long it would take, so we left our pager numbers with the clerk. We filed out of the courtroom.

Crooke, Lt. Rice, Lt. Duke and I decided to go to TGI Fridays, a chain restaurant in downtown Indy, for lunch and to wait it out. Each of these good men had worked on this case, going above and beyond their obligations. Each had spent numerous personal hours searching for Brandon, meeting with witnesses, bringing me up to speed. On the way there, I wanted feedback from Crooke. I wanted his approval, I guess, for the way that the trial had been handled. I wanted to know if my closing was good enough to have sewn all of the tiny pieces of evidence together to form a murder conviction. I wanted all of that.

What I received was Crooke's blanket conclusion. "They will never convict Michelle Engron Jones of murder." My heart was in my throat. I asked him to explain why he thought that, but he just had a feeling. I was crushed by his blunt assessment.

While we ordered, I wondered how many soccer games I had missed. My children were both involved and active, and I had been working every weekend on this case. I considered all the chores, homework, and chauffeuring that Steve, my husband, the saint, had done while I prepared for and tried this case. I had some serious making up to do.

We ordered our lunch and waited. Before the food arrived, Crooke's pager, my pager and Rice's pager vibrated simultaneously.

We had a verdict.

When we returned to the courtroom, the defendant and her attorneys were already present and seated at counsel table. There were numerous members of the public defenders' staff and deputy prosecuting attorneys in the gallery awaiting the verdict. The press was there. The tension was substantial. We stood as the jurors slowly walked into the courtroom and took their seats. None of the jurors looked at me. None of them looked at the defendant. They focused their attention on Judge Magnus-Stinson.

The Court asked the foreman, who was standing with some papers in his hands, whether the jury had reached a verdict. He said that they had. The foreman handed the papers to the bailiff, who handed them to the judge without looking at them. The foreman was seated.

The judge slowly read the verdicts to herself. When she looked up, I could read nothing on her face. The Court asked the defendant to rise. Michelle Engron Jones and her attorneys stood, facing the judge. The judge read the caption of the case, which included the name of the court, the courtroom number, name of the parties, and case number.

Then she read: "Verdict. We the jury find the defendant, Michelle Engron Jones, guilty of murder, a felony, as charged in Count I."

The Court read the name of the foreman and the date that had been handwritten on the form. Although there had been a whoosh of breath from the gallery as the verdict was read,

I saw nothing on the defendant's face. Mark Earnest looked ashen.

"Verdict. We the jury find the defendant, Michelle Engron Jones, guilty of neglect of a dependent, a Class B Felony, as charged in Count II." Again, the Court read the name of the foreman and the date: November 22, 1996.

The defense asked that the jury be polled. Each juror was asked by Judge Magnus-Stinson whether that juror agreed with the verdicts that she had just read.

"Juror number one, is this your verdict?" The juror stood and affirmed that the verdict was his verdict. The Court repeated this process, asking every juror whether the written verdicts were their verdicts. Every juror confirmed that they had voted to convict Michelle Engron Jones of murder and neglect as a Class B Felony.

Michelle Jones was remanded into custody. This did not alter her living arrangements. The defendant had not been able to post bail set by the Court following the pretrial hearings.

The judge also ordered a pre-sentence investigation and set a day for the defendant's sentencing. The defense lawyers glared as Crooke and I left the courtroom.

There can be no celebration when two young lives are ruined or lost. Brandon Sims was killed by Michelle Jones. But her life too was forever altered by her actions. Only sadness can follow that result.

While I was glad that I had convicted her, I had no desire to celebrate. The strongest emotion I felt was a longing to hug my kids and my spouse, thank my parents for loving me, and sleep for a week.

CHAPTER THIRTY-THREE

THE COURT'S SENTENCE

In Indiana, unlike many states, sentencing was not immediate after a verdict. Instead, the law required a pre-sentence investigation. This was a report completed by the probation department that provided both basic and more complex information that could be considered by a court in making a sentencing decision. In that report, the defendant could provide an unsworn statement that could be considered by the judge. The PSI, an acronym for pre-sentence investigation, would include information from friends and family, prior criminal history (if any), and requests or comments by the victims.

The court had a range of sentences that could be imposed for every crime. The law set a "presumptive" sentence in 1996. The presumptive was the standard sentence prescribed by the legislature for a given crime. A presumptive sentence served as the starting point and allowed the sentencing court some limited discretion to enhance a sentence to reflect aggravating circumstances, or to reduce a sentence to reflect mitigating circumstances. The court was required to put into writing any aggravating or mitigating factors that were applied to vary from the presumptive sentence.

The defense and the State were permitted to present evidence and argument to support their requests and arguments for leniency or a tougher sentence. The sentencing hearing, where this evidence and argument could be presented, was open to the public.

Michelle Jones was in the Marion County Jail awaiting sentencing. The Court had ordered a pre-sentence investigation as was required by law. The probation department essentially collected all available data that could be useful to the Court in imposing a sentence. These reports were confidential. Keeping them strictly under wraps from the public and others encouraged candor from the defendant and the other people who were interviewed.

The probation department did a good job in most instances, but there were also private firms that conducted pre-sentence investigations. These private firms worked for individual attorneys and, in some instances, the public defender's office, to provide additional information and perhaps more defendant friendly information to the Court.

The sentencing hearing for Michelle Jones was delayed, permitting her team of lawyers more time to prepare for her sentencing. It was held on February 28, 1997. While the reports themselves were private, the sentencing hearing was open to the public. Many of the witnesses, reporters, and courthouse observers who had watched or participated in the trial came to the sentencing.

The Court advised everyone that she had received the pre-sentence reports and had reviewed each of them in detail. Each party had the opportunity to correct information in the reports and to present additional information for the Court to consider. Frequently, the defendant had friends and family speak on her behalf. Sometimes, the defendant made a statement. The victims also had the right to address the Court.

For the defense, the defendant, Mark Earnest, and Susan Burke were present along with the private pre-sentence investigator that they had retained, Steven Brock. Kevin Sims and I were at the State's table. Sgt. Crooke was on to other murders that needed solving.

The hearing for Michelle Jones lasted several hours. Judge Magnus-Stinson started by asking defense counsel and the State if there were any corrections to Probation's PSI. There were none.

The defense called two witnesses from Michelle Jones' past. The first was Mary Armstrong-Smith. Susan Burke questioned the witness.

Armstrong-Smith was the executive director of the Vivian Smith Teen Parenting Program in Indianapolis. She had served as director for three years but had been with the agency for a total of eight years. She met Michelle Jones in 1986 when Michelle applied for a Youth Job Preparedness Program. Jones was fourteen or fifteen at the time. She was accepted, and Armstrong-Smith testified that she got to know her pretty well.

Armstrong-Smith testified about a conversation that she had with Jones' mother, Mae Engron, in about April of 1987. Mae told her that if Jones had been sexually active and if she was pregnant, that she, Mae Engron, was going to beat her up and throw her out.

Armstrong-Smith later received another telephone call from Mae Engron. She was even more enraged than before. Mae had confirmed that her daughter was sexually active and possibly pregnant and that she, Mae, was going to beat her.

Armstrong-Smith told the judge that she called the police and Jones was taken to the Guardian's home. After that, Armstrong-Smith saw her only occasionally. She saw her at Morris House. The last time that the witness had seen Jones was about two or three years prior to the hearing.

Armstrong-Smith told the Court that she had seen many angry mothers, but that she truly believed that Mae Engron meant that she would kill her daughter for getting pregnant.

"Now you're aware of the charges for which Michelle has been convicted or has had the verdict of the jury. Is there anything in her past history that you think might help the judge understand how this case came to pass?" Burke asked.

"When I read about this, I was really sick, but not really surprised. Kids who don't have support at home, who in effect have anti-support, and who don't get the kind of help they need have a lot of trouble being parents."

She elaborated on her observations. Armstrong-Smith testified that Jones had done really well in the Job Preparedness Program and became the president of the group. "I worried about her sometimes because she was kind of a perfectionist, she had extremely high standards for herself."

The witness expressed her opinion of Michelle Jones. "Her whole life has been I think a reaching out for some kind of support and validation that didn't happen at home. And if she'd gotten the right kind of help, maybe things would be different."

Armstrong-Smith wondered whether Jones had been physically abused at home, but there was no real evidence of that. She also elucidated on her belief as to why some abused children become perfectionists. She shared that she had grown up in a situation somewhat similar and she empathized.

"I was lucky. There was the right kind of support. And it was hard, but it worked out. I know she's been convicted of murder. This is awful. The baby's gone. And yet I believe with all my heart that she is salvageable. She's twenty-four. And I know she has to be punished in some way, I know that's your job." Armstrong-Smith addressed the judge, "But I hope that you take into account everything. I just don't think she's a sociopath, I don't think that she's an evil person. She made some mistakes. She did some terrible things. But I also think that she has something she can contribute to the world if she had a chance."

I was permitted to question the witness. In response to my questions, she admitted that while she had watched closely for evidence of physical abuse, she never saw any that she could attribute to Michelle's home. And she knew of only one instance where Mae Engron became so enraged that she threatened to beat Jones. On that day, Armstrong-Smith called the police.

"So that the only incident from which you have drawn all your conclusions about her mother's parenting skills is the one incident, and she was, from what you described, in an incredible rage over her daughter's pregnancy?" I asked.

"Michelle had made comments prior to that indicating some fear of her mother. She never said why, she wouldn't say why. And no, there were no bruises, so I didn't make a call to Child Protective Services."

Burke reminded the witness about a situation that Jones had related to her involving a 2x4.

"Well, a board. The night I went to her house and the police were there she said her mother beat her with a board," Armstrong-Smith replied. At Burke's urging, the witness testified that she did not believe that there was an ordinary mother/child love relationship in the family.

The next witness was Delores Mockabee, director of the Indiana Child Development Institute. (*More strong women who had been in her life*, I thought. *They'd been in the same careers from the time she was a teen. She could have called any one of these women for help with Brandon.*) In 1988, she was the director of Morris House and met the defendant. Jones lived at that group home until 1990. Mockabee described her close working relationship with Jones and how she was a success at the home, graduating from high school, getting a job, all of the concrete issues.

Mockabee's greatest fear for Michelle Jones was her lack of support. But while she was at Morris House, she received therapy. She was "very organized. I mean she was very planned." Alternatives, if her plans did not work out, "were very difficult because she had everything laid out. She was a perfectionist in many ways," Mockabee explained.

When asked by Burke why Jones was so concrete, she said she didn't know.

Mockabee's last contact with the defendant was in 1990. She testified that the defendant had no contact with Mae Engron while she lived at Morris House, but Kevin Sims, "would come for visits and interact with Michelle and Brandon. Initially, Kevin was real involved. I think he got in some trouble with the law and was incarcerated and did not follow through with visits because he wasn't able to."

Once Jones left the group home, she was involved in Mentor Mother, and for a brief time, an aftercare program that she was referred to from the group home. Mockabee did not know anything else about her support system after 1990. She saw the defendant at stores and at African Fest one or two years before the hearing.

Burke asked Mockabee if she wanted to say anything to the judge. She responded, "When I read about this, I cried. I cried for the loss of Brandon and I cried for Michelle for what she might have gone through, for that fact that there probably wasn't a lot of support for her, and what she must be going through. Michelle is a very bright young lady. And I truly feel that she has a lot to offer."

It was the State's opportunity to ask questions of the witness.

"Ms. Mockabee, you've talked a lot to the Court about support, and from what you said you really apparently have no idea of what support systems were in place for Michelle after she left your supervision, is that right?" I asked.

"Yes."

"In fact, ma'am, do you know LeTava Parker?"

"No."

"Or Kadisha Aamir?"

I wanted to remind the judge about these incredible women who truly had cared for the defendant and were there to support her. I asked Mockabee if the only support that was important was familial support.

"You're not suggesting to the Court that the only type of support that you feel is important is that of a natural parent, is it?"

"No, I'm not. What I'm saying is after Michelle left, I had no idea of what supports Michelle had," she responded.

"Brandon had a father who, at least before he was incarcerated, was actively concerned about Brandon. You saw that, didn't you?" I asked, her looking at Kevin Sims as he sat at the table in the courtroom.

"Yes, he was involved."

"And he was the one who brought Brandon to visit Michelle?"

"Yes."

"And one of the issues in terms of Michelle being at Morris House was that she make time for Brandon, and one of the processes that you were involved with or the program was involved with was trying to convince Michelle to focus on her son and less on her own projects and plans?"

"Yes."

"After Kevin went to prison, which you were aware of, his mother Arlene Blevins took over the role of bringing Brandon to visit Michelle?"

"Yes."

"And you're aware that Arlene communicated with Michelle concerning her care of Brandon and tried to be an active participant in Michelle and Brandon's relationship?"

"Yes," she agreed.

"And Arlene Blevins showed an enormous amount of care and concern for their relationship?"

"Yes."

I had no further questions. Both women, witnesses called by the defense, were kind and caring people who had graced Michelle Jones' life. Mockabee knew that Arlene Blevins was there for Jones. Just how much support was Michelle Engron Jones entitled to expect?

Burke effectively directed the witness to conclude that she only had a limited knowledge of the relationship between the defendant and Ms. Blevins. She also described that the support of friends is not necessarily enough to overcome the concrete thinking Michelle possessed. In her last statements, Ms. Mockabee said it all.

"I mean, I look at myself and can remember finishing college, and had my sister not taken me in, I would have been lost. And this is after finishing four years."

I thought that she was a very nice woman, like the many women who had befriended and helped the defendant. She was excused and Tahirah Abubakr was the defendant's next witness. Earnest would ask her questions.

Ms. Abubakr testified that she was Michelle Jones' surrogate mother from the time they met in 1993 at a Kwanzaa celebration. She testified that at about the same time, Jones met and immediately bonded with Kadisha Aamir.

"I know Michelle," she told the Court, "because with me, Michelle was able to cry. She could talk about her child without feeling that I needed to judge her. She could talk about how it feels to lose that child. But she never could talk about what actually happened. She knew that there was some responsibility and she never had intentions of ever changing that responsibility. But she always say I am not responsible for the murder of my child, but I know I have responsibilities for negligence." Abubakr was advocating as she testified.

I did not object. All the defense witnesses had been in the courtroom while the others testified. The State had the right to sequester the witnesses, but I had no issue with these women hearing each other mourn.

Abubakr believed that Jones was looking to bond with someone. She talked about the absence of unconditional love and fearing rejection, "literally beating you to the punch of getting rid herself." She shared her judgments, uninterrupted, for more than ten minutes. She seemed to consider herself an expert. Abubakr never once mentioned Brandon or his suffering.

The defense asked Steven Brock, who had prepared the PSI on behalf of Michelle Engron Jones, to testify. Brock was a frequent witness at sentencings and the Court was obviously familiar with him and his work. His report had been thorough and provided a depth of information that had not been included in the probation's pre-sentence investigation report.

Mr. Brock believed that Jones lacked "support" after leaving Morris House. Unlike the prior defense witnesses, he felt that the defendant craved support from men. He noted that as soon as she left Morris House, the defendant moved in and then married Damon Jones. Apparently, the Morris House staff were unaware that the defendant was living with Damon or that he would lead her to the Nation of Islam.

Burke asked him, "Do you know from your conversations with Miss Jones or anyone else whether the Nation of Islam had any position about the support systems that had been put in place for her previous to her joining the Nation of Islam?"

"I don't know if the Nation of Islam had anything about her particular support systems. But talking with Michelle, she indicated that the Nation of Islam wanted her to disconnect herself from some of her past resources of support. She indicated they wanted her to focus on creating relationships with other people in the Nation of Islam and that those persons outside of Nation of Islam were individuals that they would frown upon her associating with," Brock replied.

"Is there anything that you have found out that would give you any insight as to why there were the constant attempts to sort of latch onto someone?" Burke asked, referring to her client.

"Well, I've come to my own conclusions based upon looking at her social history. And her social history was one in which she had no significant relationships with any men in her life. She did not know who her father was. Her biological father was never present. And she was quite confused about who it might be, based upon conversations she had with her mother. And upon men introduced by her mother as being her father and then later discovering they were not. You find she became pregnant from a relationship she had with Mr. Sims. And, for a while, I think there was some attempt at being responsible on both their parts. Michelle was younger, much younger than Mr. Sims. And it's interesting, but at the time she was done at Morris House and completed the program, she came out and Mr. Sims was not available to her. I think the reasons are stated in the report. And you look at the way she's tried to attach herself to religions. There are three different religions that she's attempted to become involved with," Brock continued. Brock agreed with the defense witnesses who proceeded him that Michelle Jones had great potential.

The State cross-examined Brock. He agreed that Jones had worked for Eli Lilly, an excellent employer, who provided insurance, daycare, summer camps, and other child-friendly benefits to their employees. Although Brock was not personally familiar with each program, he assumed that they were provided at no cost to their employees.

Michelle Jones had broken it off with Kevin Sims before he was incarcerated. While Brock did not know the reason for the breakup, he admitted that the defendant had been dating Damon Jones while she was at Morris House. She met Damon, a musician, at a dance. Brock added that at one point, welfare was considering charging Kevin Sims with child molestation because of the age difference between the two teenagers. But they never did.

I wanted to focus on the true nature of the defendant, Michelle Engron Jones, not as reported by her, but by those that knew her well. "Mr. Brock, in compiling your pre-sentence memorandum, I noticed that it describes that in one of Michelle's placements, and again we know about one incident with her mother, but when she was placed with an aunt from July 1987 to February of 1988, something happened; and she, meaning Michelle Engron Jones, broke the aunt's nose or at least hit her in the face, do you recall that?"

"Yes."

"That it was the *defendant* who physically injured the aunt, not the other way around."

"In this report, yes." Brock was referring to verified records incorporated into his PSI.

"And in compiling this report, sir, were you also aware of the incident where police were called to Michelle's apartment where Brandon was bleeding from his head and had a swollen lip and other physical injuries?" I asked pointedly. "And she blamed it on her husband?" I added, knowing that he had not included it in his report. Mr. Brock conceded that he had reviewed the document but had not commented on it.

I concluded my questioning of Steven Brock by confirming that he had not spoken with Arlene Blevins about her willingness to support and help with Brandon. Nor had he spoken with LeTava Parker Muhammad or Kadisha Aamir. Brock said that he didn't speak with these women because he knew that the probation department would interview them.

As Brock left the witness stand, Burke indicated that they had no additional witnesses. The Court asked whether the State cared to present any additional evidence. The Court had been glancing toward the State's table. The judge had to have noticed that Brandon's grandmother, Arlene Blevins, was not present at the table or in the courtroom. I volunteered that Arlene Blevins had been hospitalized the day before the hearing and was not able to be present. Kadisha Aamir was in such bad health that she also was unavailable to testify. But I wanted to share some of what they had told me.

"First, Judge, I'd like to talk about Kadisha Aamir and what we believe she would say had she been here today. When I first met Kadisha Aamir, she talked about the guilt that she felt because she felt that she had been there for the defendant and the defendant had never taken her up on it. And I think the Court got a feel for the enormous, I guess, maternal instincts of Mrs. Aamir. And so, in the first interview, one of the few interviews before the neglect charges were filed, she was still fairly protective of Michelle."

I continued. "Mrs. Aamir, after a period of time, told me that she felt that she had been manipulated by Michelle Engron Jones. She watched Michelle abandon her and Deborah Asante, and move on to the next group, which was the group that involved Saundra Holiday, Mijiza. Mrs. Aamir told me that during the course of the proceedings as neglect charges were filed against her that she frequently saw the defendant at what's known as the Culture Club, a Black, African American dance club, and that during the time she would be dressed in what Mrs. Aamir described as tiny tank tops and tight pants, and Mrs. Aamir's perception was that the defendant flaunted what had gone on and felt that 'well, Brandon's gone and I'm going to live my life.' And in fact, told her that on occasions."

I told the Court that Arlene Blevins did not make a recommendation for sentencing. Kevin Sims sat quietly at counsel table. I told the Court that he did not want to say anything. The Court asked him, to be sure, and reminded him that he had the right to make a statement. He acknowledged with a shake of his head.

Michelle Engron Jones made a statement. These were the first words that I had ever heard her speak. I quote every word she told the Court. Susan Burke asked the questions.

"Michelle, you're the defendant in this case; is that correct?"

"Yes."

"And you asked us, you told us you wanted to talk to the judge a little bit today?"

"Yes."

"Is there anything that you want to say to the judge regarding your responsibility for Brandon's death?"

I held my breath. Kevin was silent. He was staring at her.

"Yes," she said in a clear voice. "I want to apologize to Kevin and Arlene and everybody who tried to befriend me, but I didn't let them in. Everything that's happened is horrible and I accept the responsibility for it. I know, I will just tell you, I'm not a murderer and I'll try to do the best I can with what I have left of my life. Thank you."

Everything that happened? What you *did, Michelle?* I thought. Not one word about her dead child. Not one mention of Brandon.

Defense counsel argued extensively about Michelle Jones' character. Burke said, "We don't have a defendant here who is evil." Burke blamed the pregnancy completely on Kevin Sims; he was the one who was responsible for this underaged pregnancy. Kevin Sims should have been prosecuted, Burke continued, and listed what she believed was the proper statute to convict him. Burke compared Michelle's relationship with Brandon to her relationship with Mae Engron.

"Obviously, what we have here is a picture of an overachiever who continuously sought external rewards to make up for her internal feelings of inadequacy. This is why she appeared to be such a high functioning person, and, in fact, she was," Burke continued. Her argument focused on Michelle Jones, only Michelle.

I commenced by saying, "What about Brandon? What kind of life did he have for the less than eighteen months that he lived with his mother, which from the evidence to the Court, consisted of being beaten with shoes, or you can call it hitting, deprived of food as punishment, taken away from his friends, taken away from the grandmother who loved and adored him and who wanted him and who wanted to be there. And from his father."

I reminded the Court that during all of the time that neglect charges were pending against her, Michelle Jones had not once tried to show anyone the location of Brandon's body. I shared with the Court that I hadn't realized how significant it is to a family not to have a body to bury.

I described Kevin Sims' reaction when I spoke with him before the trial. As I told Kevin, "We've charged Michelle with murder. Brandon's dead." He started sobbing hysterically. It embarrassed Crooke, who had been with us, so much that he left the room. "Because throughout all of this, Kevin Sims never wanted to admit that his son was dead, because he didn't know, and she," I said, pointing at the defendant, "kept that from him."

I was pretty emotional myself. I kept reflecting out loud what I believed the State had proven and what the Court should consider. "I think it would be inappropriate for the Court to sentence without thinking of what that little four year old, who was apparently unable to get himself food or water or help, went through before he died. When I met the friends that Michelle had, and I was fairly new to Indianapolis myself, I thought about, if only I were lucky enough to have that quality of friends."

I briefly described the State's belief that there were mitigating and aggravating factors but the facts that the Court should consider as most significant, beyond what Kevin and his mother had suffered, was what Brandon had endured.

It was time for the Court to impose a sentence on Michelle Engron Jones. She sat impassively with her attorneys, Mark Earnest and Susan Burke. Steven Brock also sat next to her.

Judge Magnus-Stinson described the charges, the presumptive, minimum and maximum permissible sentences. Murder carried a presumptive sentence of forty years. The minimum sentence that could be imposed was thirty years and the maximum sentence was sixty years. The Court would not sentence the defendant to neglect as a Class B Felony because of double jeopardy concerns. This was because conviction of neglect as a Class B Felony required proof of death. Because the defendant was already being sentenced for killing Brandon, the neglect count would be reduced to a D Felony. The presumptive sentence for neglect as a Class D Felony was eighteen months incarceration with a minimum of one and a maximum of three years.

The judge spoke directly to the defendant. "I don't think there's any case I've spent more time on in the time that I've been on the bench. Pretrial hearings and the length of the trial, both evidence that was admitted for purposes of the jury, and evidence that the Court heard in making pretrial rulings. Days and days of testimony literally that the Court heard. And I considered all that and I consider it now, as well as the evidence presented today."

The Court found several mitigating factors. She said the defendant was raised in a neglectful and abusive home. She conceded that the report written by Ms. Armstrong-Smith about her conversations with Mae Engron was disturbing.

Mae Engron said she would abandon Michelle but would beat her before she abandoned her. How had I missed the analogy? The Court apparently hadn't missed the irony. Didn't Michelle do to Brandon exactly what Michelle's mother had threatened to do to her?

The remaining mitigating factors that the Court found were that the defendant had no juvenile history nor any adult criminal history. Also, she was relatively young at the age of the offense.

But, the Court explained, there were significant aggravating factors as well. The judge looked at me, but quickly turned her head to speak directly to Michelle Jones. "And the first, and I would respond to, I guess, the question, what about Brandon, by saying there probably hasn't been a day since this case has been assigned to me that I haven't thought about Brandon. And there hasn't probably been a time, oh maybe there's been a time, but many times when my own child cries, I think about Brandon and what he must have felt, by the defendant's own admission, the four days, three to four days when he was left alone. And one of the statutory factors I'm to consider is the victim's age, and he was four years old at the time. But I also consider as an aggravator the fact that you were his mother and the person to whom he looked for care and love, and not abuse and neglect. And LeTava Parker told us, LeTava Muhammad, told us he was like any little boy and he loved his mommy and should have been able to count on you to take care of him." The Court took a breath, then continued.

"I also find as an aggravator that you had previously struck him. Several witnesses documented the beatings. Deborah Asante, Kadisha Aamir, they saw him struck with a shoe for wetting himself at the picnic just the month before, I think, the last time he was seen alive. In addition, I'm not going to take into account the testimony of Damon Jones, because I don't have to and I'm not going to—" (Damon Jones had testified, in a pretrial hearing, that the defendant had beaten Brandon Sims often. He said that once she knocked out Brandon's tooth.)

"But LeTava Muhammad also gave accounts of the beatings that he endured before. And as another aggravator I find this: I believe you're sorry for what's happened, and I believe you've stated that you've accepted your responsibility for Brandon's death, but whatever your mother did to you did not kill Brandon Sims. I'm sorry it happened to you. But it didn't kill that little boy. Your conduct led to his death and no one else's. As another aggravator, I do find there's been a lot made by the defense about lack of support, but I agree with the State and observed the witnesses themselves testify." The Court did not have to read her notes. She knew what she heard.

"First and foremost, Brandon's grandmother — who loved him, who delighted in his being her grandson, for her and the several times she offered to take Brandon back, her reluctance to even give him up in the first place, but she knew he was yours, and she knew that's what she had to do; you had custody, but she offered and you refused her help. LeTava Muhammad also offered. And in fact, offered several days before the time period, I believe, anyway, listening to the evidence that Brandon died. You had left him at her house for a couple of days, she knew you were undergoing stress, but she offered to keep him, and he was happy there and he had friends there and you refused her help too.

"And finally, the last aggravator, and this is something that runs contrary to, I think, the image that's been projected, Miss Jones, you refused to tell Arlene Blevins and Kevin Sims where that baby was for a year and a half. And you lied to them or dodged them, and then when other friends asked you where he was, you made up stories. He's with his dad, he's with his dad and his new wife, he's with his grandmother, he's in Texas, he's in Tennessee. And you created a pattern to mislead everyone about where Brandon was.

"And while your counsel has asked me to find as a mitigator that you confessed, it wasn't until Kadisha Aamir confronted you, when she received information from two sources, one from you that Brandon was with his dad, and one from his dad that no, he wasn't. I mean, these people were trying to find this little boy and it wasn't until that confrontation that the truth came out.

"I also wanted to talk a little bit about when you talk about your state of mind at or about the time this happened and when you acknowledged that you left him. You paint one picture of being tormented by the Nation of Islam and abandoned by your husband, but Deborah Asante talked about a trip to Detroit where you went to a theatre conference shortly after the Fourth of July. Now Brandon was last seen alive, I believe it was July 3rd, by Miss Muhammad. And she described you as functioning well there, having a good time, socializing, interacting appropriately, and in fact, meeting someone that you thought was a nice man.

"And apparently, all that time, this little boy was alone. So, I have considered your abusive upbringing and I've thought about it for months, and probably myself more than anyone else in this room has heard from your mother." The Court described receiving calls and letters from Mae Engron and her testimony in Court. "Maybe she's accepting some responsibility for what she did to you, but she didn't do it to Brandon.

"So, in weighing the factors, I find that your abusive childhood in youth, although they offer some explanation for your conduct, cannot erase the terrible fact that Brandon died at your hands. And as the person he trusted for love and care," Judge Magnus-Stinson retained eye contact with the defendant, "you betrayed that trust with dire consequences to him."

The Court went on to comment on the profile of abused children that Steven Brock had described as becoming perfectionist. "Everyone agrees you have that quality," the Court said. "They also argued that you have a feeling of self-contempt. I don't see that in your behavior. Rather, I look at a psychological report that was prepared at Morris House and there they diagnosed a different reaction, and this is your projection of blame on others and viewing yourself as a victim of all things. You were a victim of what your mom did to you, no one disputes that, but not everything else. But the one thing the doctor did note is that the personality trait would affect your relationships, but it wouldn't affect your thinking. In other words, I think what I took from that is: you would know better."

After discussing some of the arguments presented in the sentencing brief, written by the defense, the Court neared conclusion.

"I recall vividly the testimony of Arlene Blevins, the love in her eyes when she talked about that boy, her memories of being with him and her offers of help, and the offer that LeTava Muhammad made. You refused both offers. Brandon lost his life. And then finally, in aggravation, I want to talk about the pattern of deception that you engaged in to cover up your crime."

The Court found that the aggravating factors outweighted the mitigating factors. The Court found that an aggravated sentence was warranted. She sentenced Michelle Engron Jones to fifty years, fifty years *executed*. This meant that the Court intended for the defendant to serve the fifty-year sentence in prison. She also sentenced the defendant to three years for neglect, the maximum sentence, but ran the sentences concurrently. The Court did not impose any fines or costs.

Michelle Jones stated that she wanted to appeal her conviction. Those were the last words I ever heard from the woman convicted of murdering four-year-old Brandon Sims.

The Court turned to Kevin Sims, who was silently crying. "I want to say to you, Mr. Sims, and if you could communicate to your mom, my sorrow for your loss. And I know that you held hope for a long time, and I am very, very sorry that your little boy is gone, and I hope that you'll convey those same feelings to your mother."

EPILOGUE

The conviction of Michelle Engron Jones was appealed to the Indiana Court of Appeals. http://caselaw.findlaw.com/in-court-of-appeals/1426342.html. *Jones v. State,* 701 N.E. 2d 863 (1998). The appellate court, in a detailed opinion, summarized the facts proven at trial. It considered each of the issues raised on appeal and unanimously agreed to affirm the conviction. The court analyzed the contentions and found that there was sufficient evidence of *corpus delicti* to justify the admission of Jones' confessions into evidence; the evidence was sufficient to sustain Jones' convictions for Murder and Neglect of a Dependent; and that the trial court did not err in permitting the State to dismiss the Neglect of a Dependent charges and refile new charges of Murder and Neglect of a Dependent. The appellate court also found that Jones' enhanced fifty-year sentence was lawful and appropriate.

* * * * * * * * *

Michelle Jones served nearly twenty years of her fifty-year sentence. She was released in 2017. She is currently enrolled in a PhD program at a university in New York. She received a full scholarship.

Mahalia "Kadisha" Aamir succumbed to cancer in December 1997. She is sadly missed.

Deborah Asante remains the artistic director and founder of Asante Children's Theatre, which is still an integral part of the Indianapolis community.

Judge Jane Magnus-Stinson retained her position as a Marion County Superior Court Judge until she was appointed to the federal bench in 2010. She is currently the Chief Judge for the Southern District of Indiana.

Michael "Mike" Crooke retired from the Indianapolis Police Department in 2004. He is the Chief of Police of Cumberland, Indiana.

Cale Bradford was elected Judge of the Marion County Superior Court. He was appointed to the Indiana Court of Appeals in 2007 and remains an active appellate judge.

Mark Earnest, Susan Burke and **Steven Laudig** are attorneys in Indianapolis, Indiana.

Diane Marger Moore continues to practice law with a national civil trial firm.

Brandon Sims' body has never been located. He has never had a proper burial.

AUTHOR'S NOTE

The story of Michelle Engron Jones, her crimes, and prosecution have been subjects I have wanted to write about for years. However, life interrupted my progress and the book remained mostly in my mind under items "to do." I purchased the official transcripts years ago to be sure my memory was accurate. After I purchased them, I Googled "Michelle Engron Jones" and found nothing. But I did find an article about Jones. It was about her writing a history of Indiana's Women's Prison. In the photographs that were part of the article, she was smiling, something I had never seen in the years I observed her.

In 2017, I was contacted by a fascinating, industrious, and dedicated journalist from the Marshall Project, Eli Hager, who was writing a story about Michelle Jones. He spent time asking me my views about Ms. Jones, her incarceration, and her successes. As the prosecutor who convicted Michelle, my responses seemed to surprise him.

Michelle Jones had been in prison for nearly twenty years and was about to be released. While incarcerated at the Indiana Women's Prison, in Indianapolis, Indiana, she obtained her undergraduate degree and had audited master's degree classes. She demonstrated her intellect and talents in several ways. She had engaged other women in some of her endeavors and been unequivocally successful. And she had been granted admission to perhaps the most prestigious university in the world, Harvard, on a full scholarship to complete a PhD in history. Then Harvard withdrew its offer.

What I did not know when I spoke with Eli was the title that he would give his well- researched and intentionally thought-provoking article. He (and the *New York Times* who published it) called the article "From Prison to PhD: The Redemption and Rejection of Michelle Jones." Eli quoted me correctly in the article and for that I am grateful.

"Look, as a mother, I thought it was just an awful crime," said Ms. Marger Moore, now a lawyer at a large firm in Los Angeles. "But what Harvard did is highly inappropriate: I'm the prosecutor, not them. Michelle Jones served her time, and she served a long time, exactly what she deserved. A sentence is a sentence."

I remain firm in my conclusion that once a person convicted of a crime, any crime, has served their sentence, we must afford them opportunities to succeed. That is certainly true for Michelle Jones, who did much to improve her life while in prison. That she also helped so many others only confirms my belief in the possibility of rehabilitation.

However, redemption is a whole other story. Redemption is the province of a higher authority. So the title of the article posits a conclusion above my pay grade. But, in my view, Michelle Jones may have been rehabilitated and she is entitled to a myriad of opportunities, but there is no "redemption" for a woman who tortured and murdered her four-year-old son.

AUTHOR'S NOTES

COMPARING CASEY ANTHONY AND MICHELLE JONES

Different Outcomes — Similar Crimes
Forgive One and Condemn the Other

Compare the murder of Brandon Sims by his mother Michelle Jones with the murder of Caylee Anthony by her mother Casey Anthony. They are shockingly similar, but with different outcomes. Today, ten years after the death of Caylee Anthony, her mother remains a pariah, yet she was found not guilty of the crime. On the other hand, Michelle Jones was convicted of killing her son, and hundreds of supporters claim that "redemption" is the proper term to apply to her. Pariah versus redeemed. How do we determine which of these women is entitled to live "normal lives?"

In the early 1990s, Michelle Engron Jones retook custody of her son Brandon Sims from his paternal grandmother. For years (not days, as in the Anthony case), no one saw Brandon who wasn't old enough to attend kindergarten. Michelle lied to her friends about where Brandon was during that time, claiming that he was with his father (who was actually in prison) or his paternal grandmother in another state.

Similarly, Casey Anthony lied to friends and family about the whereabouts of her daughter, three-year-old Caylee. She claimed that a babysitter had the child or kidnapped the child or she was "missing."

Michelle Jones admitted to her friends and law enforcement that Brandon was dead but lied about where she had buried him. She did admit that she "wrapped him in a blanket and buried him in the woods." Casey Anthony also lied to law enforcement, blaming the "nanny." Casey claimed she didn't know where Caylee, alive or dead, was located. Six months later, Caylee's skeletal remains were found wrapped in a blanket in a wooded area near the Anthony's family house.

Casey Anthony was arrested for child neglect almost immediately after the child was declared missing. Michelle Jones was not arrested until more than a year after she admitted the child was dead, after she left him alone in their apartment for more than four days. Instead, detectives working with the prosecutor on the case spent the time investigating the death, locating evidence and witnesses. They took the time necessary to prepare a case.

Prosecutors repeatedly fail to learn from the first O.J. Simpson criminal trial. Rushing to trial may be gratifying, and satisfy the public, but the ultimate result of that expediency may be failure. It was certainly true for O.J. as it was for Casey Anthony.

Each of these women, single mothers, could be described as a "party girl who killed her [child] to free herself from parental responsibility and enjoy her personal life." Both seemed to continue that life after the death of their only child. Both women were attractive. Michelle was also intellectually gifted.

One difference was that Caylee's body was found. Brandon's never was. And yet Michelle Jones was convicted of murder and Casey Anthony was not.

It is certainly arguable that the Casey Anthony investigation had far more evidence: they had the victim's body. And confessions. And other physical evidence.

Both women had strong defense teams made up of three defense lawyers at trial. Both cases involved substantial pretrial publicity, although Michelle Jones' case was highly publicized only in Indianapolis and the surrounding area, unlike the national attention focused on Casey Anthony.

But Michelle Jones is lauded as an incredible success story and Casey Anthony is not. That Michelle Jones was punished for her crime, spending twenty of the fifty year sentence she received in prison, while Casey Anthony has remained free, may be one explanation. But there was no outrage that Jones served less than half of her intentionally enhanced sentence. Michelle Jones denied murdering Brandon. Casey Anthony denies killing Caylee. We know that Michelle Jones killed Brandon. What do we know about Casey Anthony that makes her so different from Michelle Jones?

For More News About Diane Marger Moore, Signup For Our Newsletter:

http://wbp.bz/newsletter

Word-of-mouth is critical to an author's long-term success. If you appreciated this book please leave a review on the Amazon sales page:

http://wbp.bz/iga

Read A Sample Next

CHAPTER ONE-*The 911 Call*

March 16, 2009
Hood River County, Oregon
6:09 p.m.

When the 911 call came into the Hood River Sheriff's Office, it wasn't so much what the caller said, but how he said it. His voice neither rose nor fell as he phlegmatically relayed the information.

911 OPERATOR: *"911, where is your emergency?"*
CALLER: *"Hello. I need help. I'm at, uh, Eagle Creek."*
911 OPERATOR: *"Okay, and what's going on there?"*
CALLER: *"My girlfriend fell off the cliff. I hiked back. And I'm in my car."*
911 OPERATOR: *"Okay. You're at the Eagle Creek Trailhead right now?"*
CALLER: *"Yeah."*
911 OPERATOR: *"Okay, and where on the trail did she fall?"*
CALLER: *"I don't know. I think about a mile up."*
911 OPERATOR: *"Okay."*

The 911 operator thought it was odd. That he was odd. Normally people calling 911 to report a traumatic event are in an agitated state with an emotional element in their speech ranging from weeping to a rapid-fire data dump to shouting or screaming. This guy might as well have been reading a manual on how to change a sparkplug.

CALLER: *"I hiked down and got her, uh, and I'm in my car now, and I don't know if I ... (unintelligible)"*
911 OPERATOR: *"Okay."*
CALLER: *"... suffering from hypothermia. I don't think it's that cold but ..."*
911 OPERATOR: *"Okay, so she fell off the trail down a cliff, and then you went down the cliff and pulled her, brought her back up onto the trail?"*
CALLER: *"No she's dead."*

There was a stunned pause as the operator absorbed his last statement; 911 callers in emergency situations tend to get to the point right away and gush with information. But this was more worried about telling her in his flat, monotone voice that he was cold than that his girlfriend had just died. And every time the operator tried to get more details about the victim, he turned the conversation back to his needs.

CALLER: *"I went down to get her. I went to the bottom. Then in the river (unintelligible) took me about an hour to get to her. I finally go over to her, then I was startin' to shake. I got too cold, so I'm, uh, now, I just got to my car, and I need someone to come and help me ... Please send someone I'm at, uh ..."*
911 OPERATOR: *"Okay, hang on just a minute ..."*
CALLER: *"... Eagle Creek."*
911 OPERATOR: *"... one second."*
CALLER: *"Okay."*
911 OPERATOR: *"And what's, what's your name, sir?"*
CALLER: *"Steve."*
911 OPERATOR: *"Okay Steve, what is, um ..."*
CALLER: *"I'm freezing. Will you please send someone?"*

911 OPERATOR: *"Um, hang on just one second for me, okay?"*

CALLER: *"All right."*

911 OPERATOR: *"Steve, what is your last name?"*

CALLER: *"Nichols."*

911 OPERATOR: *"And what's her name, Steve?"*

CALLER: *"Rhonda."*

911 OPERATOR: *"Rhonda's last name?"*

CALLER: *"Casto."*

911 OPERATOR: *"Could you spell that for me please?"*

CALLER: *"R-H-O-N-D-A ... C-A-S-T-O."*

911 OPERATOR: *"Do you need an ambulance? Do you feel like you might need medical attention?"*

CALLER: *"I don't know if I'm shaking from, I don't know ... I'm really cold."*

911 OPERATOR: *"Okay, okay, Steve."*

CALLER: *"I'm just really cold."*

911 OPERATOR: *"Are you able to start the car and get warm?"*

CALLER: *"Yeah, the ..."*

911 OPERATOR: *"Blankets?"*

CALLER: *"... car is running."*

911 OPERATOR: *"And now Steve, I know this is a difficult question for you to answer for me, but what makes you think she was deceased?"*

CALLER: *"I don't know it for sure. I stayed with her for about an hour and a half, and I gave her mouth-to-mouth, and I tried covering up her leg. There was blood coming out of her leg, and I just sat and helped her, and then I started shaking uncontrollably, so ...* (unintelligible)*"*

911 OPERATOR: *"Okay."*

CALLER: *"Had to go back, and ..."*

911 OPERATOR: *"Was she breathing when you left her?"*

CALLER: *"No."*

911 OPERATOR: *"Do you know if she had a pulse?"*

CALLER: *"Where's that?"*

911 OPERATOR: *"Hood River? Um, it's about twenty minutes away, but he's on his way, about seven minutes ago, okay, and we have an officer coming from Corbett. Do you know where that's at?"*

CALLER: *"No I don't."*

911 OPERATOR: *"He's a little closer so he'll be there shortly."*

CALLER: *"Okay."*

911 OPERATOR: *"So I'm going to stay on the phone with you. Are you getting any warmer in the vehicle with the heat on, Steve?"*

CALLER: *"No but I have it on full so that should heat up."*

911 OPERATOR: *"Are you in wet clothes at all?"*

CALLER: *"Tried to ... (unintelligible) ... up river. Uh, was too strong, so ..."*

911 OPERATOR: *"Are you able to get your wet clothes off and put something else warmer on?"*

CALLER: *"Yeah ... (unintelligible) ... shirt off."*

911 OPERATOR: *"You what? You have warmer clothes to put on or dry clothes at least?*

The caller was silent.

911 CALLER: *"Steve?*

Still no answer.

911 OPERATOR: *"... Steve? ... Steve?"*

CALLER: *"Yeah, that helps. ... How far away is he?"*

911 OPERATOR: *"He said just a few minutes."*

CALLER: *"Okay."*

911 OPERATOR: *"Are you there?"*

CALLER: *"Yeah."*

CALLER: *"Uh, no, I don't think so."*

911 OPERATOR: *"Okay, Steve, we have an officer who's on his way."*

CALLER: *"All right. How long ... how long will it take an ambulance to get here?"*

911 OPERATOR: *"It'll take just a minute. Would you like an ambulance for you?"*

CALLER: *"Uh, uh ..."*

911 OPERATOR: *"If there's a question, I can send them, and, um, then you can decide not to go with them if that's what you choose to do."*

CALLER: *"Just so cold. That's the thing, I'm cold. ... How long will it take to the police car to get here?"*

911 OPERATOR: *"They're on their way, okay? Hang on just a second. How far down the trail, how far over the cliff is she?"*

CALLER: *"Uh, I don't know, like a hundred feet ..."*

911 OPERATOR: *"A hundred feet, okay."*

CALLER: *"I don't know."*

911 OPERATOR: *"Steve, how old are you?"*

CALLER: *"Uh, 34."*

911 OPERATOR: *"I'm going to send the ambulance for you, okay?"*

CALLER: *"All right."*

911 OPERATOR: *"Hang on just a second for me. You're going to hear some silence, okay?"*

CALLER: *"Okay."*

The caller waited patiently and quietly for the 911 operator to get back on the line. When she did, she assured him that the ambulance was on its way and she would stay on the line with him until somebody got there.

CALLER: *" 'kay."*

911 OPERATOR: *"And we have an officer on his way from Hood River."*

911 OPERATOR: *"Hang on just a second for me, okay?"*

There were several more pauses over the next couple of minutes as the operator checked with law enforcement and the ambulance crew. Again, the caller patiently waited for her return and would then inquire as to when someone would be there to help him. He never once said anything about his girlfriend without being asked a direct question.

CALLER: *"What time is it?"*

911 OPERATOR: *"It's 6:18. They're going to be there in a few minutes, okay?"*

CALLER: *"Okay."*

911 OPERATOR: *"So Steve, how far up the trail did you say she is?"*

CALLER: *"I don't know. I think a mile."*

911 OPERATOR: *"Okay. What was she wearing?"*

CALLER: *"Uh, jeans. ... I don't know the top. ... She put on my shirt, but I think she put one over ..."*

911 OPERATOR: *"Okay. They're on their way, okay?"*

CALLER: *"Yeah."*

911 OPERATOR: *"Hang on one second for me, Steve, okay?"*

CALLER: *"Mm hmm."*

The 911 OPERATOR spoke to one of the responding officers: *"Brandon ... (unintelligible) ... responding? I have a hypothermic guy sitting in his car."*

The 911 OPERATOR then addressed the caller. *"They're on their way, okay."*

THE CALLER: *"Uh huh."*

911 OPERATOR: *"They're on their way. They said less than five minutes, okay? He'll be there in just a couple of minutes."*

THE CALLER: *"All right."*

The operator asked a few more perfunctory questions, such as date of birth for both the caller, January 4, 1975, and his girlfriend, July 2, 1985. The operator then attempted to gather more details about the "accident."

911 OPERATOR: *"Do you know what made her fall, Steve? Did she lose her footing, or did she get hurt? ... Do you know why she fell?"*

CALLER: *"I think she's high on something."*

911 OPERATOR: *"Have you done any drugs or alcohol today?"*

CALLER: *"No."*

911 OPERATOR: *"What do you think she's high on?"*

CALLER: *"I don't know. She always hides that stuff from me."*

911 OPERATOR: *"Okay. Are you doing okay?"*

CALLER: *"Yeah, I'm warming up a little."*

911 OPERATOR: *"Oh, you're ..."*

CALLER: *"Shaking. ... I can't stop shaking."*

911 OPERATOR: *"The ambulance is on its way. It will be there in a few minutes."*

CALLER: *"Uh huh."*

Again the 911 OPERATOR broke to speak to the responding officers: *"Are you guys aware of what's going on?"* After speaking to them, she returned to the CALLER: *"Did you leave anything on the trail showing where she went down over the cliff? ... Did you leave a backpack or anything there?"*

CALLER: *"No, I left my backpack ... (unintelligible) ... farther down, so I could go down. But then when I made my way back up, I got it. ... Only thing I left was my sweatshirt."*

911 OPERATOR: *"You left your sweatshirt there on the trail?"*

CALLER: *"No that was down by the river. ... It's close to where she is, but that's where I went in the river. ... The policeman's here."*

911 OPERATOR: *"Okay. I'll go ahead and let you go."*

CALLER: *"Okay."*

911 OPERATOR: *"Okay."*

CALLER: *"Thank you very much."*

911 OPERATOR: *"You're welcome."*

CALLER: *"Bye."*

911 OPERATOR: *"Bye bye."*

With that exchange of pleasantries, the call ended. A young mother was dead. But the important thing, at least according to the 911 call, was that her boyfriend was cold.

CHAPTER TWO—*First Responders*

Eagle Creek Trailhead
6:28 p.m.

When Hood River Sheriff's Office Deputy Marc A. Smith heard the 911 operator's radio dispatch that a woman had fallen from the Eagle Creek Trail and that her boyfriend was possibly suffering from exposure, it came as no great surprise. Every year·deputies from the sheriffs' offices in Hood River and Multnomah, the two counties responsible for law enforcement in that part of the Columbia River Gorge Scenic Area, participated in about thirty search and rescue missions to assist injured, lost, or simply ill-equipped hikers.

Sometimes people died on the trails through falls, loose rocks, heart attacks, or one of the biggest threats in that climate, hypothermia, a potentially fatal drop in body temperature due to exposure. The Eagle Creek trail had its share of fatalities due to its natural splendor, easy access, and proximity to a city.

The trailhead was located about forty miles east of Portland and a half-mile off Interstate 84, the east-west corridor that parallels the Columbia River. It's one of the most beautiful hikes in Oregon, climbing through a primordial Pacific Northwest rainforest along a 24-mile path that leads to a half-dozen waterfalls, bridges a spectacular gorge, and even burrows through 120-feet of rock behind thundering Tunnel Falls.

The trail starts off along Eagle Creek, which is a typical stream for the area—vigorous, boulder-strewn and littered with logs and debris—cutting noisily through a steep-sided gorge on its way to the Columbia. But the stream and trail soon part as the path begins to climb along a slope populated by moss-draped cedars, Douglas Fir, and a variety of hardwood trees that provide a thick and brooding canopy over maidenhair ferns and impenetrable undergrowth.

It's not a tough hike. The first four miles up to Punchbowl Falls is rated by online trail guides as an "easy to moderate" climb, gaining 500 feet in elevation, with footing that ranges from a smooth, gently-sloping forest path to broken chunks of rock that hikers must pick through to avoid a turned ankle.

This initial portion of the trail is generally safe, traveled without incident by numerous families and hikers of all ages and abilities, but there is one area that deserves caution. Slightly less than a mile from the parking lot, the trail grows suddenly steeper and narrows as it traverses a cliff 300 feet above the gorge floor. There's even a hand rail of cable and pipe fastened to the rock face on one side for those intimidated by the precipice on the other. It's with this spot in mind that the trail guides warn that children and dogs should be supervised.

If the caller, who'd identified himself as Stephen Nichols, was right, it was in that area where his girlfriend, Rhonda Casto, had fallen.

A 10-year veteran with sheriff's Office, Smith had been driving back to Hood River from the state capital of Salem and was near the town of Corbett when he heard the call come over the radio. He knew that sheriff's investigator Matt English was on his way, but realizing he was closer than his colleague, Smith had radioed that he would respond as well. Pulling into the trailhead parking lot, Smith noted there were two cars: an unoccupied, maroon-colored mini-van with Washington plates; and the blue Mazda the caller had identified. Getting out of his own car, the deputy saw a male sitting in the driver's seat of the Mazda, his head on the steering wheel. The occupant didn't have a shirt on and was covering his upper body with a blanket.

The man didn't appear to notice him when Smith walked up, so the deputy knocked on the driver's side window. Even then the occupant was slow to respond, but he at last rolled the window down partway. He was still on his cellphone with the 911 operator: "The policeman's here. ... Thank you very much. ... Bye bye."

Smith introduced himself and ascertained that the man's name was Stephen Nichols. The deputy could see that Nichols' hair and pants were wet. He wasn't wearing any shoes or socks either. The deputy cautioned Nichols to stay warm and offered his fleece coat.

"When will the medics get here?" Nichols asked.

"They're on their way and will be here in a few minutes," Smith replied. He indicated the front passenger seat. "Mind if I sit down while we talk?" Nichols leaned over and unlocked the passenger side door.

Entering the car, Smith removed a wet t-shirt from the seat and place it on the floorboard. Nichols explained that it was wet because he tried to swim upstream to reach his girlfriend, Rhonda Casto. "There's probably some blood on it from me giving her mouth-to-mouth resuscitation," he added.

"How far up the trail did she fall?" the deputy asked.

"About a mile," Nichols said before describing how he'd then run back down the trail one-half to three-quarters of a mile before he could find a spot to scramble down to the creek. He then tried walking back along the bank, he said, but it was too rough. So he got in the stream and attempted to "swim." This, too, proved difficult and he climbed back out to walk.

Nichols also repeated his story about trying to give her mouth-to-mouth resuscitation. "But she was dead."

At one point during their conversation, Nichols' cellphone rang. He looked at the Caller ID but didn't answer. He told Smith that the caller was Rhonda's mother, Julia Simmons, who was watching the couple's nine-month-old daughter, Annie.

"I don't know how to tell her or Rhonda's sister, Melanie, that Rhonda's dead," Nichols said.

Smith assured him that either he or some other law enforcement official would inform Rhonda's family. "You don't need to talk to them right now."

While questioning Nichols, the deputy noted that the young man seemed withdrawn and didn't readily offer any information, but rather had to be drawn out with questions. He also alternated between a somber expression and sobbing.

An ambulance from the Cascade Locks Fire and EMS arrived. Nichols got out of the car and headed for the medical team. In the ambulance, paramedic Wayne Overcash took five tympanic (ear) temperature measurements between 6:34 p.m. and 6:52 p.m., all of them either 36 degrees or 37 degrees Celsius.

Normal tympanic body temperature is 35.5 to 37.5 degrees Celsius. Readings of 32 to 35 degrees is considered "mild hypothermia" with symptoms being shivering and slurred speech, but alert;" 28 to 32 is considered "moderate" and symptoms of "sleepiness" but no shivering; and 20-28 is severe. The body temperature of Nichols, who Overcash noted was "verbal and alert," was normal.

When Nichols exited the Mazda to go to the ambulance, Smith got out as well and looked at the back seat. He saw a pair of wet hiking boots and a woman's purse on the floorboard in the back; a backpack that also appeared to be wet was sitting on the seat.

Soon after Nichols got in the ambulance, Deputy Matt English arrived. He spoke briefly with Smith and got Nichols' account of the "accident." Then, while Smith joined Nichols in the ambulance to continue the questioning, English talked to Cascade Locks Fire Chief Jeff Pritcher, who was preparing to hike up the Eagle Creek trail with a Cascade Locks Fire department volunteer, Zach Pardue, to locate the victim.

Both men were also members of the Hood River Crag Rats, the oldest volunteer search and rescue organization in the United State, and especially trained for technical rock-climbing and avalanche rescues. With twilight fading and night falling, the pair left the parking lot at 6:38 p.m.

Back in the ambulance, Smith asked Nichols what his girlfriend had been wearing. He was given a brief description of "jeans" and that she had blond hair. The deputy then asked what happened to cause her to fall.

"She must have been high on something," Nichols said. "She was just flying around."

Rhonda had been about fifty feet in front of him, Nichols explained, and heading down the trail. He said he was trying to catch up to her when she suddenly plunged off the cliff. He said that when he reached that spot he looked over the edge and saw her "lying in the water" and screamed. That's when he ran down the trail to find a place where he could get to the stream.

Nichols also gave a rough description of the spot where his girlfriend fell, saying it was between two sets of cables attached to the rock face along the trail. He said she fell about 3 p.m.

After providing his and Rhonda's personal information, and stating that they lived together, Nichols was asked if he knew what made her "high." He said he didn't know but that she'd had a drug problem in the past.

Detective Sergeant Gerry Tiffany, the senior detective on the small Hood River Sheriff's Office staff, arrived. After obtaining Nichols' consent, he and Deputy English began to search the car while Smith continued his interrogation.

Nichols told him that he'd known his girlfriend for about four and a half years, living together for four of it. He also said that he and Rhonda had hiked the trail before, and that she had been on it "frequently" prior to knowing him. "She used to come up here to drink vodka and take pills," he asserted.

At that point, the ambulance crew said they'd be taking Nichols to the hospital for further evaluation. Nichols asked if he could retrieve his cellphone from his car, but Smith told him that he'd bring it and his wallet to him at the hospital. The ambulance then departed at 7:03 for the twenty-minute ride.

Smith then returned to Nichols' car where the other officers were searching the contents. They gave him a bottle for a prescription made out to Rhonda Casto that had been located in her purse. They'd also located a checkbook belonging to Nichols, noting he'd recently written a check to the Oregon Department of Revenue for more than $20,000, and that was another check $1600 check for "child support." The searchers also found a small card from a jewelry store with various diamond cuts and sizes on it.

Taking the prescription bottle, as well as Nichols' wallet and cellphone, Smith was about to leave for the hospital when Tiffany told him to question Nichols again about his relationship with his girlfriend.

Arriving at the hospital, Smith was met by emergency room doctor Phil Chadwick, who asked about weather conditions at Eagle Creek and Nichols' physical behavior when he was being questioned. The deputy reported that Nichols shivered, though not all of the time, and that he switched back and forth between an oddly flat demeanor and voice, and sudden sobbing.

Smith showed Chadwick the prescription bottle for *Gabapentin* and was told it was an anti-seizure/anti-depressant medication. The deputy then asked to speak with Nichols.

When Smith entered the examining room, he handed over the cellphone. Nichols looked at it and told the deputy that Rhonda's mother, Julia Simmons, had tried to call several times and had texted once asking where they were. He again expressed concern about her being told of her daughter's death.

Smith asked for Simmons's address so she could be notified. But Nichols said he didn't know it, though he could personally find her house in Hillsboro, Oregon.

The deputy then asked Nichols to again go over the events leading to Rhonda's fall. Nichols said that they'd arrived at the trailhead about 2 p.m. "We're trying to lose some weight by hiking," he said.

They got as far as Punchbowl Falls before turning around and heading back down the trail. On the way back, he said, Rhonda started acting like "Super Girl," running down the trail, forcing him to hurry to catch up. Then when he reached her, she'd take off again. He repeated his assertion that she was "high" on something and that she'd run ahead fifty feet when she slipped and went over the edge at a narrow place on the trail.

Again, he recounted how he'd looked over the edge and saw her lying "in the water," not moving. After scrambling down to the stream, he said he got in and attempted to "swim" upstream for several minutes but that the current was too strong. He claimed that he then got up on the bank and made his way to her body where he gave her mouth-to-mouth resuscitation. But he soon realized she was dead and returned to the trailhead where he had cell service and called 911.

"What were the weather conditions like?" Smith asked.

Raining at times with some hail, Nichols replied. There was even snow on the sides of the trail, which he described as "wet and slippery." However, he noted, they both were wearing hiking shoes that were good for the conditions.

When Smith asked about his hiking activities, Nichols said he didn't do much. It was his fourth time on that trail but only the second time with Rhonda. He repeated his story that she'd been there frequently to drink vodka and take pills.

"How did you know she was high?" Smith asked.

Nichols said that he'd known her to do "everything under the sun," but she hadn't done drugs to his knowledge since the birth of their child. He wouldn't elaborate on the types of drugs she'd allegedly used.

"What about today specifically?"

Nichols shrugged. He hadn't seen her take, drink or smoke anything. However, he said, whenever she acted as she had prior to her fall, she was "usually on something."

Smith asked if Nichols knew if Rhonda was taking any prescription drugs. At first, Nichols denied it, but a few minutes later said she was taking something for post-partum depression. When the deputy showed him the anti-seizure medication bottle, he said he didn't know anything about it.

Moving on, Smith asked about his relationship with Rhonda. Nichols replied that the relationship was a good one. They'd had their arguments like any couple, he said, but denied they'd been fighting lately. He also said he'd never been physically abusive to her.

The deputy wanted to know if Rhonda had any injuries before her fall. "She was clumsy," Nichols answered. "Just this week she fell down for no reason in the bedroom. Two weeks ago she fell down the stairs and hit her head hard. ... She was always tripping and falling."

Other than the issue with post-partum depression, Rhonda was in good health, Nichols said. She'd seen her doctor a week earlier, but Nichols didn't recognize the doctor's name on the prescription bottle.

The interview ended with Smith asking what the couple did for a living. Nichols said he was a day trader; Rhonda mostly stayed home and took care of Annie.

About this time, Deputy English arrived, and Smith asked him to question Nichols again while he listened from another room. Nichols repeated his answers without deviating, except for one item.

When Nichols noted that Julia Simmons had continued trying to contact him, Smith told him that law enforcement had not been able to find her at the location he'd given them. Now, however, Nichols suddenly remembered that she was staying at his house watching Annie.

"Did she know you and Rhonda were going hiking?" English asked.

"She just knew we were going out for a few hours," Nichols replied, adding that Simmons didn't know they were going to hike on the Eagle Creek Trail.

Both Smith and English would note in their subsequent reports that throughout the questioning that Nichols had remained withdrawn and somber. He'd answered their questions unemotionally and without volunteering any information unless they asked a direct question.

After English finished questioning him, Nichols asked if he could make a call from his cellphone. He was told he could make any call he pleased.

Nichols said he wanted called his father, Stephen P. Nichols Sr., who lived in Bend, Oregon, a mid-sized city in Central Oregon about a three-and-a-half hour drive from Hood River. Nichols placed his call and reached some unknown person with whom he made some small talk as the deputies listened. He then told the person on the other end that he needed to talk to his father because Rhonda had died. The call was brief, as was Nichols' crying during it.

After he hung up, he asked if Rhonda's mother had been notified of her death. And if he was free to go.

About 8:30 p.m., Dr. Chadwick said Nichols could go. His body temperature readings had all been normal, and other than a small bruise on the palm of his left hand, he had no other injuries despite "scrambling" down a steep incline, attempting to swim a vigorous, debris-filled stream, and then working his way through brush, fallen trees and rocks to reach his girlfriend.

English and Nichols left the hospital to return the latter to his car at the trailhead. On the way, the detective called the Washington County Sheriff's Office and requested that they contact Simmons at Nichol's house.

During the drive, Nichols said he wanted to drive home. English replied that the deputies were concerned with him operating a motor vehicle after all he had been through. But Nichols assured him that although he was "sad like when my mom died" and depressed, he was fine to drive. He said he just wanted to go meet his father so that he could help him with Annie.

Upon arriving back at the trailhead, English and Nichols found Sheriff Jerry Wampler waiting. He was there to check on the search and recovery effort.

Wampler and English reiterated the concern with Nichols driving. However, when he insisted, the sheriff said that English would follow him as far as Cascade Locks to observe how he did on the road.

"I want you to wait for me there until we hear from Washington County that Rhonda's mother has been notified," English added.

When they reached Cascade Locks, Nichols parked near the deputy who could see him making phone calls. English called the Washington County Sheriff's Office and spoke to Corporal Scott Mikkelson, who told him that there'd been a holdup contacting the family because they couldn't locate a chaplain in case the family needed spiritual help. Mikkelson told him that Rhonda's family had filed a missing person report.

After waiting several more minutes, Nichols asked if he could leave. English said yes on the condition that he not go into his apartment until Rhonda's family had been notified. He promised to wait outside if he arrived before then.

English returned to the Hood River Sheriff's Office where he was contacted by Mikkelson a short time later. The other deputy told him that Rhonda's mother, Julia Simmons, had been notified "and things are not going well."

Without having been told any details beyond that she'd fallen from a cliff while hiking with Nichols, Rhonda's family believed that he was responsible for her death. "Apparently, he took a million-dollar life insurance policy out on her recently," Mikkelson said. "And they're saying that she told some of them that if something happened to her, or she died, he was responsible."

Hanging up with Mikkelson, English then asked dispatch to call Nichols and tell him the family had been notified. He then called Tiffany and Wampler to tell them about the insurance policy and the family's accusations.

Just three hours after Nichols called to report an "accident" that claimed the life of his child's mother, it was appeared that there might be an entirely different theory about what happened that afternoon on the Eagle Creek trail.

http://wbp.bz/savinganniea

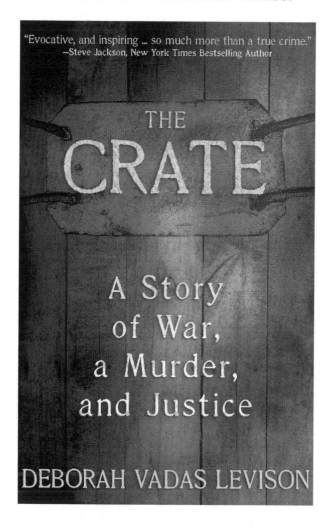

Chapter One

NATURALIZATION

Even in my darkest nightmares, I'd never imagined the words my brother would whisper in my ear.

My family and I had arrived at the hotel minutes earlier. Already the suite lay in a state of chaos, so that when my cell phone rang it took me a few moments to trace the sound and find the device, buried under boarding passes, sunglasses, and baseball hats on the kitchenette counter. I answered with one hand and loaded bottles of Gatorade into the refrigerator with the other.

The kids were arguing, staking their claims for pullout couches and cots in the spacious living area surrounding the kitchen, jostling for the best view of the TV.

"Hang on, I can't hear," I yelled into the phone, slamming the refrigerator door. "For God's sake, can someone turn the air conditioner down? It's like the Arctic in here." I turned around to see the boys poised for a pillow fight, and braced for the inevitable howls. Fourteen-year-old Jake would never allow himself to be bested by his eight-year-old brother, Coby.

Jordyn, our oldest, was seventeen. Coolly, she snatched the cushion out of Jake's hand before he could strike.

I turned my attention back to the phone. A familiar number shone on the screen. "Hey, Pete."

My brother Peter's voice came through muffled by the racket in the room. Still, he sounded strained, and a wisp of apprehension fluttered over me.

"Are Mum and Dad okay?" I shouted over the noise. My parents were eighty and eighty-four, increasingly frail, and with mounting health concerns. They lived in Toronto, hundreds of miles away, and I constantly imagined the worst.

"They're fine, Deb," my brother said, somber, with no hint of his usual chipper tone. I drew back a heavy curtain and unlatched the glass door, seeking the quiet of a balcony. In front of me lay a gorgeous screened lanai furnished with a large wooden dining table and chairs. Another world shimmered outside here on the deck in Florida: bright, mild, calm.

"Now I can hear you better," I said into the phone. "What's going on?"

"Everyone's okay," Peter repeated. He paused. "How about you guys? When do you leave for Florida?"

I glanced around. Beyond the table stood a row of recliners on an open-air balcony that wrapped around the lanai. I pulled a second door closed behind me and walked barefoot to the iron railing, gazing out on a magnificent, unobstructed view of blue Gulf waters.

"We're here! Just checked into the hotel. I'm looking at the ocean now, actually. Are you at work?" That might explain the tension in his voice, I thought; my brother's medical practice involved harried hours of examinations followed by long evenings of dictation, often leaving him stressed and exhausted. He still had a block of patients to see, he confirmed.

I continued, "I know you hate the heat, but it would be nice for you to get away from the hospital for a few days and relax. You sound like you're on edge. When did you last swim in the ocean?" I chattered on, my unease dissolving as I basked in the sunshine and told my brother about our trip.

My husband, Craig, our kids, and I had arrived in Fort Myers that afternoon with Jake's travel team, Xplosion, for an elite baseball tournament that would pit us against some of the best high school ballplayers in the country. Initially, I had not wanted to stray out from under the luxurious green and leafy canopy surrounding our New England home, where the woods near our house beckoned, shady and cool, just like those in which I'd spent my childhood in Canada. I dreaded the prospect of Florida in July; "hot, thick, and humid" constituted my least favorite climate.

Peter paused again before answering my question. "The last time we were at the ocean? Probably when we came down to visit you last fall."

"Oh, that's just the Sound." I referred to Long Island Sound, the swirling gray bathtub of fresh and saltwater that rings the north shore of Long Island and the southern shores of Westchester and Connecticut. To my surprise and delight we'd found, though, an hour's drive from our home to the corner of Rhode Island, the open Atlantic rippling outwards in an endless spread of mint jelly, and dotted along the coast, quaint seafaring villages with weathered wooden piers like wrinkled fingers pointing out to sea. The discovery of this maritime scenery helped soften my docking in America.

I'd felt ambivalent about the whole move. Torontonians typically are not a migratory species. For the most part, those who hatch in Toronto nest there, attend college somewhere close, and settle in the suburbs for the long haul. That life, I had imagined for myself, too. When we moved away, I felt guilty, selfish for leaving my parents. They'd been immigrants themselves. Surely when they landed in Canada in 1956 they assumed that their family would huddle there together forever. When Craig and I left with two of their grandchildren, we effectively took away half of their family.

I'd cried when we all sat down at my parents' kitchen table to break the news. My mother had nodded slowly and said, "Anyvay. You have to do vhatever is best for your family." My father stood up quietly and walked out, but not before I saw that his eyes were wet.

But still, the company that Craig worked for, Trans-Lux, had offered him a good job and we were flattered that they seemed willing to go to great lengths to move us to the States. The tight economy in Toronto in the mid-nineties meant that another, equally good job might not be so easy to find. I'd left my own job in public relations to stay home full-time with Jordyn, a toddler then, and Jake, a baby. In the end, Craig and I agreed: We'd be a Swiss Family Robinson of sorts. We would embark on a year-long adventure, and after that we would come home. One year, we gave ourselves.

Trans-Lux sent a team of movers, and I watched as they packed our tidy little life into boxes and onto a moving van bound for the border.

Craig had wanted to live in or as close to New York City as possible since he would be working on Wall Street for three weeks out of each month, while the fourth week would be spent in Norwalk, Connecticut, the headquarters of Trans-Lux. To Craig, New York held all the allure of Oz: a furious pace, vast business opportunity, endless entertainment, and a spinning kaleidoscope of humanity that appealed to his adrenaline-junky personality.

I had no interest in living in Manhattan. Even though metropolitan Toronto bustled just as much, I perceived New York to be dirty and dangerous. I wanted more living space, not less. I hated traffic jams and parking hassles. And I wanted a stroller-friendly front porch, fresh air, and lots of green grass for our kids. We expanded the home search progressively north of New York City, moving along the Hutch to the scenic Merritt Parkway in Connecticut. As the numbers on the exit signs increased, the property prices decreased.

Eventually, our real estate agent brought us to Trumbull. Our agent had pegged Craig as a huge sports fan. When she pulled up in front of Unity Field, the town's main baseball complex, the sun appeared from behind the clouds and shone down, brilliantly illuminating a banner at the entrance. The sign read, *"Welcome to Trumbull, home of the 1989 Little League World Champions."* Craig practically drooled. I could almost hear a chorus of angels burst into song. *Well, that's that,* I thought. *Here's home.*

In 1996, when my husband and I and our young family first arrived in Connecticut, I'd heard some new friends say to their kids, "Let's have a catch." The phrase rolled around in my head. You "have" a headache or you "have" an appointment, I thought. My dad never said to me, "Let's have a slalom" when we went skiing. But having a catch seemed to be what people in Fairfield County, Connecticut, did on their wide, manicured lawns.

We found a sprawling, if dated, house on a flat acre of land with towering oaks and spacious rooms. Bigger than anything we could afford in Toronto, Craig said. Great bones, I said. Surely, with some modern finishes, we could turn a profit in the twelve months we planned to live there before flipping the house and returning home to Canada. It felt, as we say in Yiddish, *bashert:* fated, meant to be.

And it seemed safe, this little town. A keep-the-front-door-open, leave-your-car-unlocked, let-your-kids-play-outside kind of town. Where all sorts of townsfolk, Jewish or not, drove to the local temple every Monday night to play Bingo. We signed on the dotted line.

Somehow, as we settled into a warm and welcoming community, a wide circle of friends, and a comfortable routine of school, work, and family life, that one year stretched into two, then five, then ten. In 2010, we had been in the States for fourteen years.

In that time I had morphed into an all-around Trumbullite: Suburban mom, carpooling in a minivan and hosting cookie-baking play dates and sleepovers, birthday bashes and after-sports pool parties for the kids and their friends. And publicist, earning media for an eclectic clientele throughout the Northeast. And journalist, interviewing movers and shakers around the state for a local paper. And volunteer, member of this committee and that, fundraiser for this project and that, room mother for this class and that.

I transformed from *alien* to *citizen* on April 8, 2005, my husband by my side, both of us eager to obtain dual citizenship, to vote, to give our children opportunities that came with being American. I didn't want to be an alien. I wanted to belong. I pledged allegiance to the flag of the United States of America, learned the words to the Star Spangled Banner, and celebrated Thanksgiving with all its trimmings ... a holiday that in Canada, as Jews, we'd ignored.

Gradually, and without meaning to, I dropped my Canadian identifiers, shedding *"aboot"* for "about," "Mummy" for "Mommy," "pop" for "soda." I understood what the kids meant when they asked for my "pocketbook," not purse, so they could buy "cotton candy," not candy floss, or a "candy bar," not a chocolate bar. *Runners?* Sneakers. *Duotang?* Folder. *Eaves troughs?* Gutters. *Garburator?* Garbage disposal. I took care not to ask for homo milk, and soon I became accustomed to buying it in jugs rather than bags. I lost track of Canadian exchange rates and Members of Parliament and stopped loading up on Canadian-brand groceries during visits to the place I still called home. And I gave birth to a third child, an American.

I connected more to being Jewish than I had earlier in life, an aspect of my persona that I had minimized as my parents worked hard to assimilate. Perhaps my own marriage and motherhood had provided the impetus, or perhaps my yearning for a sense of community had propelled me along. Whatever the reason, trying on Judaism for size reminded me of standing in a dressing room surrounded by dozens of rejects, zipping the one thing that – at last! – fit perfectly.

And I embraced baseball.

After years spent on the bleachers at Unity, I'd finally figured out the game. I'd come a long way from the days of yelling "SLIDE!" to a runner headed for first, or referring to the dugout as a penalty box. I could recite the rules, use the lingo, follow the plays. I shouted "Give it a ride!" to the batter or "All right, one, two, three!" to the pitcher. I felt comfortable speaking *baseball;* it was yet another language I had learned.

Craig and the kids seemed thrilled to be here in Florida, and now, standing in the mild breeze on the terrace, I felt excited, too. During school vacations, three or four times a year, we invariably returned to Toronto to visit our families – a marked contrast to this rare junket due south. Here, we'd swim in the sea and bask on the beach. In downtown Fort Myers, we'd treat the kids to ice cream cones, browse the surf shops. Jordyn would try on straw hats. Jake and Coby would ask for necklaces with a shark's tooth. Something for everyone.

It would be a great vacation.

"You should come down for a few days," I urged my brother on the phone. "A change of scenery would do you good. It's a pretty hotel."

I leaned on the railing and gazed out at the tops of swaying palm fronds. The surf rippled, crystal clear and glistening in the late day sun. Gulls circled in the sky. Sailboats and ships floated across the horizon. Pastel colored umbrellas polka-dotted the coastline and little kids with plastic shovels dug for shells in the sand. I tilted my face upward to catch the sun's rays. *Ahhhh.*

Over the phone, my brother suggested I sit down. Slowly I lowered myself to the edge of a chaise lounge.

"Something's happened," Peter's voice dropped low.

The needles of anxiety returned to prick at me. "Peeps. For God's sake. What is it?"

"There's been a murder ... at the cottage."

http://wbp.bz/cratea

1.

July 25, 2003

The monster stirred inside him. Most times, he could tame it. Keep it hidden. Silence its screams. But tonight, the beast demanded release.

She lifted her head up. "You're taking too long. I'm done."

He pressed her head back down. "You're done when I say you're done ..."

She wriggled beneath the firmness of his grip. "No!" she protested, forcing herself up from his lap. She stared him straight in the eyes—defiant and unafraid. "That's all I'm doing for you, Devin."

His calloused fingertips nervously tapped the upholstered backbench and his spine tingled with an odd mixture of excitement and fear. The beast was rising. There was no going back. Not now. Not ever. "Rape her," the monster instructed. "Rape the whore!"

*

It had been a long night of hustling for Nilsa Arizmendi and Angel "Ace" Sanchez. Maybe it was the hot weather, but the regular johns were being especially cheap and irritable, and Nilsa was forced to negotiate smaller fees. Ordinarily, she charged $30 for a half hour, but tonight's tricks were turning a maximum of only $20 and some demanded blowjobs for a measly 10 bucks. Like shrewd customers at a turn-of-the-century street market, the johns knew that the vendor in question was desperate for cash.

Ace loitered around the corners of New Britain Avenue, where his girlfriend worked. He stared glumly at the filthy surroundings, trying not to think about Nilsa's activities. He did not like their lifestyle. In fact, he despised it. But how else could he and Nilsa score drugs? The couple's shared habit was not cheap. In July 2003, they were each smoking about 20 to 30 pieces of crack per day and shooting up a bundle-and-a-half of heroin, which translated to about 10 to 15 bags on the streets. Sometimes, Nilsa used up to three bundles of heroin a day, depending on the amount of crack she smoked. It was a nasty cycle. The crack got Nilsa and Ace ramped up and wired and the heroin brought them down. They needed both to survive.

Without the drugs, sickness set in. Being drug sick was terrible—worse than having the flu. In the darkness of their motel room, the childhood sweethearts huddled together in sweat-soaked sheets, shivering with nausea and chills. Every joint and bone ached as invisible bugs furiously crawled beneath the surface of their skin. In between fits of vomiting, their bowels loosened and the bed became soiled. Nilsa kept the curtains drawn and placed the Do Not Disturb sign on the outside door handle for days at a time. The room was a mess. Their lives were a mess. Besides the incessant and all-consuming craving for heroin, she felt shame.

"This shit has to stop," Ace thought as he watched Nilsa emerge from the back seat of an old man's car. She walked toward him, tucked her tie-dyed T-shirt into her dungaree shorts and offered a faint smile. Normally 140 pounds, the 5'2", dark-haired woman was now only skin and bones. "I'm tired," she said. "Let's go home."

On the walk back, Nilsa briefly disappeared and scored a blast of crack at Goodwin Park in Hartford. She returned to Ace and attempted to take his hand. He pulled away. "I'm done with this shit. You gotta go to rehab, Nilsa. We both gotta go."

She acted like she did not hear him. It was usually the best way to avoid a fight.

But tonight, Ace would not let up. "I'm done with the fucking drugs," he mumbled, running his hand through his greasy dark hair. Normally, he kept it long, but a few days before, he had cut it short. "Done with the hustling. Fuck. Fuck this shit."

Their shadowy figures forged into the night, softly illuminated by the neon lights of outdated motels. Rolling hills of forest stood far in the distance, strangely comforting and yet somehow sinister. When Nilsa's high wore down, they started to quarrel. This time, Ace would not take no for an answer. They both had to go to rehab in the morning.

Nilsa was reluctant. She had been in and out of rehab for years and it never did her any good. Still, she loved her four children and desperately wanted to be done with the drugs and get clean forever and for good. Overhead, the night sky opened and a warm drizzle began to fall. The blue rock watch on Nilsa's frail wrist ticked into the early morning hours. They walked southbound along the pike, past Cedar Hill Cemetery containing the corpses of Connecticut's affluent class, including legendary actress Katharine Hepburn, and then a smaller cemetery containing the remains of lesser-known citizens.

Ace gently elbowed Nilsa. "You gonna start singing?"

She sometimes sang Christian hymns that she learned in childhood as they walked along the pike. It passed the time and gave them both a sense of comfort in the midst of all the pain. She smiled beneath the foggy moonlight. "You want me to?"

"You know I like your voice," he replied.

Her smooth, clear voice chimed like a bell into the darkness of the night:

O Lord my God, When I in awesome wonder,
Consider all the worlds Thy Hands have made;
I see the stars, I hear the rolling thunder,
Thy power throughout the universe displayed.

By the time they reached the parking lot of the Stop & Shop in Wethersfield, Ace had persuaded Nilsa to agree to the plan. Nilsa was worthy of a long and healthy life. After all, Ace needed her. Her mother needed her. Her children needed her. She vowed to never turn another trick again or inject poison into her veins. The party was over and fuck her if it had not been the party from Hell.

Nilsa eyed a lone vehicle parked in the far corner of the store's lot. "That's Devin's van."

"Let's get back to the motel," Ace said.

"I'm just gonna say hi."

Nilsa walked across the lot to the beat-up blue van owned by their mutual acquaintance, Devin Howell. They had met Howell a few months before. At the time, he was pumping gas at the Exxon gas station on the corner of Broad Street and New Britain Avenue. The rain was heavy and Ace and Nilsa were soaking wet as they approached Howell's van and asked for a ride to their motel room on the Berlin Turnpike in Wethersfield. "We'll give you five bucks," Ace said.

Howell had to go to Lowe's to price out some supplies for an upcoming job. He was driving in that direction anyway, so it was not a problem to assist two near-strangers who appeared down on their luck. "Yeah, sure. The door's unlocked."

Nilsa and Ace squeezed into the bucket seat on the passenger side. Nilsa used her street name, Maria, when she introduced herself to Howell. As they drove to The Almar Motel, Howell told the couple in his mild Southern drawl that he had a lawn-care business. Ace glanced over his shoulder at the back of the van. The space was large, with a long bench sofa littered with lawn service tools and clothing. The stench of body odor pervaded the vehicle's interior.

When they arrived at the motel, Ace and Nilsa invited Howell into their room to hang out. Howell brought some beer and marijuana. Nilsa and Ace offered to share a little crack, but Howell refused. He was a weed and booze guy. Together, the three got high on their poisons of choice. Howell told them that he was living in his van and he often parked it at the Stop & Shop parking lot in Wethersfield. He left the motel less than an hour later. As he drove back to the Stop & Shop lot to bed down for the night, he glanced at the open ashtray and saw that a $20 bill rolled up inside of it was gone. "No fucking good deed goes unpunished," he cynically thought. Ace and Nilsa had ripped him off.

In the months that followed, the occasional contact with Howell proved beneficial to Nilsa and Ace. The couple had lived on the Berlin Turnpike for the last 18 months or so, first at The Elm Motel and then at The Almar. Their daily routine involved walking from the motel on the pike to the familiar section of New Britain Avenue in Hartford where Nilsa turned tricks, about 1½ miles from The Almar. Ace had not worked a job for seven or eight months and he no longer had a vehicle of his own. Especially in the cold weather, Nilsa and Ace relied on acquaintances to spot them walking along the busy roadway and offer a lift. Occasionally, they had money for a cab, but that meant less money for drugs.

Howell also proved useful in assisting Nilsa and Ace to cop drugs. He did not mind driving them to local dealers living 15 to 20 minutes away. He would not get high with them when they scored. He seemed content to do them a favor by giving them a ride in exchange for a few dollars. All told, Howell served as the couple's makeshift Uber driver on about five occasions over the course of one month.

At approximately 2:45 a.m. on July 25, 2003, Ace watched Nilsa's skeletal form traipse across the empty parking lot. It was hard for him to believe that this was the same woman whose weight had sky-rocketed to 180 pounds when she was last released from federal prison—all beefed up by the cheap, starchy food. Nilsa stopped at the van and appeared to talk to Howell, who sat in the driver's seat. Then she walked around the van and got into the passenger side. Howell turned on the engine and slowly drove away. It was the last time Ace would see Nilsa alive.

*

When Christ shall come, with shout of acclamation,
And take me home, what joy shall fill my heart.
Then I shall bow, in humble adoration,
And then proclaim: "My God, how great Thou art!"

Nilsa "Coco" Arizmendi, Jan. 29, 1970–July 25, 2003
Rest In Peace

http://wbp.bz/hisgardena

 WILDBLUE
P R E S S

See even more at:
http://wbp.bz/tc

More True Crime You'll Love From WildBlue Press

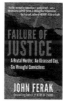